Young People on Margins

Our society leaves too many young people behind. More often than not, these are the most vulnerable young people, and it is through no fault of their own. Building a fair society and an equitable education system rests on bringing in and supporting them. By drawing together more than a decade of studies by the UK's Centre for Education and Youth, this book provides a new way of understanding the many ways young people in England are pushed to the margins of the education system, and in turn, society.

Each contributor shares the personal stories of the young people they have encountered over the course of their fieldwork and practice, combining this with accessible syntheses of previous studies, alongside extensive analysis of national datasets and key publications. By unpicking the many overlapping factors that contribute to different groups' vulnerability, the book demonstrates the need to understand each young person's life story and to respond quickly and collaboratively to the challenges they face. The chapters conclude with action points highlighting the steps individuals, institutions and policy makers can take to bring young people in from the margins.

Young People on the Margins showcases first-hand examples of where these young people's needs are being addressed and trends bucked, drawing out what can and must be learned, for teachers, leaders, youth workers and policy makers.

Loic Menzies is Chief Executive of the Centre for Education and Youth (CfEY), England's "think and action-tank". Before founding CfEY he worked as a teacher, school leader, a youth worker and as a teacher trainer.

Sam Baars is Director of Research at CfEY. He has extensive experience designing, managing and conducting research projects drawing on a range of methods, from film–based participatory research to systematic literature reviews and statistical analysis of large-scale survey data.

'This important book shines a light on a section of the pupil population too often overlooked, yet often in most need of our help. The book combines analytical rigor with humane concern, weaving pupils' voices with analysis of national data. Each chapter explores a different sub-group of young people at risk, but the authors also expose the connections between them of poverty, trauma, disruption, and discrimination. *Young People on the Margins* avoids easy criticisms of schools in favour of constructive reflection and recommendations on how we might do better in working with these young people to protect and include them'.

Professor Becky Francis, CEO of the Education Endowment Foundation and former Director of the UCL Institute of Education

'This is a detailed, compassionate and insightful work that tackles head on the challenges facing this country's most disadvantaged young people. I read it cover to cover as there is so much to hear from young people in this book'.

Dame Rachel De Souza, Children's Commissioner and Former Chief Executive of the Inspiration Trust

'Loic and his team highlight sobering accounts portraying the experiences and realities of marginalised young people within education. It is well researched, unique and insightful. This book is a must read and is calling *everyone* within the education sector, to action. It has made me ask questions of myself as a teacher and reinforces my decision to work within alternative provision. For busy people, the taking action section at the end of each chapter provides a summary of what needs to be done in order to make necessary changes. Yet, no matter how busy you are, this is a book that needs to be read from cover to cover'.

Bukky Yussuf, Senior School Leader, Science teacher and coach

'As policy makers and school leaders wrestle with a Covid-19 world and its aftermath, here's a "must-read". The case for more inclusively minded secondary schools and a revival of youth services has never been more urgent. By cleverly interweaving powerful analysis with suggested changes for practice, Loic Menzies and the contributors he has assembled illustrate their arguments with vignettes of troubled youngsters which should persuade even the faint-hearted that the time to act on their good intentions is now'.

Sir Tim Brighouse, Former Schools Commissioner for London

'*Young People on the Margins* is a book that should certainly not be on the margins when it comes to educational practice. There is so much of value here for all who work with children and young people. The multiple examples and perspectives of what creates and contributes to marginalisation and disadvantage provide so much food for thought. The fact that this is articulated in such an accessible way with clear implications for practice makes it a must read for practitioners, academics and policy makers alike'.

Professor Sam Twiselton OBE, Director of Sheffield Institute of Education at Sheffield Hallam University

'A typically thoughtful and thought-provoking book from the team at CfEY, going beyond cliché and generalisation to explore the biggest challenge our system faces'.

Ed Vainker OBE, CEO, Reach Foundation

'*Young People on the Margins* presents us with a challenge. It asks the questions that reside in the space between policy and narrative. Every country talks endlessly about supporting the most vulnerable and marginalised yet very rarely do we see profound impact. What this book does is to give a voice to those people who often, as a result of the hand that they have been dealt, do not make the same gains in educational attainment, or the same progress in career opportunities as their more advantaged peers. If we consider the impact that Covid-19 has had on our most vulnerable communities, there could not be a better time for this publication to help sharpen our resolve to create a more socially just society'.

Sir David Carter, Executive Director System Leadership at Ambition Institute and former National Schools Commissioner

'This is a great piece of work in a messy, difficult area. Tackling these topics is courageous and *Young People on the Margins* makes the issues very accessible'.

Lisa Cherry, Speaker, Trainer and Author

'This book is a timely and important contribution to debates and discussions some would rather society did not continue to have. Those debates are decades old, so it's clear we have not solved the issues raised. Which means we need to go on exploring them, and as this book does, doggedly seeking solutions that will bring justice, dignity, equality and peace into vulnerable lives. Some of their voices ring out, clear and brave and fearless, in this book. There is otherwise little for the comfort of those who would rather we didn't pay due attention to children we have somehow placed in the margins of our concerns for far too long. It is informative, research backed, and rich in evidence. Its challenges to all of us need to be addressed – in policy, and in practice'.

Maggie Atkinson, Former Children's Commissioner for England (2010–2015)

Young People on the Margins

Priorities for Action in Education and Youth

Edited by Loic Menzies and Sam Baars

Routledge
Taylor & Francis Group

LONDON AND NEW YORK

First published 2021
by Routledge
2 Park Square, Milton Park, Abingdon, Oxon OX14 4RN

and by Routledge
52 Vanderbilt Avenue, New York, NY 10017

Routledge is an imprint of the Taylor & Francis Group, an informa business

British Library Cataloguing-in-Publication Data
A catalogue record for this book is available from the British Library

Library of Congress Cataloging-in-Publication Data
Names: Menzies, Loic, editor. | Baars, Sam, editor.
Title: Young people on the margins : priorities for action in education and
   youth / edited by Loic Menzies and Sam Baars.
Description: Abingdon, Oxon ; New York, NY : Routledge, 2021. | Includes
   bibliographical references and index. |
Identifiers: LCCN 2020043678 | ISBN 9781138360457 (hardback) | ISBN
   9781138360464 (paperback) | ISBN 9780429433139 (ebook)
Subjects: LCSH: Children with social disabilities--Education--Great
   Britain. | Youth with social disabilities--Education--Great Britain. |
   Education and state--Great Britain. | Community and school--Great
   Britain.
Classification: LCC LC4096.G7 Y68 2021 | DDC 371.826/940941--dc23
LC record available at https://lccn.loc.gov/2020043678

ISBN: 978-1-138-36045-7 (hbk)
ISBN: 978-1-138-36046-4 (pbk)
ISBN: 978-0-429-43313-9 (ebk)

Typeset in Melior
by SPi Global, India

Contents

Contributors

Abi Angus is a Research Associate at The Centre for Education and Youth. Abi Angus spent over ten years working with marginalised groups of young people and their families. In this time, she supported young people with additional needs to access play and youth projects, ran a national education support project for Gypsy, Traveller and Roma families and designed support plans for young people displaying high-risk behaviour in care and youth work settings. Abi holds a BA in Community Development and Youth Work as well as an MA in education policy and society.

Sam Baars is Director of Research and Operations at The Centre for Education and Youth. He has extensive experience designing, managing and conducting research projects drawing on a range of methods, from film-based participatory research to systematic literature reviews and statistical analysis of large-scale survey data. Sam has authored numerous publications in peer-reviewed journals and books and has particular interests in youth research, area-based inequalities, social science impact and local economic development. He has written for the Guardian and the New Statesman, written and produced a short film on the garden cities movement, and runs a regular podcast for Worthing Museum and Art Gallery. Sam holds a PhD and ESRC-accredited Masters from the University of Manchester, and a degree in philosophy, politics and economics from the University of Oxford.

Kate Bowen-Viner was a Senior Associate at The Centre for Education and Youth. Kate led a variety of research projects and impact evaluations for charities working with young people. She also co-authored reports about a range of issues in the education sector, including leadership in Multi-Academy Trusts and young homeless people's experiences of education. Kate has been working in education since she left university. She began her career in Liverpool and went on to teach English in West London and Bristol. She also has experience of policy delivery in central government through her role at the Office for the South West Regional Schools Commissioner (Department for Education). There, she worked with Local

Authorities and education providers to deliver free schools. Kate is particularly interested in how education, and policy discourses shape attitudes towards gender. She has an MSc in policy research at the University of Bristol, as part of which she wrote her dissertation on girls' experiences of menstruation in school. She is now studying for a PhD.

Loic Menzies is Chief Executive of The Centre for Education and Youth (CfEY). He has authored numerous high-profile reports on issues ranging from youth homelessness to teacher recruitment, all based on detailed qualitative and quantitative research. He works closely with practitioners and policy makers to communicate research's implications, for example by presenting to the Education Select Committee in Parliament or working with civil servants on approaches to tackling disaprities in achievement. Loic was previously a teacher, youth worker and tutor for Canterbury Christ Church University's Faculty of Education. He has been a school governor and a trustee of a number of youth and social entrepreneurship charities.

Will Millard is Head of Engagement at The Centre for Education and Youth. Will has authored major studies on careers education and work experience, educational assessment, oracy and the achievement of disadvantaged groups. Will presents and blogs extensively on a wide range of issues affecting children and young people. A qualified teacher, Will began his career working in a large secondary school in North West London. He is a founding trustee of the charity 'I Can Be', and has two Masters degrees in public policy.

Ellie Mulcahy is Head of Research at The Centre for Education and Youth. Her specialist areas include widening participation in higher education, Gypsy, Roma and Traveller (GRT) young people's education, Early Years and child development, and, the nature and impact of bias. She is the co-author of a series of reports on inequalities in higher education as well as a number of studies of youth homelessness. Ellie also specialises in supporting education and youth organisations to develop their practice and has conducted impact evaluations for a range of social enterprises. Ellie previously worked as an Early Years teacher and as a researcher for Teach First and the Behavioural Insights Team.

Alix Robertson is an Associate at The Centre for Education and Youth. In 2018 she authored a report exploring the barriers that Latin American young people face in accessing UK higher education for King's College London. She has also worked with the National Association of Special Educational Needs to produce a series of training videos on twelve different conditions. Alix began her career as a secondary school English teacher. She then moved into journalism, working for sister papers FE Week and Schools Week where she won awards for her investigations and reporting on subjects including college finances, multi-academy trusts, and the experiences of women and LGBT people in education. Alix volunteers with the charity Keen London, helping to organise and run activities for young people with disabilities.

Bart Shaw is Head of Policy at The Centre for Education and Youth and has spent the last 14 years working in education. He combines experience of policy making at the heart of central government with hands-on experience as a teacher and middle leader in school. He has authored numerous studies focusing on special educational needs, as well as a major study of ethnicity gender and social mobility for the Social Mobility Commission. Previously Bart worked for the Department for Education and Skills as part of the Civil Service Fast Stream. There he developed, delivered and evaluated national policies including the £13 million subsidy pathfinder which helped disadvantaged students access after-school activities. From 2008 to 2009 he was seconded to the Cabinet Office. In 2011 he left the Civil Service to work directly in schools as a geography teacher, data analyst and Head of Department in a secondary school in rural Derbyshire. Bart holds an MA in governance and development from the University of Sussex.

Acknowledgements

We would like to thank the many thousands of individuals who have participated in our research and, in doing so made this book possible. You have opened up and shared deeply personal stories from which we have learned a huge amount and we are deeply grateful to you for your time and trust.

We would also like to thank the peer reviewers who kindly took the time to read through our draft chapters and offered invaluable comments and advice.

Chapter 1: Vanessa Joshua
Chapter 2: Rob Webster
Chapter 3: Jo Taylor and Dean Johnstone
Chapter 4: Ruth Lupton
Chapter 5: Chelsea McDonagh and Chris Derrington
Chapter 6: Hannah Collyer, Lisa Cherry, and Rosie Boggis
Chapter 7: Beth Watts and Lauren Page-Hammick

Finally, we would like to thank the many clients who supported and funded the research publications we have drawn on to write this book.

Introduction

Young People on the Margins

Loic Menzies

In the summer of 1998, all the pupils in my form group at Chesterton Community College in Cambridge received a leaflet. Apparently, the City Council wanted to know what we, the young people of the city, thought would make our lives better. That moment was when my journey in the education and youth sector, and towards editing this book, began.

A hasty email led me to join in with a series of local 'action groups', meeting young people I never normally got to know properly. Some of them attended the same educational institution as me, but perhaps in different streams or sets. Others went to different schools.

Free of the normal constraints that come with an institution trying its best to educate 2,000 young people, we embarked on joint endeavours, putting on music nights for young people in our community and addressing our local councillors on issues of concern to us and our peers.

This was exciting and eye-opening, but even more fascinating were some of the youth workers I met; people like Lisa Sibley and Jo Mathieson, who had an amazing knack for drawing out stories from the young people they worked with. These exceptional professionals – who were so open to learning about marginalised young people's lives – built relationships that changed my life, and the lives of many other young people in our community.

I did not belong to one of the marginalised groups that this book focuses on. In fact, I am aware that one day a debate kicked off in Cambridge Youth Service's office about whether I was sufficiently marginalised to deserve the time and resources that were being invested in me. However, a year later I took my first steps towards coming out, and in those days of state-sanctioned discrimination against gay pupils in schools, youth workers quickly realised that I might appreciate them being by my side on that journey.

A few years later I was handed an employee's badge for my first proper job beyond a paper round; I too had become a youth worker. Then, a few years later, I received my next badge, this time as a secondary school teacher in North West London.

In the nearly twenty years since I embarked on my journey through the sector, I have become familiar with many young people's stories, each unique but with numerous overlaps. This book is about those overlaps; the overlaps that reveal the missed opportunities to stop marginalised young people from falling through the gaps.

At first glance, what is in your hand is a collection of discrete chapters representing different groups of young people, each of whom might be given a different label. Yet on closer inspection, the distinctions become less clear cut. For example, in Chapter 1 we ask who is more likely to be excluded from school. The answer: pupils growing up in poverty; pupils from certain ethnic minorities, pupils with special educational needs; pupils living on the fringes of homelessness. Then, in Chapter 2 we ask who is more likely to be identified as having a special educational need. The answer: pupils growing up in poverty, pupils from certain ethnic minorities.

In Chapter 7, we ask who is more likely to end up homeless. The answer this time: pupils growing up in poverty, pupils who have been in care or who have needed support from social workers (explored in Chapter 6), pupils with mental health problems (Chapter 3), and pupils who are LGBT+ (who, incidentally, are also more likely to have mental health problems).

With every chapter, and with every research project I have worked on as Chief Executive of the Centre for Education and Youth (CfEY), the web of interactions between factors contributing to marginalisation gets tighter, and the overlaps more striking.

So why are so many young people being pushed to the margins of our society?

Time and again, research demonstrates that different services have different responsibilities and different "thresholds for need" determining young people's eligibility for support. And these thresholds are almost always too high. Tightly prescribed remits and a lack of coordination and collaboration drive a tendency for services and professionals to "process cases" according to the service's particular responsibilities; too rarely the young people's needs.

In 1988, another teacher turned researcher, James Pye published a book called *Invisible Children* in which he describes the pupils he remembers, alongside the many he has forgotten. With the benefit of hindsight, Pye reflects on what he wishes he had done to support Alasdair, one of his former pupils:

> What I now think should have happened, is that we should have united to try and crack his enigma; should have surrounded him... Had we talked and thought, perhaps we would have agreed on a common approach to him, with powerful unanimity[1]

Identifying. Pupils at risk is not rocket science, but what is much harder is taking the sort of collaborative approach that Pye advocates; delving into a young person's life story and finding ways of supporting them and their family. I suspect few readers will read the stories in this book without recognising the desperate need for such an approach, despite the fact that more than a decade of cuts and fragmentation have made it so much more difficult.

Young People on the Margins therefore proceeds as follows. The first chapter explores one of the most concrete manifestations of marginalisation: school exclusion. In it I set out exclusion's long-term consequences for young people and society as a whole. Then, in the next three chapters, my colleagues explore some of the underlying factors that affect these young people, including special educational needs and disabilities, poor mental health and local geographical context. Finally, in the last three chapters Will Millard, Ellie Mulcahy and Kate Bowen-Viner zoom in on specific groups of young people to show how they are marginalised. The first group we explore are Gypsy, Roma and Traveller young people, a group who are defined as such at birth through ethnicity. The second group, "children in care and in receipt of social services' support", acquire their status in response to their childhood experiences, and the third – young homeless people – through their outcomes in late adolescence.

The risk factors described in each of the seven chapters all coalesce around a pernicious mix of socio-economic deprivation, challenging personal and family circumstances and undiagnosed or unmet needs. Thus, whilst this book comprises seven discrete chapters, it is a book about overlaps, and the good news is this: the crossovers mean that work we do to tackle marginalisation on one front, or for one group, will almost always have transferable and mutually reinforcing benefits for others. Indeed, the four main areas for action with which we conclude in Chapter 8 are not specific to any one group but instead have the potential to bring far more of the young people we have had the privilege of meeting, teaching and learning from; in from the margins.

Reference

1 Pye, J. (1989). *Invisible Children: Who are the Real Losers at School?* Oxford: Oxford University Press.

Pushed out and left out

Understanding school exclusion

Loic Menzies and Abi Angus

1.1 Introduction

In the late 2000s I worked in a school in North West London. It was a tiny site packed in behind tall fences and across the road were more fences. Behind those, on an old playground, lay some portacabins, and inside these sat a transient group of pupils.

This was the school's "inclusion unit", where pupils on the fringe of exclusion were brought to learn, or at least be contained. Some of the time it "worked", and pupils were successfully reintegrated; other times, it was a staging post on the way to more formal exclusion. This chapter explores the story of pupils like Francis who I taught there on my weekly trips across the road.

Every week when I arrived at the unit, Francis had taken another step down the road towards exclusion. But why? Surely something could have stopped what felt like an inexorable slide away from the mainstream.

This chapter sets out what I have learned since my days in the unit. It begins by outlining the implications of being "pushed out" of the mainstream, both for young people and society as a whole. We then explore how young people are pushed out, arguing that both formal and informal exclusion play a role. It is clear that formal and informal exclusion affect some young people more than others; I therefore highlight which young people are most likely to be excluded, but go beyond traditional analyses of excluded pupils' demographics by investigating the underlying reasons why these young people are at greater risk of exclusion. I argue that this is crucial in order to understand how these young people's life chances can be improved. Finally, I set out a number of changes that would ensure fewer pupils like Francis were pushed onto the margins.

1.2 Why do these young people matter?

Francis and his peers' journey into, and on from, the unit were not unique. No one knows exactly how many pupils are in a similar position, but it is clear that the personal and social costs of school exclusion are huge.

1.2.1 The personal cost of exclusion

Chris Henwood is co-founder of Foundation Futures, an alternative education provider that supports excluded young people to re-engage with education. She explains the toll exclusion takes on many of the young people she works with, saying:

> This is from their mouths… they feel excluded, forgotten about, tossed on the scrapheap, nobody gives a toss about them… some of the places in which they're taught are horrible… one is in the back end of an old primary school and when you go in the door, you can see the damp up the walls and it's got that horrible damp smell and the paint's peeling… So, what these young people feel is that they're not worth anything, nobody cares, they can't fit in to an academic classroom, so they're turfed out and they're just pushed out and pushed aside and they haven't got a voice at all [1].

National data on excluded pupils' experiences paints a similarly bleak picture: nearly a quarter of pupils in PRUs and AP are educated in provision judged less than "good" by Ofsted, and in some areas such as the West Midlands this rises to over 50% [2]. On top of this, as we will see later in this chapter, many excluded young people unofficially 'disappear' from records. Whilst there are serious questions as to whether Ofsted judgements provide a meaningful and reliable measure of quality in the AP sector, it is clear that many excluded young people end up with little or no formal education, as was the case for Emily:

Emily is a 19-year-old from Newcastle. Growing up, Emily had an unstable family home. She would often argue with her mother and would be asked to leave the house. This resulted in her frequently drifting between her mother's and her father's houses and staying in each one temporarily.

At the age of 11, the death of one of Emily's cousins devastated and deeply affected her and this had a serious impact on her education. Finding it difficult to deal with her emotions, Emily exhibited behaviour issues at school, and this eventually led to her exclusion from two schools.

Emily became homeless when her mother told her that she could no longer stay in the family home. At this time, she did not want to live with her father because none of her siblings would join her.

She is currently living in a hostel and explains that:

> When I moved in to [Pupil Referral Unit], I started going with people who would cause trouble on a daily basis and then I didn't want to get kicked out because that was the last school I would go to, so I changed, but then I ended up getting kicked out for something else. I didn't go to school then; I went to the library for 45 minutes a day [3].

1.2.2 The social cost of exclusion

Estimates suggest that the cost of school exclusion can amount to at least £370,000 per pupil [4]. However, too much credence should not be given to such estimates, since most analyses of the social cost of exclusion are correlational, in other words, they highlight the link between exclusion and factors such as joblessness, or incarceration. There is, therefore, a considerable methodological difficulty here, in that as we argue throughout this book, these outcomes and characteristics tend to be interrelated, and links are not necessarily causal. Thus, the same factors that result in a young person being excluded from school (such as drug use or violence) might also increase their chance of being incarcerated – independently of exclusion.

On the other hand, those who have experienced exclusion frequently describe highly plausible causal links between their exclusion and later life events as summarised in the diagram below. We therefore should not dismiss links simply because we do not have the experimental studies needed to provide stronger "proof" of causality.

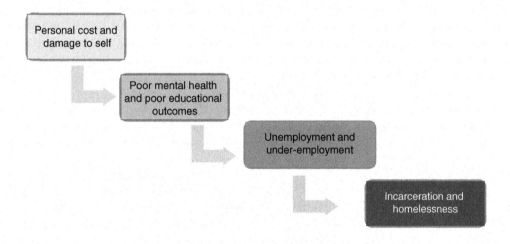

The social cost of school exclusion can be categorised according to four domains [5]:

1.2.2.1 Qualifications

Most young people who are excluded from school are not enrolled to take two core GCSEs in English and Maths and only 1.5% of students in LA Alternative Provision achieve good GCSEs in these subjects [6]. Meanwhile, in one study, nine out of ten young people who had never been excluded from school achieved level two qualification by the age of 20, whereas only 3 in 10 excluded young people did so [7].

1.2.2.2 Employment

Lacking qualifications has a knock-on impact on future employability. In 2018 the Department for Education published data on young people not in education, employment or training (NEET), looking at the characteristics of those who had been NEET for a year in the three years following Key Stage 4. The report showed that only around 1 in 20 young people from this cohort were NEET for a year, the proportion rose to 1 in 4 when looking at young people who had attended a PRU or Alternative Provision [8].

1.2.2.3 Criminality

Schools are not to blame for young people offending but many of the risk factors for youth violence or criminality overlap with risk factors for exclusion, for example being male, growing up in a deprived area and a history of low educational attainment. It is therefore not surprising that nearly two-thirds of prisoners in a 2012 Ministry of Justice Study reported having been temporarily excluded when at school and nearly half had been permanently excluded. The study also found that prisoners who had previously been excluded from school were more likely to be repeat offenders compared to other prisoners [9]. On the other hand, exclusion may act as a tipping point for many young people, moving them decisively towards the path of criminality.

1.2.2.4 Health

Evidence suggests that exclusion can increase the risk of long-term psychiatric illness, with research from the University of Exeter showing that young people excluded from school were not only more likely to already be affected by poor mental health, but were also more likely to show signs of psychological distress following an exclusion [10]. Researchers tracked a sample of young people between 2004 and 2007, and reported that "levels of psychological distress were consistently higher among children reported to have experienced exclusion at any time point compared to their non-excluded peers."

1.3 How are pupils excluded?

Young people can be pushed out of school either through official means (namely an authorised permanent of "fixed-term" exclusion), or through unofficial means, often referred to as "off-rolling".

Gill et al. summarise the five main forms of exclusion as follows (2017, p.11):

Official Exclusion
- Permanent exclusion
- Fixed term exclusion

Unofficial Exclusion
- Managed move
- Offsite alternative provision
- Illegal exclusion

In addition, previous studies have argued that some young people who never begin to attend school (for example, because they are educated at home) are also de facto excluded from school [11]. Meanwhile, De Pear argues that young people can be excluded even when they attend school because they are marginalised, permanently taught in "units", or because they are unable to access what others take for granted. We therefore explore below how institutional practices, informal exclusion and formal exclusion can all contribute to pushing learners out.

1.3.1 Institutional practices

Norms and practices that facilitate mass education underpin most schools. These "institutional practices" lead to expectations around compliance that can result in exclusion when pupils deviate. Views as to whether fixed expectations and enforced compliance are desirable or not depend considerably on values, ideology and theoretical standpoint.

Institutional practices are not the main focus for this chapter and, for reasons that will become clear, I disagree with the view that the link between school structures and exclusion makes structures and expectations of compliance undesirable in general. However, it is worth summarising five different perspectives on the link between compliance and exclusion.

According to Marxist sociologists. teaching compliance simply serves the needs of a capitalist elite, reinforcing values based on a hierarchy of authority by engendering motivation to complete tasks that may be repetitive or unimaginative through external rewards [12]. This view can also be found in widespread critiques of a "neoliberal education system" that prioritises instrumentalism and the servicing of employers' needs [13]. A neoliberal education system might therefore be argued to place "greater importance on pupil attainment and testing, leading teachers to prioritise subject and whole-class teaching rather than the needs of individual pupils" [14]. Thus, exclusion may be used to ensure young people who do not behave as expected do not hamper achieving such goals.

Compliance can also be criticised from a progressive standpoint, a school of thought that takes its roots in the late nineteenth century work of writers like Dewey. Dewey criticised traditional education particularly, for prioritising the transmission of knowledge, conformity, docility, receptivity and obedience [15]. According to this school of thought, enforcing compliance is illiberal and inherently conservative and schools should instead play a less directive role, leaving pupils free to express themselves and pursue their own paths. Meanwhile, Foucault draws striking comparisons between schools and prisons as means of ensuring order and obedience [16].

It might also be argued that compliance-enforcing practices prioritise the needs of a "normal" majority to the detriment of a minority who struggle to conform. Advocates of this view frequently call for an inclusive school system that is more responsive to special educational needs and shaped around equality rather than "what works" for the majority [17]. Similarly, proponents of the social model of disability commonly argue that, at their most extreme, institutional practices result in the disabling of certain young people [18].

On the other hand, from a behaviourist perspective, enforcing expectations is developmentally and socially desirable. Indeed, Didau and Rose [19] rightly point out that "students need to be helped to make good choices sometimes, and will benefit from being reminded of the consequences of poor choices." Teaching young people to comply with institutional expectations is therefore a key part of preparing pupils to function in society. and teaching some degree of compliance could therefore be one of schools' primary functions, as agents of socialisation.

In the short term, schools' enforcement of compliance may also be desirable in order to create a safe environment and to facilitate learning for as many pupils as possible. as Peter Hughes, Chief Executive of the Mossbourne Federation explains:

> I wouldn't allow and I would never allow one child to upset 29 others in a classroom and I would say for too long education has done that or has allowed that to go on. We're seeing many failing schools around the country where everyone talks about the child; no one's talking about the other 29 children in the room. 'We need to adapt and do this', 'we need to do this for this and this' – and by the time you look at the list of that child's stuff, the rest of the children have spent half the lesson not learning. For me, fundamentally, the mainstream school is to address the vast majority of students as best you possibly can [20].

According to this view, a failure to ensure compliance might itself drive exclusion by failing to provide a safe environment. Thus, whilst some argue that "negative behaviour communicates an unmet need" [21, 22] which is no doubt the case for many pupils, in other cases, poor behaviour may simply be a "normal" response to chaos and *laissez-faire* conditions. Tom Bennett, the government's "behaviour tsar" who has become a lead protagonist in an increasingly popular campaign against progressivism, therefore argues that young people are often marginalised by schools where behaviour is poor and standards are not robustly established [23]. It is also worth noting that where schools do not create a safe environment, this can itself be particularly problematic and marginalising for pupils at greater risk of bullying such as LGBT+ young people and those with disabilities. On the other hand, others might argue that these are exactly the young people who are "pushed out" as a result of rigid expectations around compliance. For my own part, I certainly found endemic homophobic bullying and unchecked pressure from peers far more marginalising than any expectation that the school ever enforced, even back in the days of Section 28.

In some schools, a desire to establish order can lead to the implementation of "zero tolerance" and "no excuses" approaches. These approaches to behaviour management take their roots in a 2000 book by Samuel Casey Carter [24]. They then gained popularity in England when they were adopted by high profile London Secondary Schools such as Mossbourne Academy in Hackney and King Solomon Academy in Westminster.

However, Didau and Rose [19] distinguish between "zero tolerance" in the US and "no excuses" in the UK, arguing that the predominant model in the UK focuses on tackling low-level disruption, whereas the US approach has questionable effectiveness. and emerged as a specific response to high levels of violence.

In England, successive education ministers have praised "no excuses" schools, but in 2018, Parliament's Education Select Committee argued that:

> The evidence we have seen suggests that the rise in so-called 'zero tolerance' behaviour policies is creating school environments where pupils are punished and ultimately excluded for incidents that could and should be managed within the mainstream school environment [25].

The "zero tolerance" approach has also received considerable criticism in the US, with Heitzeg drawing attention to a "school to prison pipeline" [26] and Hirschfield arguing that young people who break rules and are viewed as "trouble-makers" within schools are "defined as criminals—symbolically, if not legally—and treated as such in policy and practice" [27] something that is particularly likely to happen to pupils from ethnic minorities due to structural racism and prejudice.

On the other hand, head teachers like Peter Hughes point out that "no excuses" and "zero tolerance" policies can play a valuable role in enforcing expectations and creating a safe environment, something most pupils benefit from. Thinking back to the "unit" I taught in Francis, I can certainly think of pupils like Ruby for whom this was the case. Ruby was hugely charismatic and loved being the centre of attention, so, whilst chaos was the school's norm, misbehaving was an effective way of maintaining her dominance and protecting herself from others. However, having originally taught her in the unit, I later went on to teach her back in the mainstream once she moved back across the road. I asked her about the change in her behaviour and she told me that once order was established in the school, it had become clear that disruptive behaviour was not the way to secure respect. She therefore switched to excelling academically.

We return to the question of balancing "no excuses" and inclusion in Section 1.4, arguing that whilst some institutional practices, enforced in certain ways might contribute to exclusion, consistent and predictable enforcement of norms and expectations need not result in pushing young people out.

1.3.2 Unofficial exclusion

Unofficial exclusion is hard to define, but the following account from Head Teacher Jarlath O'Brien's book *Don't Send him in Tomorrow* [22] hints at the iceberg of unofficial exclusion that sits below official exclusion figures. Jarlath tells the story of an instance when he tried to organise a visit to see a primary school pupil, only to be told that his visit would have to be in the morning because the pupil went home every day at 11am when they became "unmanageable". His curiosity piqued: he asked how many fixed-term exclusions the pupil had had. The conversation proceded as follows:

> "Er, none. Why do you ask?"
> "When a child is sent home during the day as a result of their behaviour, that is a fixed-term exclusion," I explained.
> "You'll need to talk to the head teacher about that. Look, we're an academic school. We're not set up to deal with this sort of thing".

This type of unofficial exclusion frequently acts as a first step along the road to more permanent, official exclusion, or a pupil "disappearing" from the system. Briggs' work [28] on the impact of "off-site provision", which is often provided by a separate institution, found that pupils who return to the mainstream after being taught elsewhere like Ruby are unusual. Similarly, older research by Stirling on school exclusions and young people in care reported that unofficial exclusions frequently resulted in young people not returning to mainstream education. In a sample of 60 children living in children's homes, 32 young people were out of education, however, only 2 of these children had received formal school exclusions, with the remaining 30 leaving education following unofficial exclusions [29].

Although unofficial exclusion might sound like a euphemism for "illegal" exclusion, this is not the right way of thinking about it, as there is in fact a considerable grey area. For example, "Managed Moves" take place where parents and schools agree for a child to have a "fresh start" in another school [30]. These arrangements have long been presented as a preferable *alternative* to official exclusion. Despite this, managed moves can quickly stray into the realm of the illegal if parents are pressured to accept a move as an alternative to formal exclusion. Furthermore, even where such moves are conducted in legitimate ways, removing pupils from a school results in considerable disruption to their education and, in many cases, pupils find themselves being moved around numerous times.

Parents in England also have the right to educate their child at home. However, it is illegal for schools to encourage parents to register their child as "home educated" in order to remove them from the school roll. Yet freedom of information requests show that the number of pupils educated at home appears to have nearly doubled between 2011/12 and 2016/17, and when journalist Jess Staufenburg investigated this trend further she found that unresolved issues with behaviour were becoming an increasingly common driver behind home education [31]. A simple "legal" or "illegal" binary is therefore an insufficiently nuanced taxonomy of exclusion.

A more incontestably unethical exclusionary practice is pre-exam "off-rolling"; in other words, removing pupils from the school roll in advance of national exams to boost the school's position in league tables. Evidence of such practices comes from a combination of teacher, parent and pupil anecdotes, as well as analysis by Philip Nye and Dave Thomson. In their "Who's left" research, Nye and Thomson showed that between Years 7 and 11, an estimated 7,000 young people across the country "disappear" from their schools' roll each year [32]. Nye's earlier research [33] also revealed that some schools' league table positions were considerably improved due to pupils leaving the school role.

Whilst critics of league tables might seize on this research as evidence that high-stakes accountability systems drive exclusion, it is important to note that not all schools off-roll. Ultimately, school leadership teams are active agents in deciding whether to engage in such practices, and shifting responsibility for unethical practices onto the system rather than individuals and schools is somewhat disingenuous.

Off-rolling tends to take place near the end of pupils' school careers, but schools can also contribute to exclusionary practices during school admissions by gaming or skewing their intakes. Oversubscription criteria set out formal processes for prioritising pupils' access to limited school places and these rules can legally give preference to children living close to the school or, children of a particular faith. However, there is also widespread anecdotal evidence of schools making themselves undesirable to "certain types" of pupils, for example by requiring pupils applying to take "banding tests" that may not be easy for families to access [34], or even by suggesting to parents that their child would be better suited to the education provided elsewhere.

Partly as a result, Becky Allen and Meena Parameshwaran showed that 10% of schools have a school population that is unrepresentative of their local area. This is more likely to be seen in London and other urban areas, and particularly in faith schools [35].

Exclusionary admissions practices are particularly likely to affect pupils with special educational needs, but can also result in the exclusion of some ethnic or socio-economic groups. Analysis of school intakes by Matthew Weldon at Lancaster University shows that certain minority ethnic groups are less likely to gain access to church schools and that catchment areas are more easily "gamed" by parents with more social and financial capital [36]. The inevitable correlate of state-sanctioned institutional practices which give some groups an advantage in securing admission to the best schools is that less-favoured groups often end up in a subset of schools, often unfairly labeled "sink schools". These frequently struggle to support the skewed mix of pupils who end up attending, with a knock-on impact on formal and informal exclusion. In order to combat young people being "pushed out", policy makers therefore need to go well beyond reducing formal exclusion, starting with reformed admissions procedures that ensure all schools are truly comprehensive.

1.3.3 Official exclusion

As we have seen above, Francis and his peers' first steps towards being "pushed out" began long before they joined the ranks of England's formally excluded pupils. Indeed, formal exclusion is rarely the first step a pupil takes on the road to exclusion. However, what makes formal exclusion distinctive is that regulation and legislation govern the process, and there are explicit rules to ensure parents and their children have the right to appeal decisions. There are different rules to govern permanent and fixed-term exclusions, but government regulations [37] stipulate that:

> Whenever a head teacher excludes a pupil they must, without delay, notify parents of the period of the exclusion and the reason(s) for it. They must also, without delay, provide parents with the following information in writing:

> - the reason(s) for the exclusion;

> - the period of a fixed-period exclusion or, for a permanent exclusion, the fact that it is permanent;

> - parents' right to make representations about the exclusion to the governing board (in line with the requirements set out in paragraphs 52 to 60) and how the pupil may be involved in this;

> - how any representations should be made; and

> - where there is a legal requirement for the governing board to consider the exclusion, that parents have a right to attend a meeting, to be represented at that meeting (at their own expense) and to bring a friend.

1.4 Who is "pushed out"?

Efforts to quantify and analyse school exclusions have traditionally been based on official fixed-term and permanent exclusions – figures that can easily be found in government statistics. These figures reveal a gradual fall in the percentage of pupils excluded each year between 2006/7 and 2012/13. This trend was then reversed, and in 2016/17 the permanent exclusion rate was broadly similar to a decade prior [38].

However, given the prevalence of "unofficial" exclusion, official statistics only tell a very partial story. Over the last few years, Kiran Gill, the founder of "The Difference", (a new programme to improve Alternative Provision and reduce exclusion), as well as researchers at Education Datalab have therefore sought to gauge the extent of unofficial exclusion.

Gill's approach has been to combine data from a range of sources including freedom of information requests, surveys and analysis of school inspection reports.

Based on this extensive detective work, she points out that 48,000 pupils were educated in the Alternative Provision sector and that this is five times the annual total of formal exclusions (p.7 [39]).

Meanwhile, Datalab have used England's National Pupil Database to track pupils' moves between institutions [32, 40]. This approach reveals that in 2017, 22,000 pupils left mainstream state schools at some point between Year 7 and Year 11 but were not recorded in state education again, a figure which raises questions about where all these pupils are going.

Studies of exclusions at primary level are less widespread, in part due to the smaller number of pupils affected. In the school year 2016/17, only 255 primary school pupils were recorded as being permanently excluded in England (0.03% of the total primary cohort) [38]. While this is a far smaller proportion than secondary pupils, receiving a school exclusion remains a disruptive and challenging situation for all the children and families involved. As with secondary age pupils, the number of primary children educated in PRUs and Alternative Provision remains consistently higher than the number of formal permanent exclusions issued. DfE data shows that in January 2018, 5,575 children aged 10 years or younger were being educated in these settings, either part-time or full-time and 289 of these pupils were under five years old [41].

Regardless of how exclusion is measured, some groups of pupils are more likely to be excluded than others. Researchers can take two approaches when describing which young people are at particular risk of exclusion. The first is primarily demographic, because it focuses on pupil groups – for example ethnic groups, genders and age groups. However, this approach is not ideal because it misses much of what matters most, as Dr Sam Baars and I argued in our 2015 report for the Inclusion Trust [42]:

> 'Pushed out' learners may fall into any number of categories, whether in care, with special needs or in poverty, but these, and any other label attached to them, matter less than the common factors that act as a barrier to their inclusion.

After setting out some key demographic trends I will therefore provide an alternative approach that instead focuses on underlying characteristics or "risk factors". This approach is preferable because it moves beyond descriptions of *who* is most at risk and helps identify *why* they are at increased risk.

1.4.1 Demographics

As the later chapters in this book show, pupils from certain ethnic groups, with special educational needs or with mental health problems; boys; poor pupils; pupils in care; and pupils growing up in deprived areas are all more likely to be excluded than their peers.

Intersecting combinations of these factors are also important, since many of these characteristics are interrelated. For example, there are clear links between poor mental health and family difficulties [4, 43] as well as between poverty and special educational needs [4, 44].

Despite its drawbacks, the demographic approach is not without value, since it demonstrates the scale of disparities and reveals some of the structural inequalities in society which underpin the problem of school exclusion and which are often profoundly linked to the relationship between ethnicity, deprivation and racism.

1.4.2 Underlying factors

Beneath surface-level pupil characteristics lie common factors that underpin the reasons why some young people are more likely than others to be excluded from school [42]. We now explore three of these underlying issues.

1.4.2.1 Gaps in basic needs

It is undoubtedly hard for young people to engage in education when their basic needs (such as food, safety, adequate shelter, sleep and basic love and care from parents or carers) are not met. Factors such as poverty, being brought up in care and many of the issues explored in other chapters of this book make it more likely that pupils' basic needs will be unmet, and this can mean educational priorities fall by the wayside, or that practical and emotional barriers stand in the way of learning [45, 46].

Whilst there is mixed evidence for the validity of Maslow's famous hierarchy of needs that places basic needs at its base [47], studies in a number of global contexts have shown that when pupils are provided with regular nutritious meals, not only are they more able to learn [48], but they also show improvements in attainment [49]. An Education Endowment Foundation study of Breakfast Clubs echoed those findings by demonstrating impact on Key Stage 1 attainment, and, importantly, suggesting that the mechanism of impact may not simply be the provision of food, but also the social support that such clubs provide [50].

1.4.2.2 Difficulties with socialisation

As Jarlath O'Brien explains through the example of Dean, who had been abused by his mother, it can take detailed unpicking to understand why a young person is struggling in a school environment.

> I taught Dean and his classmates to use Bunsen burners so that we could carry out some investigations in chemistry. For almost all the students this was an exciting thing to be doing... [however] Dean promptly upped and left at the beginning of one lesson, to be found a short time later at the top of the fire

escape in tears. We had developed a very solid relationship and had got to the point where we could always talk things through candidly after an incident. After a significant investment in time (and time spent with children is always an investment), and some deep questioning, this is what I learned:

- Dean was very excited at the thought of using a Bunsen burner;

- Dean really wanted to learn how to use it safely;

- Dean knew he could learn to do it;

- Dean did not like the feeling that excitement gave him in his belly;

- Dean got the same feeling in his belly when he was scared;

- Dean was unable to tell the difference between the two feelings;

- Dean wanted help to know the difference [22].

Poverty, growing up in care, crowded living conditions and hectic parental work patterns can all lead to a difficult home life. In such environments, young people can struggle to develop typical or expected social skills, and this can make it hard for them to function within schools, eventually leading to exclusion as Dr Sam Baars and I explain in our 2015 report.

Functioning in a school requires the ability to negotiate basic interactions – for example to walk... from one room to another through a thousand other people or to be able to sit in a room quietly with other people [42].

There is increasing awareness that difficulties with socialisation can result from "insecure" or "disorganised" attachment with care-givers in the early years of a child's life.[1] According to attachment theory, the relationships formed between a child and their primary caregiver in early childhood form the basis for how an individual understands and maintains relationships throughout their life. Growing up within a difficult family situation or in care can therefore result in young people lacking secure attachments and this unmet needs can be manifested through challenging behaviour, particularly around self-regulation and understanding of social situations.

Young people who grow up in care or in a chaotic home with abusive or negligent parents are particularly likely to suffer from attachment difficulties, with estimates suggesting that around 40% of young people who grow up in care have a Reactive Attachment Disorder [51]. However, as Didau and Rose point out [19], attachment problems are complex psychological disorders and teachers should resist the temptation to diagnose these or to attempt to substitute for a lack of attachment to primary care-givers.

Atypical social skills can also result from certain special educational needs (some of which are themselves linked to poverty and unmet basic needs, as we explore in chapter 2). On the other hand, definitions can sometimes be somewhat circular here, since "challenging, disruptive or disturbing behaviour" can itself be classified as a form of SEND ("Social Emotional and Mental Health needs" or SEMH). Difficulties with socialisation are therefore at times treated as a symptom of SEND, and at others, SEMH needs are treated as the cause of socialisation difficulties.

As I have already touched on and will explore further below, there is considerable debate about the extent to which mainstream schools should accommodate young people who do not conform to social expectations, or whether alternative providers and special schools are better placed to provide support where this needs to be more intensive.

1.4.2.3 Gaps in basic skills

Difficulties with basic skills such as speech and language, numeracy or literacy can result in profound and long-lasting barriers to young people's ability to succeed, or function within schools [52, 53].

Undiagnosed special educational needs often lie behind gaps in basic skills, as Fiona McFarlane, a clinical psychologist at London's Great Ormond Street Children's Hospital explains:

> A situation that I've just come across again and again is the child who's had massive behaviour problems from primary school, all the way through and the focus has always been on the behaviour and they're not learning because of their behaviour and then actually, come 16, for some reason we manage to get a cognitive assessment... and we discover they had severe dyslexia or they had a working memory of a tiny size [42].

This was the case for Owen, another of O'Brien's pupils who had been excluded from a mainstream school and did not seem to listen. Although some of Owen's needs had been diagnosed, the school was not aware of the full range of issues he faced, they were therefore surprised when a local authority hearing specialist visited and they discovered he was death in one ear.

As O'Brien goes on to explain, pupils who lack basic skills such as reading frequently behave disruptively in order to cover up their needs [22].

1.5 What can be done about it?

Given the personal and social costs of exclusion, there is no doubt that exclusion needs to be minimised and that the support provided to "pushed out" young people needs to be improved. I now turn to a number ways of doing this.

According to some, the bottom line is that schools should never exclude and that instead, they should find ways of supporting all pupils, including the most challenging pupils. Others believe that exclusion can generally be avoided, but concede that in extreme cases – for example where pupils are violent towards teachers – exclusion may be necessary.

One apparently simple way of reducing exclusion would be for policy makers to make it harder for schools to exclude pupils. This could be done in a number of ways, for example by strengthening the right to appeal or by using the school accountability system to incentivise inclusion [25]. However, these approaches would do nothing to tackle illegal exclusion; indeed, making formal exclusion more difficult could have the unintended consequence of increasing the number of hidden, illegal exclusions.

Unlike the Education Select Committee, England's Children's Commissioner has therefore focused specifically on illegal exclusion [54]. The Commissioner argues that greater awareness of the law is needed, and that there should be much tougher sanctions for illegal exclusion. The Commissioner has also called for governing bodies to have a designated member with responsibility for behaviour and exclusions (in the same way that they tend to for special educational needs and certain other issues). They suggest that this member should have a remit to:

> ...examine the school's policy and practice on behaviour management, including exclusions, and should receive mandatory training to support them on this. Governing bodies should have a responsibility to review the school's behaviour policy... as they do with numerous other school policies, and a responsibility to ensure that it complies with the law.

On the other hand, simply making it harder for schools to exclude, whether illegally or legally, still does nothing to tackle the reasons why young people are pushed out in the first place, and if nothing is done to address the behaviour that is leading to exclusion, no one benefits. Dr Sam Baars and my 2015 report therefore presented three different approaches to supporting pushed out learners that might minimise the damaging effects of exclusion.

1. Bringing "pushed out" learners into the mainstream structure

2. Innovating within the mainstream structure

3. Working outside of the mainstream structure.

We now explore these three approaches in turn.

1.5.1 Bringing "pushed out" learners into the mainstream structure

A lack of safety, security and good order often underlies why young people like Ruby behave in ways that ultimately lead to their exclusion; the most cursory observation of the average university freshers' week quickly shows what happens when eighteen-year-olds suddenly find themselves without structure and discipline. It should therefore hardly come as a surprise that *Lord of the Flies* style consequences soon follow when younger teenagers find themselves in schools without boundaries, and Head Teacher Peter Hughes is right to argue that "once you remove the chaos then you can start to dig down as to why the behaviour is happening". Providing a safe, structured and well-ordered school environment is therefore the first step in tackling the root causes of behaviour that might otherwise result in exclusion.

On the other hand, although changing school norms shifted many of my own pupils' behaviour, the transformation was far from universal. What I believe my school could have done better was responding to pupils whose unmet needs were more complicated than a need for institutional order. Indeed, Peter Hughes himself recognises that simply focusing on order and discipline can mean prioritising 29 pupils in a class over one pupil who is unwilling or unable to conform to expectations. Hughes might argue that this is a reasonable, if regrettable trade-off, but it risks bedding-in a one-in-thirty (or 3%) exclusion rate which is incompatible with a belief in social justice and inclusion. Schools therefore need to marry a safe and well-ordered environment with one that responds to needs if the terrible costs of exclusion are to be reduced.

Doing this requires schools and teachers to recognise the difference between "reasons" for poor behaviour, and "excuses". In other words, investigating and understanding the causes of poor behaviour to identify the most appropriate response, without allowing these reasons to make the poor behaviour acceptable or excusable [55]. As Jarlath O'Brien puts it, "it is not a sign of weakness to seek to understand the causes of negative behaviour; it is a self-evident professional strength". Similarly, despite sympathising with her former teachers, Yasmin, a young homeless person who was excluded from school, explains that she wishes teachers had made more effort to understand what was happening in her life:

> I think that teachers didn't understand the change [when I became homeless]. So, instead of working with me going through the change, they decided to judge me. And I've had teachers call me a gangster, I've had teachers call me a thug, and then you kind of just have this mentality you are like, well, forget school, then, I will go and be what you're telling me I am... So, if a child's acting like some kind of negative thing in society, maybe you can help to understand why... because there's probably a reason why they're like that [1].

On the other hand, understanding why a young person is behaving in a particular way should not result in lowering expectations or accepting disruption to others' learning. As Nancy Gedge, a primary teacher and special needs expert whose eldest son has Down's Syndrome, explains:

> The labels we apply to children carry negative as well as positive power and, as well as opening doors to specialised support, can cause us to unwittingly limit our expectations... Take a child with ADHD, for instance. Can they be expected to behave themselves and follow the same rules as the rest of the class? Of course they can. You may have to adapt the rules or routines of the class in order to conform, but a diagnosis shouldn't become an excuse [56].

What constitutes an "appropriate response" to the reasons for a young person's misbehaviour varies, and in some cases, the "hook of success" may play a role. In other words, identifying a domain in which a young person at risk of exclusion is successful can provide a means of re-engaging them. Many youth programmes use sports to engage "disengaged" learners and research with young people involved in DJ-ing provides just one example of how even the most disengaged young people can be incredibly diligent and hard-working when it comes to activities they are passionate about [57].

However, providing engaging activities can quickly result in tracking pupils onto alternative pathways. Many "naughty" pupils find themselves on a conveyor belt of graffiti projects and street-dance programmes. These risk stereotyping, labelling and separating them from their peers and from academic learning (often in problematically racialised ways), leading to de facto exclusion from the mainstream. There is also a risk that focusing on what is "relevant" to marginalised young people fails to expand their horizons and traps them in what is familiar rather than helping them access new and unfamiliar content and activities – thus reinforcing, rather than challenging, inequality.

Hooks should, therefore, *draw young people in,* rather than channelling them towards an alternative. This can be seen in some schools' efforts to use "idealistic aspirations" (such as becoming a footballer) as a "hook" to begin conversations about how these occupations might require skills that also transfer to other opportunities, as well as other options [58].

A safe, structured environment combined with the "hook of success" may be effective in building engagement, but as we saw above, deep and complex underlying factors frequently lie behind the behaviour that leads some young people to be pushed out. This behaviour is unlikely to be resolved until underlying causes have been identified, understood and addressed.

Schools should, therefore, deploy a range of strategies, such as:

- Effective classroom practice by skilled and trained practitioners;

- Specialist support from SENCOs, Speech and language, mental health experts;

- Family and home outreach;

- Effective safeguarding and child protection, including liaison with other specialist agencies.

Historically, a sharp rise in education spending under the Labour government, combined with policies such as "Every Child Matters" and "Extended Schools" sought to ensure pupils received considerable support like this. However, after a decade of austerity things have changed dramatically, as Laura McInerney, a former London teacher, explains:

> I recently encountered the pupil who tried to stab me. He's now in his mid-twenties and a lead earner in a blue-chip company, having got a degree from a top university. We didn't exclude him. We showered him and his family in pastoral support. Keyworkers, housing help, attendance officers picking

him up when his attendance dropped low. How? Because it was the mid-2000s: cash was liberal and the curriculum flexible [59].

As McInerney puts it in a later article, "There is a long road from a teenager misbehaving to them being so disruptive a school can't keep them. At one time that road involved a lot of support and intervention. Now, with services cut to the bone, it is shorter" [60].

McInerney's emphasis on wider economic policies, government spending and social support is crucial, and there is a clear need for policy makers to ensure that schools (and the services that support them) have the resources required to respond to young people's needs. Her argument also underlines the need for preventative early intervention, a recurring theme throughout this book.

A small tweak to school funding arrangements which we first proposed back in 2016 could encourage and facilitate preventative action [44]. When pupils are excluded, alternative providers or special schools receive additional funding to cater for these pupils' needs. However, if a mechanism could be found for mainstream schools to access the cash *before* pupils were excluded, they might be able to secure more of the intensive support that McInerney's blue-chip pupil benefitted from.

Money spent early on prevention could bring considerable cost savings further down the line and make a real difference to pupils' lives.

1.5.2 Innovating within the mainstream structure

As we saw above, some argue that exclusion is an almost inevitable by-product of dominant institutional practices in schools. According to this view, mainstream systems need fundamental reform if schools are to stop pushing pupils out. Some people therefore argue that it is time to "break" or "revolutionise" the mainstream, but I am unconvinced.

People often base their arguments for revolutionary educational reform on a belief that a changing world has made traditional schools and schooling redundant often suggesting that this irrelevance is the root cause of disengagement and exclusion. The late Sir Ken Robinson, a famous international education speaker and former professor of arts education is well known for arguing that "factory schools" need to be replaced with innovative, individualised and creativity-enhancing approaches to education, which would re-engage and include all young people [61].

Examples of alternative approaches to mainstream education include greater use of technology, project-based learning and pupil-led learning. However, despite their perennial popularity, such approaches have been criticised from a number of angles. Firstly, it is unclear how they tackle gaps in basic needs, basic skills or difficulties with socialisation; factors that we saw earlier tend to lie behind exclusion. Secondly, the evidence base to justify a switch to such approaches is at best patchy, and at worst, fully contradicts Robinson's view [19, 62, 63].

Alternatively, innovation could take place at a system, rather than school level with some arguing that reducing the focus on academic attainment would reduce exclusion. Professor Twining of the Open University, for example, argued in our 2015 report that measures of "subjective wellbeing" should sit at the heart of an overhauled accountability system. Yet it is unclear what this would mean in practical terms since wellbeing has, in some form or other, featured in most, if not all of Ofsted's inspection frameworks. Meanwhile, including more objective, quantitative measures of wellbeing in accountability system would risk creating perverse incentives, compromising their validity.

Nonetheless, there are elements of innovative practice in some mainstream schools that could play a role in bringing pushed out learners back in. These include closer links to employers to create more opportunities for "real world" learning [64] as well as nurture classes, in which small groups of vulnerable pupils follow a tailored or adapted programme that helps them access the mainstream (an approach which should be used with caution given the mixed evidence base) [65]. Resources permitting, schools can also move beyond their traditional remit by employing or commissioning specialist school-based mental health services or providing support to pupils' families and communities [43]. A famous example of this approach is Harlem Children's Zone, which takes a holistic approach to supporting young people by providing a range of services that meet the local community's needs. This support takes a variety of forms including after school clubs, employability support and extra staff trained to provide academic support and mediation when needed. The approach has since been brought to the UK, notably through the Reach Children's Hub in London.

1.5.3 Working outside of the mainstream structure

Orderly environments, improved support and elements of innovation within the mainstream all have the potential to reduce school exclusion. However, it would be a mistake to focus exclusively on reducing exclusion and to ignore what happens when pupils *are* excluded. Indeed, the Education Select Committee's report on exclusion noted that "going into Alternative Provision was the best outcome for some children" [25].

This is particularly the case where pupils have such complex needs that providing sufficient support within the mainstream is unfeasible. Thus, moving outside of the mainstream, into settings where pupil-to-staff ratios are lower and more specialist support is available can be a positive experience, setting some pupils on the path to a more positive future. Indeed, Kiran Gill's report highlights examples of pupils like Khadija/Jenni (below), who benefitted considerably from high quality Alternative Provision.

Khadija/Jenni's story

Khadija was asked to leave her mainstream school in Year 9. She arrived at her AP school with no records. Throughout her first year there, she was known as Khadija. Her mother had converted her to Islam and changed her birth name, after a new boyfriend had moved in with the family. Khadija did not smile, make eye contact or engage in class. On her first day at the AP school, teachers noticed signs of self-harm and prompted an urgent referral to social care and child and adolescent mental health services (CAMHS). An investigation into the family produced evidence that both Khadija and her brother were subject to child protection orders in two boroughs and her mother had a history of moving them with no forwarding address to avoid agency involvement. Khadija and her brother were witness to domestic violence at home.

Although her home life was not improving, Khadija began to settle in and enjoy her new school. Her attendance gradually improved and she developed relationships first with staff, and eventually with other students. After a year at the AP school, Khadija gradually became less aggressive and started to engage in her CAMHS sessions. At this point Khadija asked staff at the academy to start calling her by her original name, Jenni, which they did. Jenni opened up to staff about being bisexual and wanting to "come out". At home, her mother said that homosexuality was disgusting and she was banned from talking about it. Jenni was particularly vulnerable at this point. She started missing school and engaging in risky, self-destructive behaviours - the school alerted social services when Jenni was seen by another student getting into a car with some older men. One day Jenni came in and had a knife in her bag, which was discovered by staff. She said that she had forgotten the knife was in there but that she had hidden it from her step-father, who had threatened to stab her and her brother. The school asked for an urgent referral from the local authority, saying that they believed Jenni's life was in danger. Jenni was taken into care and was placed with a foster carer with whom she could build a supportive relationship, and begin to process some of the abuse she had suffered in her birth family. At school, Jenni's attendance returned to normal and she began to become more confident. She got a new haircut and some piercings, and became open and more comfortable about her sexual orientation, talking with other students about it. She stopped self-harming, and her attainment increased. Jenni did so well on her coursework that she was entered for higher papers at GCSE.

Unfortunately, the quality of education outside of the mainstream is variable, and a number of challenges need to be overcome if it is to consistently help young people flourish and succeed. Research particularly highlights four areas for development that would improve provision outside of the mainstream [4, 66, 67].

1.5.4 Better evidence

Gill argues that if more research and evidence were available regarding Alternative Provision, policy makers and professionals would be better placed to support pupils in these schools:

> There has been very little research into what works in engaging and improving the trajectories for excluded pupils. In fact, there is no consensus over what 'success' looks like in AP... the sector has very little access to an understanding of the knowledge base that does exist in the mainstream sector. Experts and practitioners interviewed for this research agreed that professional development in AP rarely focuses on teaching, assessment or pedagogy; the most common training in AP schools covers 'positive handling' to reduce behaviour escalation, and safe ways to physically restrain pupils.

1.5.5 Improved workforce

Pushed out learners have some of the most complex needs in our education system, yet they are often left to be taught by the least qualified practitioners. As a proportion of all teaching posts in the sector, vacancy rates in special and Alternative Provision schools are 100–150% higher than in mainstream secondary schools, and the number of vacancies has increased rapidly in recent years leading to widespread use of supply teachers and unqualified teachers, such that pupils in Alternative Provision are twice as likely to be taught by an unqualified teacher, and twice as likely to be taught by a supply teacher [68]. Research for the Department for Education by Professor Martin Mills and Professor Patricia Thomson therefore suggests that bringing more teachers into the sector is crucial in improving the quality of education in Alternative Provision, since, unlike in the mainstream, difficulties recruiting staff, rather than problems with staff retention, lie at the heart of the problem [66].

1.5.6 More appropriate accountability and oversight

Greater transparency is needed regarding where pupils are being educated since an opaque system means that at present there is little accountability and oversight when it comes to excluded young people's education. This is a particular problem in unregistered Alternative Provision.

Re-weighting all schools' results to include all the pupils who have been educated there, in proportion to the amount of time they have spent in that school could help, and the government has indicated that it will move in this direction. This change would also discourage schools from off-rolling their pupils and might provide a market-based mechanism for improving Alternative Provision, since schools would be incentivised to commission high quality provision. This would be an invaluable change, since most schools do not evaluate the quality of the AP they commission [67].

Furthermore, if mainstream schools retained accountability for pupils it might encourage them to work more closely with Alternative Providers for example by forming partnerships such as multi-academy trusts. Staff might then find it easier to move between school types and it would be easier to reintegrate pupils into the mainstream where appropriate.

On the other hand, any changes to accountability in the Alternative Provision sector should take into account the question of what we expect the sector to deliver. Parker and Levinson (2018), criticise an increased focus on academic qualifications in Pupil Referral Units, arguing that this:

> ...changes their purpose from being alternative to being part of the main-stream system. No longer is the intention to provide different types of environment for students who struggle to fit into mainstream settings; the purpose becomes to replicate the activity in those mainstream settings as far as possible [69].

Addressing pupils' deeper, underlying difficulties may therefore be a more appropriate focus for Alternative Provision. The charity "Right to Succeed" has therefore established four principles for effective AP, which include "a strong diagnostic baseline and regular assessment of progress" and "robust, standardised measures (of a range of outcomes) where feasible".

1.5.7 Joint working

Exclusion should not be a one-way street, and Alternative and Mainstream Providers need to establish closer links. Professors Mills and Thomson were commissioned by the Department for Education to research good practice in the use of Alternative Provision, and – based on extensive interviews with teachers across both sectors – they concluded that close links and communication are critical.

> AP providers considered that referrals worked best where full information about the circumstances of the referral were disclosed upfront; where they were able to get comprehensive information on the pupil's background and prior attainment; where any SEND were already identified, or identified early in the transition; where there was a gradual or phased introduction to the AP setting; and where the pupil's parents/carers and mainstream school remained closely involved. Overall, AP providers reported that referrals worked best where schools referred children directly to their settings, typically for short-term placements. Referrals for permanent exclusions usually came through

the LA. Where this was the case, AP providers received limited information about children's needs or backgrounds and there was no opportunity for a gradual induction process [66].

Mainstream schools should therefore carefully vet any provision they are commissioning to make sure it is of the highest possible quality. They can then build up relationships with high quality providers and work together to prepare a "soft landing" for pupils once they arrive in AP. This could include a phased transition, pre-visits (involving parents where possible) and sharing information (not just about curriculum and where a pupil has reached in their studies, but also their interests and hobbies), so they can be made to feel at home.

Once a pupil moves into AP, it is essential to do all that is possible to avoid closing the door, so that reintegration is possible in the future if appropriate. This might mean a link teacher visiting the pupil and keeping up to date with progress and what approaches seem to be working best in meeting the young person's needs. Reintroduction can then take place in a phased way, combined with additional monitoring, carefully planned support from a key point of contact, alongside a combination of academic and behavioural targets [70].

Of course, the difficulty is that many of this guidance relies on high quality, local AP being available – which it often is not. For this reason, in 2014 the National Foundation of Educational Research (NFER) and Institute of Education (IOE) provided a series of examples of how schools were innovating to increase the supply of provision; for example, by pooling resources across schools to commission new provision, or even setting up new AP within mainstream MATs. One case study highlights a partnership between a number of schools that jointly commissioned provision for pupils at risk of exclusion:

> The partnership was structured as a limited company and the secondary headteachers and the college vice-principal were company directors. A company manager was employed on a part-time basis, with a key part of this role involving coordinating the monthly Fair Access Panel meeting, ensuring that the partnership collaborated to provide pupils at risk of exclusion with access to the most appropriate provision. The partnership purchased AP on behalf of its members with AP commissioned under a common contract and costs negotiated to ensure maximum value for money. Through negotiation the company had been able to secure a larger number of places at a lower cost price. A national provider was commissioned to provide full-time KS3 and KS4 AP provision. Close links existed between the commissioners and providers of AP, enhancing the oversight and monitoring of the provision. The company manager held weekly meetings with AP managers to discuss the progress made by pupils and lesson observations were carried out on a regular basis. Staff from the partnership schools had regular contact with AP providers to discuss attendance, behaviour and attainment issues.

Ultimately, if we accept that at least some pupils will occasionally need provision outside of the mainstream, and that these are likely to be some of the most vulnerable pupils with the most complex needs, effective provision of AP needs to become a far higher priority.

1.6 Conclusion

When I think about why the issue of exclusion matters so much, I immediately think back to Francis who we first met in this chapter's introduction, as he slid ever closer to exclusion.

I think the reason Francis stands out for me above all the other pupils I have known in similar situations is the circumstances I last saw him in. Let me therefore return to his story, before summarising what could change to ensure the odds are improved for pupils like him.

Francis had actually been one of the first pupils I met, back in 2006 when I took a day out from sunny coastal Kent, where I was training as a teacher, to visit the school I would work in, come September.

Arriving at the school – a small, Catholic Secondary – the first thing that struck me was how few pupils there seemed to be in the building. The school was heavily undersubscribed at the time, and even the pupils who were there did not seem to spend a lot of time in lessons.

A nun who worked there at the time took me on a tour, and the last stop was the lunch hall where she introduced me to a fourteen-year-old pupil with piercing green eyes. This was Francis.

Briefly releasing one of his peers from a headlock, Frances looked straight at me, shook my hand with remarkable decorum and responded, "Yes, Miss", to the nun when she said "You pretty much run this school, don't you, Francis"

A few months later Francis was in my Citizenship class. The difficulty was that there were 37 students in my lesson, but I only had 28 chairs. Luckily, Francis was on hand to help. "I'll sort it out, Sir, I'm sure I can find some more". Of course, he did. Less fortunately, he also found time to run up and down the corridors unleashing mayhem all the way. As I grew to know him better, I realised this was typical; moments of mayhem punctuated most of what Frances did, yet somehow his norm remained this strikingly polite, authoritative and helpful contradiction.

Soon enough, Frances was in "the unit" where I continued to teach him on odd occasions. I learned a little more about his life, but not much. I gathered a grandparent, was bringing him up, for various difficult reasons. I also learned just how smart and – in some ways, motivated he was. Recognising this and realising he might not have long before he slipped away from the school, I decided to enter him for a GCSE in combined humanities a year early, on the grounds that it would give him something to work towards. Over the next few months, we worked on his coursework and on some basic underlying concepts and principles behind the GCSE he would be sitting. When his coursework (which explored the Israeli–Palestinian conflict) was finished, I took it to the photocopying room and asked Mary, the kind and gentle lady working there, whether we could do something special with it. She bound it beautifully, and when we presented to him, he stared at us and said, "This is the first thing I've done in my life that I'm really proud of".

A few months later, it was the day of the exam, and we could not find Francis anywhere. He was eventually dragged in from who-knows-where, and ended up achieving an F or a G grade. It was by no means a great qualification, but as far as I know, it remains the only qualification he sat, since he was rarely in school the next year.

In fact, the next time I saw him was in a hospital bed. He had been stabbed whilst stealing a car.

On this occasion, he was ok, but I have no idea what has happened to him since and my usual optimism fails me.

Francis' behaviour was completely unacceptable in school. The pupil he put in a headlock needed protecting from him, the mayhem he caused on the corridors whilst fetching chairs disrupted everyone else's learning and he only completed his coursework because I sat supervising him one-to-one in my free periods – hardly a sustainable approach within a mainstream school. Yet I am left wondering what it would have taken to ensure he did not disappear from education completely, or end up in that hospital bed.

I still do not know the answer and I think at its roots, the profound social issues that left him needing to be put in the care of his grandparent lie at the heart of it all. However, my hope is that the research presented in this chapter points the way to some actions individual practitioners, institutions and policy makers can take to help pupils like Francis go on to a better future.

I have argued that exclusion is sometimes necessary and, in some cases, in the interest of the young person themselves. However, I have also called for far closer examination of the reasons why a young person might be excluded – not because this provides a reason for not excluding them, but because it offers clues as to how to avoid needing to exclude them.

I have also argued that the stakes should be lowered by improving the quality of provision outside the mainstream, so that young people who do end up excluded are guaranteed an education that will fully cater for their needs. Although there are pockets of excellence, for now, a move outside the mainstream too often means a move to a second-class education. This needs to change.

1.7 Taking action

As Kiran Gill points out:

> There are two key areas where reform is pressing if we are to rewrite the story of worsening school exclusion: the capacity to prevent exclusion and the capacity to improve trajectories for excluded pupils.

The ideas presented below would tackle both.

1.7.1 Policy makers

- In making spending decisions and shaping economic policy, politicians should recognise the short-sighted nature of decisions that result in cutting-back support and early intervention for vulnerable young people.

- Policy makers should develop funding mechanisms that allow mainstream schools to access some of the additional funding that is available once pupils are excluded. This would help them respond to pushed out learners' needs before they are excluded, without having to take this life-changing step. It is absurd that head teachers and parents are on occasions agreeing that exclusion is the best option for a child because it is the only way of accessing the funding that child's needs.

- Policy makers should finally implement reforms to school performance tables that would include results for all the pupils who have been educated at a school in its results, in proportion to the time they spent there.

- Inspection of Alternative Provision should be sensitive to the unique and specialist functions that these institutions serve.

1.7.2 Institutions/organisations

- Schools should examine their institutional practices to assess whether they isolate and remove pushed out learners or whether they also address the factors that push them out.

- Schools, social services, mental health teams and other specialist services should develop strong partnerships and meet regularly to identify opportunities for joint working in order to respond to pupils' needs.

- Schools and alternative providers should develop federations, multi-academy trusts or other partnerships to make it easier for staff and expertise to move between different types of provision. This would also help pupils to access specialist support from within the mainstream, or to be reintegrated after leaving it. Where high quality AP is lacking, mainstream schools should work together to set up or commission better provision.

- Rather than simply focusing on pupil-premium eligible young people, or those with identified special needs, schools should be sensitive to the full range of factors (explored throughout this book) that might lead to a pupil being "pushed out".

1.7.3 Individual practitioners

- Teachers should recognise that a calm, safe, orderly environment is the first line of defence in minimising exclusion.

■ Teachers and school leaders should work alongside other professionals like social workers to investigate any gaps in basic needs, socialisation and skills in order to identify the underlying reasons why pupils behave in ways that lead to exclusion. They should see these as reasons that point to solutions – such as working with specialist practitioners – rather than as excuses or reasons to lower standards.

■ Teachers should look for opportunities to "hook in" disengaged pupils through activities that appeal to their passions and interests. However, these should be "ways in" rather than alternatives.

Recommended reading

Making the Difference Breaking the Link Between School Exclusion and Social Exclusion: Gill, K., Quilter-Pinner, H., & Swift, D. (2017). *Institute for Public Policy Research.* Retrieved from www.ippr.org/publications/making-the-difference.
The Alternative should not be Inferior: What now for "Pushed OUT" learners?: Menzies, L., & Baars, S. (2015). *Inclusion Trust and LKMco (CfEY).*
Don't send him in Tomorrow: Shining a Light on the Marginalised, Disenfranchised and Forgotten Children of Today's Schools: O'Brien, J. (2016).
"Always Someone Else's Problem": Office of the Children's Commissioner's Report on illegal exclusions. (2013).

Note

1 See for example "Attachment Aware Schools".

References

1 Small, I., Mulcahy, E., Bowen Viner, K., & Menzies, L. (2017). *A Place To Call Home Understanding Youth Homelessness*, Retrieved from www.cfey.org p62.
2 PRUs: concern over numbers in underperforming AP | Tes (2019). Retrieved May 12, 2020, from https://www.tes.com/news/exclusive-numbers-low-grade-prus-underestimated.
3 Small, I., Mulcahy, E., Bowen Viner, K., & Menzies, L. (2017). *A Place To Call Home Understanding Youth Homelessness*, Retrieved from www.cfey.org p47.
4 Gill, K., Quilter-Pinner, H., & Swift, D. (2017). *Making the Difference Breaking the Link Between School Exclusion and Social Exclusion*, Institute for Public Policy Research. Retrieved from www.ippr.org/publications/making-the-difference.
5 *ibid.*
6 *Ibid.*
7 Department for Education (2011). *Youth Cohort Study and Longitudinal Study of Young People: 2010 – GOV.UK*, Retrieved May 12, 2020, from https://www.gov.uk/government/statistics/youth-cohort-study-and-longitudinal-study-of-young-people-in-england-the-activities-and-experiences-of-19-year-olds-2010.

8 Department for Education (2018). *Characteristics of Young People who are Long-term NEET*. Retrieved November 20, 2020, from https://assets.publishing.service.gov.uk/government/uploads/system/uploads/attachment_data/file/679535/Characteristics_of_young_people_who_are_long_term_NEET.pdf.

9 Ministry of Justice (2014). *Prisoners' Childhood and Family Backgrounds. Results from the Surveying Prisoner Crime Reduction (SPCR) Longitudinal Cohort Study of Prisoners*, Retrieved from www.justice.gov.uk/publications/research-and-analysis/moj.

10 Ford, T., Parker, C., Salim, J., Goodman, R., Logan, S., & Henley, W. (2018). The relationship between exclusion from school and mental health: A secondary analysis of the British Child and Adolescent Mental Health Surveys 2004 and 2007. *Psychological Medicine, 48*(4), 629–641. https://doi.org/10.1017/S003329171700215X.

11 Pear, S. (1997). Pupils' views Excluded pupils' views of their educational needs and experiences. *SupportforLearning, 12*(1), 19–22. https://doi.org/10.1111/j.1467-9604.1997.tb00493.x.

12 Bowles, S., & Gintis, H. (1976). *Schooling in Capitalist America: Educational Reform and the Contradictions of Economic Life*, New York: Basic Books.

13 Mccafferty, P. (2010). Forging a "neoliberal pedagogy": The "enterprising education" agenda in schools. *Critical Social Policy, 30*(4), 541–563.

14 Hedegaard-Soerensen, L., & Grumloese, S. P. (2020). Exclusion: The downside of neoliberal education policy. *International Journal of Inclusive Education, 24*(6), 631–644. https://doi.org/10.1080/13603116.2018.1478002.

15 Dewey, J. (1938). *Experience and Education*, New York: Kappa Delta Pi.

16 Foucault, M. (1977). *Discipline and Punishment: The Birth of the Prison*, New York: Pantheon Books.

17 Biesta, G. (2010). *Good Education in an Age of Measurement*, New York: Routledge.

18 Holt, L. (2010). Children with mind–body differences: performing disability in primary school classrooms. *Children's Geographies, 2*(2), 219–236.

19 Didau, D., & Rose, N. (2016). *What Every Teacher needs to know about Psychology*. Melton: John Catt Educational Ltd.

20 Menzies, L., & Baars, S. (2015). *The Alternative Should Not be Inferior: What Now for "Pushed out" Learners?* Inclusion Trust and LKMco (CfEY), Cambridge.

21 Frey, L. M., & Wilhite, K. (2005). Our five basic needs: Application for understanding the function of behavior. *Intervention in School and Clinic*, https://doi.org/10.1177/105345 12050400030401.

22 O'Brien, J. (2016). *Don't Send him in Tomorrow: Shining a Light on the Marginalised, Disenfranchised and Forgotten Children of Today's Schools*. Independent Thinking Press, Bancyfelin.

23 Bennett, T. (2013). '*The TWO biggest Problems in Education that no one takes Seriously*,' Retrieved April 20, 2005, from http://community.tes.co.uk/tom_bennett/b/weblog/archive/2013/11/16/the-two-biggest-problems-in-education-that-no-one-takes-seriously-1-behaviour.aspx.

24 Carter, S. C., & Heritage Foundation (Washington, D. C. (2000). *No Excuses: Lessons from 21 High-Performing, High-poverty Schools*. Heritage Foundation, Washington DC.

25 House of Commons Education Select Committee. (2018). *Forgotten Children: Alternative Provision and The Scandal of ever Increasing Exclusions Fifth Report of Session 2017–19 Report*, together with formal minutes relating to the report The Education Committee. Retrieved from www.parliament.uk.

26 Heitzeg, N. A. (2009). Education or incarceration: Zero tolerance policies and the school to prison pipeline. *Forum on Public Policy: A Journal of the Oxford Round Table, 9*.

27 Hirschfield, P. J. (2008). Preparing for prison?. *Theoretical Criminology*, *12*(1), 79–101. https://doi.org/10.1177/1362480607085795.

28 Briggs, D. (2010). "The world is out to get me, bruv": Life after school "exclusion". *Safer Communities*, *9*(2), 9–19. https://doi.org/10.5042/sc.2010.0222.

29 Stirling, M. (1992). How many pupils are being excluded? *British Journal of Special Education*, *19*(4), 128–130. https://doi.org/10.1111/j.1467-8578.1992.tb01383.x.

30 Woodley, H. (2017). *"Managed Move" Or A Shifting Of The Problem?* Retrieved May 13, 2020, from https://www.teachertoolkit.co.uk/2017/02/24/managed-move-or-a-shifting-of-the-problem/.

31 Staufenburg, J. (2017). *Home Education Rises, with Schools left to "Pick up Pieces"*, Retrieved May 13, 2020, from Schools Week website: https://schoolsweek.co.uk/home-education-doubles-with-schools-left-to-pick-up-pieces-when-it-fails/.

32 Nye, P., & Thomson, D. (2018). *Who's Left 2018, Part One: The Main Findings – FFT Education Datalab*, Retrieved May 13, 2020, from FFT Datalab. https://ffteducationdatalab.org.uk/2018/06/whos-left-2018-part-one-the-main-findings/.

33 Nye, P. (2017). *Who's Left: The Main Findings – FFT Education Datalab*, Retrieved May 13, 2020, from FFT Datalab. https://ffteducationdatalab.org.uk/2017/01/whos-left-the-main-findings/.

34 Noden, P., West, A., & Hind, A. (2014). *Banding and Ballots: Secondary school admissions in England: Admissions in 2012/13 and the impact of growth of Academies.*

35 Allen, R., & Parameshwaran, M. (2016). *The Sutton Trust's Caught Out Research - April 2016*, Retrieved May 13, 2020, from https://www.slideshare.net/SirPeterLampl/the-sutton-trusts-caught-out-research-april-2016.

36 Weldon, M. (2018). *Secondary School Choice and Selection Insights from new National Preferences Data*. Department for Education, London.

37 Department for Education (2017). *Exclusion from maintained schools, academies and pupil referral units in England Statutory guidance for those with legal responsibilities in relation to exclusion*. Department for Education, London.

38 Department for Education (2018). *Permanent and Fixed-Period Exclusions in England: 2016 to 2017 – GOV.UK*, Retrieved May 13, 2020, from https://www.gov.uk/government/statistics/permanent-and-fixed-period-exclusions-in-england-2016-to-2017.

39 *Ibid.*

40 Allen, R. (n.d.). *Schools Should be held Accountable for all the Pupils They Teach - FFT Education Datalab*, Retrieved May 13, 2020, from https://ffteducationdatalab.org.uk/2016/01/schools-should-be-held-accountable-for-all-the-pupils-they-teach/.

41 Department for Education (2018). *Schools, Pupils and their Characteristics: January 2018 – GOV.UK*, Retrieved May 13, 2020, from https://www.gov.uk/government/statistics/schools-pupils-and-their-characteristics-january-2018.

42 Menzies, L., & Baars, S. (2015). *The Alternative should not be Inferior: What now for "Pushed Out" learners?* Inclusion Trust and The Centre for Education and Youth (LKMco).

43 Menzies, L., Bernardes, E., & Huband-Thompson, Billy, (2018). *Schools and Youth Mental Health: A Briefing on Current Challenges and Ways Forward*. Minds Ahead and The Centre for Education and Youth (LKMco), Cambridge.

44 Shaw, B., Bernardes, E., Trethewey, A., & Menzies, L. (n.d.). *Special Educational Needs and their Links to Poverty*. The Joseph Rowntree Foundation and The Centre for Education and Youth (LKMco), York.

45 Ridge, T. (2011). The everyday costs of poverty in childhood: A review of qualitative research exploring the lives and experiences of low-income children in the UK. *Children & Society*, *25*(1), 73–84. https://doi.org/10.1111/j.1099-0860.2010.00345.x.

46 Mazzoli Smith, L., & Todd, L. (2019). Conceptualising poverty as a barrier to learning through 'Poverty proofing the school day': The genesis and impacts of stigmatisation. *British Educational Research Journal*, *45*(2), 356–371. https://doi.org/10.1002/berj.3506.

47 Tay, L., & Diener, E. (2011). Needs and subjective well-being around the world. *Journal of Personality and Social Psychology*, *101*(2), 354–365. https://doi.org/10.1037/a0023779.

48 Orazem, P. F., Glewwe, P., Patrinos, H., & Bank, W. (2009). *The Benefits and Costs of Alternative Strategies to Improve Educational Outcomes*, Retrieved from http://lib. dr.iastate.edu/econ_las_pubs.

49 Afridi, F., Barooah, B., & Somanathan, R. (2013). *School Meals and Classroom Effort: Evidence from India School Meals and Classroom Effort: Evidence from India.* International Growth Centre, London.

50 Magic Breakfast | Projects | Education Endowment Foundation | EEF, (2019). Retrieved May 13, 2020, from https://educationendowmentfoundation.org.uk/projects-and-evaluation/projects/magic-breakfast/.

51 Lake, P. (2005). Recognizing reactive attachment disorder. *Behavioral Health Management*, *25*(5), 41–44.

52 *The Long Term Costs of Literacy Difficulties*, 2nd Edition. (2009). Every Child a Chance Trust, London.

53 Lee, W. (2013). *A Generation Adrift*. The Communication Trust, London.

54 *"Always Someone Else's Problem": Office of the Children's Commissioner's Report on Illegal Exclusions*, (2013). Office of the Children's Commissioner, London.

55 Menzies, L. (2017). *No Excuses Versus Inclusion: Impossible to reconcile? – CfEY*, Retrieved May 13, 2020, from https://cfey.org/news-and-events/2017/03/no-excuses-versus-inclusion-impossible-reconcile/.

56 Gedge, N. (2016). *Inclusion for Primary School Teachers*, London: Bloomsbury Education.

57 Stahl, G., & Dale, P. (2013). Success on the decks: Working-class boys, education and turning the tables on perceptions of failure. *Gender and Education*, *25*(3), 357–372. https://doi.org/10.1080/09540253.2012.756856.

58 Baars, S., Shaw, B., Mulcahy, E., & Menzies, L. (2018). *School Cultures and Practices: Supporting the Attainment of Disadvantaged Pupils*, Retrieved from http://www. academia.edu/download/57299562/London_Effect_Qual_Research_-_Research_Report_ FINAL_v2_1.pdf.

59 McInerney, L. (2018). *Blame Cuts – not Headteachers – for School Exclusions | Laura McInerney | Education | The Guardian*, Retrieved May 13, 2020, from https://www. theguardian.com/education/2018/sep/18/blame-cuts-not-headteachers-school-exclusions-laura-mcinerney.

60 McInerney, L. (2020). *The Tories are Hiding from Blame for Youth Crime. That's not on, The Guardian*, Retrieved May 13, 2020, from. https://www.theguardian.com/education/2020/ jan/21/tories-hiding-from-blame-youth-crime-cuts-schools-support?fbclid=IwAR2PlenHu 82Rxv7i-98Nza1Oq3gqTHuDfzInF-bCL0SAwlhx08VzU8q80ZA.

61 Robinson, K., & Aronica, L. (2015). *Creative Schools: Revolutionizing Education from the Ground up*. Penguin, London.

62 Christodoulou, D. (2014). *Seven Myths About Education*, Retrieved from https://www. amazon.co.uk/Seven-Myths-About-Education-Christodoulou/dp/0415746825.

63 Willingham, D. T. (2010). *Why don't Students like School?: A Cognitive Scientist Answers Questions about how the Mind Works and What it means for the Classroom*. Jossey-Bass San, Francisco.

64 Millard, W., Bowen-Viner, K., Baars, S., & Menzies, L. (2019). *MORE THAN A JOB'S WORTH: Making Careers Education Age-Appropriate.* Founders4Schools and The Centre for Education and Youth (LKMco), Cambridge.

65 *EIF Guidebook: Nurture Groups,* (2017).

66 Mills, M., & Thomson, P. (2018). *Investigative Research into Alternative Provision. October 2018.* Centre for Social Justice, London.

67 Centre for Social Justice. (2018). *PROVIDING THE ALTERNATIVE How to Transform School Exclusion and the Support that Exists beyond,* Retrieved from www.centreforsocialjustice.org.uk@CSJthinktankDesignedbySoapbox, www.soapbox.co.uk.

68 *ibid.*

69 Parker, R., & Levinson, M. P. (2018). Student behaviour, motivation and the potential of attachment-aware schools to redefine the landscape. *British Educational Research Journal, 44*(5), 875–896. https://doi.org/10.1002/berj.3473.

70 *ibid.*

2 Special educational needs and disabilities

Bart Shaw

2.1 Introduction

Working as a geography teacher in a secondary school, I remember the day it dawned on me that I had become part of the problem.

James arrived at the school I taught in midway through Year 11. He had autism and seemed to be struggling at GCSE. He wrote well but seemed not to understand the concepts I was trying to teach. In those days we were encouraged to tier GCSE entries into higher and foundation papers, with those taking foundation papers limited to a C grade at best. My instinct was that James would be out of his depth on the higher paper so, thinking it was for the best, I suggested he take the foundation paper. Of course, I was wrong and James' mother knew that. Determined to advocate for her son, James' mother persuaded me to enter him for the higher paper. Over the next few months, I provided him with extra work and had the genuine pleasure of sitting with him after school, providing the extra support he was so keen to receive. Later that summer, the annual ritual of results day came around, and James clasped the exam board's verdict proudly. He had achieved the A* that he and his mother knew he was capable of.

I felt chastened but relieved by the experience and from then on have never doubted the critical importance of collaboration between parents and the services that support their children.

For thousands of young people with SEND, challenges with far more than an A* at stake are a daily occurrence. Every new professional, and every new service that comes into the young person's life, can mean a new hurdle to overcome. Far too often, young people and their parents have to "prove" the extent of a congenital disability or lifelong learning need on an annual basis. It can feel as though the system is designed to avoid "cheats" rather than to provide the best support possible for those with real needs.

Psychologically, as well as in terms of time and finance, battling for support is draining. Health, wellbeing and outcomes can all be compromised as a result. This is the problem I was part of. Advocating for your child's additional needs, and individualised support should not feel like a battle. Those from low-income backgrounds, or whose poverty or class, ethnicity, gender or sexual orientation often face additional discrimination which leads to further marginalisation, and that is unjust and unfair.

This chapter explains how SEND is managed in the English school system, and sets out the various barriers that are, sometimes unintentionally, placed before young people with SEND, and which lead to their marginalisation. It shows how, despite well-intentioned policy, and well-intentioned professionals like myself, young people like James can be let down by the education system.

The challenge in writing this chapter is to capture the diversity of experience within this group. Perhaps more so than any of the other marginalised groups included in this book, young people with SEND are diverse and heterogenous. Individual needs or disabilities vary hugely. Young people with SEND come from all sorts of socio-economic, ethnic and cultural backgrounds (although disproportionately, many are from low-income backgrounds). All these factors add layers of complexity to the puzzle of how to provide effective support.

This chapter therefore begins by introducing key themes in SEND policy before exploring the range of ways young people are marginalised in and outside of school and finally sets out a range of ways the situation could be improved.

2.2 SEND policy

Around 15% of children in primary and secondary schools in England are identified as having some form of SEND [1].

The 2014 Children and Families Act defines young people with SEND as being those who have:

> significantly greater difficulty in learning than the majority of others of the same age, or ... a disability which prevents or hinders him or her from making use of facilities of a kind generally provided for others of the same age in mainstream schools or mainstream post-16 institutions [2].

It is easy to see the subjectivity in such a definition. SEND should arguably be understood as a continuum rather than a binary either/or. Imagine one girl with multiple co-morbidities. This imagined young person might, for example, be 14 years old; have severe learning difficulties that limit their cognitive abilities to the extent that they are not able to grasp the concept of addition and subtraction; have a visible physical disability that confines them to a wheelchair; and health needs that require daily medication, such as a heart defect or epilepsy. It is likely that health, social care and educational professionals would agree this young person has "significantly greater difficulty in learning than the majority of others of the same age", or indeed, that her disabilities are likely to "hinder her from making use of facilities in a mainstream school". As a result, there is likely to be widespread professional agreement about this fact that this young person needs additional resources, if necessary funded by the state, to support her education.

On the other hand, consider a less clear-cut case: an eight-year-old boy whose needs do not come with a medical diagnosis yet, but who will go on to be diagnosed with a neurodevelopmental disorder in his teens. For now, they are cognitively able, but struggle to concentrate in class and are demonstrating some challenging behaviour. This young man's teachers are finding it hard to manage his needs and his mum suspects he may have ADHD. His GP feels similarly, and he has therefore been referred to a specialist for an assessment. On the other hand, his teacher, and the school SENCO, are less sure and perhaps without voicing their doubts, feel sceptical about the validity of an ADHD diagnosis in any case [3].

Is this young man demonstrating "significantly greater difficulty in learning than the majority of others of the same age"? Is he likely to receive additional support that meets their needs? Who should pay for this support? Is their classroom teacher trained and supported enough to meet his needs in a way that means he can thrive in his mainstream classroom, without disruption to others in the class? Should the school's already stretched pastoral staff spend time with him, or with another boy in his class who has anxiety? He may see a specialist and receive a diagnosis, but this medical confirmation might not change much in terms of the support he receives at school and he may still miss out on the support he is entitled to.

Whether or not a child is identified as having SEND (and therefore qualifies for additional support in their education) is thus not always straightforward. Over- and under-identification of SEND can have considerable negative consequences. Under-identification deprives children of support which they are entitled to, while over-identification (labelling a child as having a "disorder" when they may simply be making less progress than expected for other reasons) can divert resources away from children whose needs are greater. Over-identification may also lead to lowering of teacher expectations, or even contribute to children experiencing social stigma or bullying. Over-identification also runs the risk of schools missing the possibility that teachers themselves or specific teaching practices may be at least part of the picture when analysing the difficulties a child may be having with their education.

2.2.1 How have definitions of SEND changed over time?

At a system level, questions about defining the "boundaries" of SEND have been debated since the publicly funded education began. Shortly after the 1891 Elementary Education Act [4], which first introduced free, publicly funded education between the ages of 3 and 15, Gladstone's government of 1893 passed a bill requiring school boards and local government to provide education for deaf and blind children [5]. Six years later, in his third and final spell as Prime Minister, Lord Salisbury's government passed the "1899 Elementary Education (Defective and Epileptic Children) Act [6]" to ensure that local government identified and provided education for children meeting that description. Shortly before the outset of WW1, Asquith's government added a "Mentally Defective" category in its 1913 Elementary Education Act [7].

2.2.1.1 The medical model of disability in education

The system Lord Salisbury's government set up, alongside that for deaf and blind children, was thought of as entirely separate from mainstream schooling. Attitudes towards disability were firmly rooted in a "medical" or "deficit" model of understanding disability. This model frames disabilities in terms of what an individual is *unable* to do as a result of their condition. Mitigating problems for that individual therefore requires treatment of the condition through specialist practices (such as medicine). Understanding disability in this way can lead to marginalisation both in education and society, as schools, organisations and decision makers see individuals with disabilities as requiring specialist treatment separate from those without disabilities. For mainstream schools and teachers in particular, the medical model can reinforce the idea that educating a child with SEND is the responsibility of an expert or specialist.

Towards the end of the Second World War, the Conservative government of the time began to set out its vision for public services in peacetime. As part of this vision, Education Minister Rab Butler (who went on to be remembered as "the creator of the modern educational system") stood before Parliament to announce the creation of special schools under the 1944 Education Act. His announcement exemplified the medical model:

> A duty is laid upon local education authorities to ascertain all children who, because of disability of mind or body, need special attention... Our object is to provide the necessary flexibility, so as to enable advantage to be taken of new developments in medical education or psychological diagnosis and practice [8].

2.2.1.2 The social model of disability in education

By the late 1970s, education policy had begun to reflect a growing consensus amongst academics and disabled activists that disability reflected not only individual's bodies, but also the inflexibility of society and its institutions in allowing disabled people to come in from the margins. The term "social model of disability" began to be used to persuade policy makers to switch their focus away from treating individual's impairments, and instead to focus on changing environments and reducing barriers for disabled people [9].

The 1978 Warnock Report reflected this new way of thinking. It rejected previous categories of "handicaps" and instead used the phrase "special educational needs" to encourage schools and policy makers to focus first on learning needs rather than on individual learning disabilities. The report also brought together a small number of studies that attempted to quantify the number of children that might meet the new SEN category. The report concluded that an estimate of 1 in 6 might represent a "reasonable judgement". This estimate has had lasting power in guiding SEND policy. The 1981 Education Act required local education authorities to find places for children with SEND in mainstream schools where possible, and stated that when choosing schools, the wishes of parents and children themselves should be taken into account [10].

Education policy in England over the next decades retained the terminology of SEN, and reflected more of the social model of disability than education policy pre-Warnock, with at least a partial focus on inclusion in mainstream settings. The 1993 Education Act attempted to widen the net of support for SEND by setting out guidelines for identifying needs, particularly in the Early Years [11]. The Special Educational Needs Act 2001 further cemented the principle of inclusion by requiring that all pupils without a statement (the highest category of need) be educated in mainstream schools [12]. The Act reflected the "social model" of disability by requiring schools and other educational settings to provide adaptations to support pupils with SEND, and to reduce discrimination [13]. The Act also set a guideline of 20% of the population for what proportion of young people might be considered to have SEN at any one time (reflecting the influence of the Warnock Report more than two decades later).

2.2.1.3 Fractured oversight and ongoing marginalisation

Between 2010 to 2020 the government implemented considerable reform to the SEND system. There were a number of different drivers behind this including the desire to give more autonomy to schools in meeting needs, and a desire to simplify the system for young people with complex needs by bringing together health, social care and education in one package of support. Young people with complex SEND would now transition from the "Statements of Need" introduced after the Warnock Report in 1978, to a new system of Education, Health and Care Plans (EHCPs) in which parents and young people could set out bespoke support, partially paid for with a personal budget.

In 2014, the Parliamentary Under-Secretary of State for Children and Families, Edward Timpson, announced new legislation setting out reformed funding arrangements and support for young people with SEND, accompanied by a code of practice for schools and local authorities. Timpson argued that "the [SEND] system, despite so much effort, became too disjointed, complex and adversarial". The positive intention behind the new reforms was to place parents and young people at the heart of decision making around support for SEND. Timpson went so far as to address parents directly in his foreword to the Code of Practice, a document ostensibly aimed at professionals working with children:

> What you as parents think, feel and say is important. You should be listened to and you need to be fully involved in decisions that affect your children. That's what the new system is all about [14].

> *Edward Timpson*

The reforms also extended the reach of SEN categorisations to include young adults between 19 and 25 years old rather than just those aged 18 or younger.

Whilst the intentions behind the reform were positive, the policy changes created upheaval that many local authorities were simply not equipped to manage. The reforms landed in the middle of a dramatic scaling back of local authority capacity. Six years after the 2008 global financial crash, and four years into a coalition government committed to reducing public spending, local authorities had seen their funding slashed and staffing reduced. Many lacked the staff numbers to handle the paperwork involved in transitioning from statements to EHCPs. In some local authorities, an already adversarial relationship between parents and the gatekeepers of support, local authority (LA) SEND services, became more fraught as vulnerable young people were left in limbo.

Policy has shifted over time towards greater recognition of the education system's potential to support and include young people with SEND. The current system also carves out more space for young people to be involved in decisions that affect them. However, despite the progress that has been made over the longer term, many young people with SEND continue to be marginalised by the school system.

2.3 Marginalisation in mainstream schools

Part of the reason young people with SEND find themselves marginalised is because negative attitudes to disability, stigma and discrimination within society play out in schools as they do everywhere else. Three problems in particular highlight the ways in which young people with SEND find themselves on the margins in mainstream schools:

1. Social ostracisation by peers.

2. Informal exclusion from lessons.

3. Relatively low prioritisation of young people with SEND by school leaders.

2.3.1 Social ostracisation by peers

Young people with SEND are much more likely to be unhappy while at school than those without SEND because of isolation from friendship groups, and bullying from their peers. For example, a survey that gathered data from 253,755 children in 3699 schools across the UK exposed very different experiences of social life at school for young people with SEND and those without. The survey found that a much smaller proportion of children with SEND reported themselves as having friends at school (59% compared with 92% without SEND) and being happy at school (59% compared to 67%). At the same time children with SEND were disproportionately worried about bullying (38% compared with 25% without SEND [15]).

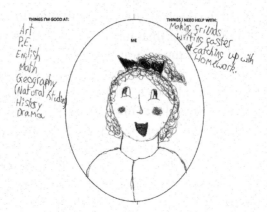

Figure 2.1: Self-portrait of a young person created as part of fieldwork for CfEY and Disability Rights UK's research on the experiences of young people with SEND in education.

Young people with SEND have shared innumerable experiences that underpin these statistics during the research I have undertaken with them. Working with a researcher from Disability Rights UK, my colleagues and I spent two terms speaking to young people in mainstream and special schools across the country. We carried out focus groups in which we heard about young people with SEND's school experiences and compared these with findings from focus groups held with young people without SEND. The findings were stark. Young people with SEND described small or non-existent social groups, resonating with previous research [16]. These groups and relationships often felt precarious as one participant explained:

> The [one] friend that I have now I've been friends with him since Year 1 so if I was like to move school or anything like that, I'd probably not have friends.
> *Young person with SEND in a mainstream school*

The young people we spoke to during our research also reported specific incidents of being bullied. Distressingly, these young people directly linked the bullying to their SEND saying:

> I'll walk into a class and I'm met with horrible comments because I walk differently because I have mobility... I walk with my feet turned out and I'm met with "penguin" or "retard", stuff like that.
> *Young person with SEND in a mainstream school*

Such experiences are all too common for young people with SEND. The Millennium Cohort Study is a major study tracking the lives of young people born in the year 2000. It found that young people with SEND were more likely than others to answer "all the time" to the questions about how often they experience bullying [17].

Schools need to be aware that social ostracisation is common for young people with SEND. As a result, schools' behaviour and anti-bullying policies should recognise the specific vulnerability of young people with SEND. Schools should encourage more active interventions by teachers to address bullying, name-calling and discrimination of young people with SEND, in similar ways to other forms of discrimination. At the same time, schools should put in place support with socialisation for young people with SEND, including support for dealing with the emotional and mental consequences of experiencing bullying. The evidence base for interventions to support socialisation is thin but growing. The Anti-Bullying Alliance highlights a number of practices that have some basis in evidence: some schools use "buddying" systems, whilst others use wider peer-education initiatives, such as encouraging peers to be supportive bystanders discouraging bullying by others [18]. Such interventions should form part of schools' toolkits for supporting young people with SEND. At the same time these interventions require evaluation to develop schools' understanding of how effective they are in reducing the vulnerability of young people with SEND.

2.3.2 Exclusion within schools (informal exclusion)

Inclusion of young people with SEND in lessons can be illusory since support for SEND pupils can lead to them having minimal contact with qualified teachers or peers without SEND.

Rob Webster is a SEND researcher based at UCL Institute of Education in London. Together with Professor Peter Blatchford, Rob has spent much of the last decade following a group of young people with EHCPs' experiences in education, together with a comparison group of average attainers. This study is the largest ever observation of young people with SEND in England and delivers uncomfortable findings.

Rob found that, even when young people with SEND are nominally included within mainstream schools, their experiences within the classroom and social time are often characterised by segregation and separation. For example, young people with SEND have far fewer direct interactions with teachers, far fewer interactions with peers, and are often placed in bottom sets which impact on their progress. The story below, taken from a blog [19] written by Rob, neatly encapsulates a typical experience for a young person with SEND:

Meet Reece. We join him in Year 5. He has a global learning delay and his expressive and receptive language skills are underdeveloped for his age. Each day, Mandy, a teaching assistant (TA), takes Reece out of the classroom with Sula and Nathan to work on their social language. They practise important skills such as greeting people, talking in turns and not interrupting.

But here's the thing: Sula and Nathan have communication difficulties, too. And while Mandy does a great job of trying to initiate and sustain conversation among the three children, progress is slow.

Fast forward to Year 9. Reece is sat with Jacqui, another TA, at his designated table in bottom-set science. His teacher is explaining that Mars's orbit of the Sun is almost twice as long as Earth's orbit.

It's not dissimilar to the teachers' orbit of the classroom. Because Jacqui is on hand to help, the teacher checks in with Reece about half as often as he does with other pupils.

And these are just snapshots of Reece's time in school. If you were to sit with him every day, you would witness a journey through the education system that is pock-marked with separation, segregation and unintentional outcomes [20].

This story highlights a second important finding from Rob's research: a system-wide over-reliance on non-teaching staff (Teaching Assistants or TAs) to teach young people with SEND. TAs are generally used to support individuals or small groups in class, to take intervention groups outside of the classroom, and support pupils with preparation for life beyond education [21].

In their earlier research, Rob, Peter and colleagues found that for many young people with SEND, the majority of their interactions in school are not with teachers or friends, but instead with a TA. Indeed, the more time a young person with SEND spent with a TA, the less time they had with a teacher. This arrangement was decisive in explaining findings that these pupils made less progress compared with their average-attaining peers, who did not receive support from TAs [22].

TAs themselves are skilled, valuable members of staff, the problem here is with the model of SEND support in mainstream schools, where funding is spent on "hours" of one-to-one support from a TA, and strategic decisions about how TAs are used are often counter-productive. It is all too easy to treat "hours of support" as the predominant currency of support rather than thinking carefully about how best to support each young person with their individual needs. Secondly, as Rob has shown, TA time can lead to "informal exclusion" within what should be an inclusive environment. Thirdly, this model of support only works if teacher and TA work together to tailor lessons and resources to individual children with SEND. However, a lack of time set aside for this planning, together with frequent changes of a child's TA often prevents shared planning from happening at all.

All mainstream schools need to rethink their use of staff to support children with SEND. This is an issue of prioritisation. Accountability pressures mean that school leaders understandably seek to improve the outcomes on which they are measured. For many school leaders, ensuring that the majority of children in the school meet or exceed the national average in exam results (particularly pupils from low-income backgrounds), takes precedence. Children with SEND are sometimes the least likely to meet national averages. Yet instead of being prioritised and placed in classes with the strongest teachers, alongside additional support and feedback from those teachers – they are often marginalised. Thus, they receive lower quality teaching than those who might progress more easily.

Beyond accountability, children with SEND's negative experiences and unhappiness at school should provide compelling reasons for school leaders to prioritise and champion children with SEND within their schools. Perhaps this is a question of system as well as school leadership. How often do you hear education ministers mentioning, challenging, or celebrating SEND provision in schools? How often do you read about anything other than the failings of children with SEND in newspapers? SEND should be placed closer to the centre of practice in mainstream schools. In doing so, we might then avoid the pitfalls that occur when children with SEND are marginalised from the school system altogether.

2.3.3 Exclusion from schools

Grace is 11 years old. I came across Grace whilst on the phone, interviewing her mother, Jill, as part of a research project. This research aimed to help a local authority rebuild damaged relationships with parents and restore trust in the system. Grace was at home on a Tuesday because she did not have a school, and was being "educated at home". Neither Grace nor Jill wanted this.

Grace had been asked to leave several primary schools, none through "formal exclusion", but in each case when Jill was persuaded that the school was unable to meet Grace's needs. Things had not turned out well for Grace. Both she and Jill felt that the social isolation of home schooling had had a damaging effect on their mental health. Jill had had to leave work to care for Grace, and their relationship, which had previously been strong, was now fractured, as Jill tried to balance her new-found dual role as mother and teacher. In the end, Jill decided that her relation with Grace had to win out. As a consequence, there were fewer conflicts, but also less learning. Yet at the time of our conversation, the local authority had been seeking a school place for Grace for over a year.

Part of the reason that young people with SEND are marginalised is that, like Grace, they are more likely to be excluded from or denied access to education. As was noted in Chapter 1, young people with SEND are three times more likely to be excluded from school than those without SEND, and official exclusion rates, as bad as they are, probably mask an even greater issue of informal exclusions, as Ofsted Annual Report in 2017 recognises:

> Some parents reported that they had been asked to keep their children at home because leaders said that they could not meet their children's needs. This is unacceptable [23].
>
> *Ofsted Annual Report 2017*

School admissions can also provide ample opportunities for young people with SEND to fall through the gaps, even before they start school. Perverse incentives for schools, whereby headteachers are judged to succeed or fail on the strength of academic exam results, lead to a temptation to discourage pupils who might find it harder to progress from applying. In my research I have come across countless examples of young people with SEND facing barriers when applying to schools. For example, one teacher told me about her school asking SENCOs *not* to attend open evenings, because they wanted parents to believe there was less support for pupils with SEND in the school than there was in reality. Another told us of teachers being told not to encourage parents of young people with SEND to apply to a school "because they already have enough of this type of learner". Unfortunately, such practises appear to be widespread across the country.

This should not happen. Schools need better support, sooner, in order to meet all their pupils needs. As the inappropriate use of TAs exemplifies, school leaders do not always have a secure understanding of how to meet children with SEND's needs. Yet at the very least, school leaders should:

- Emphasise individual teachers' responsibility for every child in their class/ setting

- Ensure teachers in mainstream settings plan effectively for pupils with SEND, taking more a more personalised approach that they would otherwise, including:

  - Individualised assessment that allows teachers to understand progress and gaps in learning.

  - Continuous reflection on what strategies or approaches work for an individual pupil with SEND, and which do not.

This reflective process has been termed "the graduated approach" [24].

- Share clear expectations regarding appropriate deployment and roles for teachers and support staff

- Ensure all staff receiving training on:

  - Working effectively with parents, building productive relationships.

  - Working with health and care professionals.

  - Where to find specialist support, such as speech and language therapy, for specific needs.

2.4 Marginalisation in the wider education system

Whilst the issues described above affect pupils in almost all English schools, for some young people, the extent of their need means that they attend schools outside the mainstream, either at special schools, in alternative provision, hospital schools, or outside the school system altogether. Many special schools and alternative providers are outstanding, and serve the children that attend them extremely well. However, alternative providers and special schools face a number of additional challenges which result in these institutions, and thus the young people that attend them, on the margins of the education system.

2.4.1 Special schools on the margins

Over time, there has been a gradual move away from special education, to a greater focus on including children with SEND in the mainstream. The 1980s and 1990s saw a steady decline in the number of special schools in England. Since the turn of the millennium however there has been a slight increase, mainly in the independent sector, with a continuing reduction in the number of state-funded special schools [25].

In the early 2000s, a number of studies set out to answer the question of whether children with SEND receive a better education in special or mainstream sector but failed to reach a firm conclusion either way. Ofsted focused its study on children with learning difficulties and found effective provision in both the special and mainstream sectors. A study by Reed et al. (2012) focused on children with Autism Spectrum Disorders, concentrating on comparing social outcomes. Reed et al. concluded that children in special schools made greater progress [26]. Clearly, there is no simple answer and we should recognise that such studies only show the relative merits of the sectors as they stand, rather than as they could be if all settings embodied best practice.

Overall, I would argue that special schools play a hugely important role in educating children with the most complex needs but are themselves marginalised within our education system, with negative impacts for the children that attend. These are children whose needs are currently not met by mainstream schools and whose parents, in many cases have chosen specialist provision (or have felt there was no choice other than a special school). Yet, despite the sector's importance and the particular challenges that children who are educated in these schools face, special schools rarely feature in the policy discourse, and numerous key documents fail to even mention them. For example, in 2019 the Department for Education published a new teacher recruitment and retention strategy [27]. However, despite special schools facing worrying staff shortages, the strategy failed to mention special schools at all. This omission, like many others, appeared to place special schools on the margins of the system.

Yet, one way of improving special schools' standing in the minds of existing and prospective teachers is to encourage more movement between special and mainstream providers. This would allow more cross-pollination of ideas and improve practice for children with SEND *and* children without SEND. Mobility could be encouraged by developing:

- Pathways for career development that involve placements in special schools for mainstream teachers and vice versa.

- SEND qualifications with additional salary attached that require experience in both settings.

- Fast-track leadership courses that require experience in both settings.

Furthermore, teacher recruitment should itself be inclusive with adverts featuring both special and mainstream schools. This would both help tackle recruitment difficulties in special schools, but might also widen the pool of potential teachers by appealing to those with experience working with young disabled people, or with a particular interest in working in special schools.

Accountability is another thorny issue facing special schools. Accountability can serve different purposes, and the relative importance of each purpose is heavily disputed. Earley and Weindling (2004) differentiate between four types of accountability: moral; professional; contractual; and market accountability [28]. For schools, therefore, accountability can be seen as serving four purposes:

- Driving improvements in schools in order to produce better outcomes for pupils.

- Identifying schools that are struggling, and in need support.

- Ensuring state funding is spent on the purposes it is intended for.

- Enabling parents to choose between schools.

For most mainstream schools the accountability system serves at least some of these purposes, at least in part but this is not the case for many special schools since many of their pupils do not take exams such as GCSEs and SATs. Thus, special schools sit at the margins of accountability system leaving pupils, schools, government and parents without a strong understanding of whether provision is good, and how it could be improved.

Despite their important role in educating some of the most vulnerable young people, policy discourse has little to say about either the quality of, or the challenges faced by special schools and special and mainstream schools too often operate in discrete silos. More therefore needs to be done to attract teachers to the special school sector and to build bridges.

2.5 Transitions to adulthood

The need for support in making the transition to adulthood after the age of 18 is often greater for young people with SEND. Once young people with SEND move out of the education system, they are at increased risk (compared to those without SEND) of being frozen out of the world of work as well as social groups and activities. Jarlath O'Brien, in his book on the pitfalls of inclusion and exclusion of young people with SEND, "Don't Send Him in Tomorrow", highlights a number of stark outcomes for adults with learning difficulties and SEND. Those with SEND are twice as likely as others to live in poverty, three times as likely to end up in prison, four times as likely to experience mental health problems, seven times less likely to find paid work, and are likely to die 15 years younger on average [29].

Although policy is beginning to recognise this greater need, society and the state do not yet support young people with SEND adequately, and this results in their being marginalised as they transition to adulthood.

Preparing young people with SEND for life after education is especially important. We know that adults with disabilities face discrimination in the workplace, meaning that they are less likely to be working, and more likely to be in low-paid jobs [30]. Meaningful careers education and work experience is therefore particularly important for young people with SEND. Yet research by the Careers and Enterprise Company suggests that young people with SEND do not get the kind of longer-term, personalised and co-designed support that evidence suggests is most likely to help them. Instead, transition support is often short-term and not targeted at each young person's individual needs. Young people with SEND are therefore more likely to leave education without qualifications, and with a lower likelihood of fulfilling their potential [31].

The further education (FE) sector is a common destination for young people with SEND after the age of 16. However, colleges are not set up well enough to support young people with SEND and many of these young people find themselves dropping off a cliff edge of support (both pastoral and academic) when they start college.

Young people with SEND may need study programmes that include content related to learning to live independently and, as at school, they may need tailored learning support. Meanwhile, outside of study programmes, life at an FE college can be unstructured and self-directed. Interactions with other young people can be difficult.

These needs appear not to be met in FE. In 2016, Ofsted published a review of SEND provision in Further Education [32]. Their conclusions were damning. While they found some pockets of effective provision, generally, young people with SEND were being let down. Often, providers lacked staff with expertise and skills to support young people's needs. Study programmes did not always meet young people's individual needs, with tutors complaining that they were not always able to access information about young people's needs from other professionals. Oversight was also patchy, with many local authorities, and the Education Funding Agency unable to evaluate the impact of SEND support in FE.

Part of the cause of these difficulties lies in the perfect storm of local authority restructuring combined with thread-bare funding and SEND reforms requiring LAs to act as commissioners and coordinators of services. Ofsted's 2016 report makes this clear, explaining that extensive restructuring in "almost all" Local Authorities since 2010 had led to:

> the loss of experienced staff with specialist expertise in working with young people with SEND... Only a few local authorities had sufficiently prioritised provision for young people with high needs following the introduction of the Children and Families Act 2014 [33].

Ofsted 2016

2.6 Conclusion

Young people with SEND's educational experiences are too often wholly unsatisfactory. For every young person like James, who achieves well, despite mistakes made by teachers like me, there are a number of children like Grace, who are let down by the education system in ways that are likely to contribute to real difficulties later in life.

> Children with SEND ... often have a much poorer experience of the education system than their peers [34].
>
> *Ofsted Annual Report 2017*

SEND permeates every chapter in this book. For children in each group, combinations of poverty, health and social marginalisation leads to higher than average rates of SEND. Interlinked with this is the challenge for schools of meeting an ever-widening range of individual learning needs. Over decades, the education system has become better at meeting these needs, but a huge gap remains and ultimately even if England's education system produces relatively good outcomes on average, this is not the case for most children with SEND.

As we have seen, the story for children with SEND does not end when they leave school. How will James, who is clearly academically able to succeed at a higher level, and who might choose to pursue a degree course, be supported through Higher Education, and into graduate employment? Will it be left to his mother who advocates for him at every turn for the support which she knows will help him, but he finds hard to articulate? How responsive will employers be to those aspects of his potential that need a different approach than they are used to providing, in order for him to realise that potential.

What will the future hold for Grace? How will her negative experience of schooling affect her interactions with professionals, carers or support workers in her adult life? How sustainable, in the longer term, is the support that she currently receives almost exclusively from her mother?

These questions are outside the scope of a book on the education system, but the extent which we are alive and responsive to SEND in the education system can provide a more stable platform for the children that experience it. How then, can we better support children with SEND, and ensure that our education system truly works for all, not just those that fit in?

2.7 Taking action

- For a long time, the special school sector has been separated or siloed from the mainstream sector. One quick win for the both the mainstream and special education sectors would be to encourage more movement of teachers and support staff between special and mainstream provision. This would allow more cross-pollination of ideas improving practice for children with SEND *and* children without SEND. A number of steps could be taken to ensure this happens:

- Placing mainstream teachers in special schools and vice versa as part of career development pathways.
- New specialist SEND qualifications that require teachers to have experience in both sectors.
- Fast-track leadership courses that require experience in both settings.

- Both mainstream and special schools struggle with staff recruitment. Recruitment campaigns should feature career opportunities in special schools in order to encourage recruits to work in these schools as well as to widen the pool of potential teachers by attracting those who have experience working with young disabled people, or an interest in special schools.

- Provision for SEND pupils is often a lower priority in mainstream schools compared to provision for pupil eligible children. This is despite the fact that both groups overlap, and include a similar proportion of pupils, as well as the fact that outcomes for SEND pupils are poor and they have additional vulnerabilities.

  - School leaders in mainstream schools should therefore be encouraged to prioritise SEND provision more highly. There are a number of ways to achieve this:

- More consistent emphasis on SEND across all areas of the Ofsted framework (including leadership, teaching and learning, pastoral care).

- Recruiting and training inspectors with a better understanding of SEND.

- Politicians raising the profile of SEND by talking more about inclusive schools, special schools. SEND pupils and their achievements.

- New awards, similar to the Pupil Premium Award and the nasen awards for schools with excellent SEND provision.

- Professionals need enhanced training to understand how their practice impacts on children with SEND. Many leaders do not know how to improve outcomes for SEND, while teachers and SENCOs are often unaware of resources that could help guide their practice.

- Given the wide range of needs that fall under the SEND umbrella, support and development should focus on key fundamentals that underpin good practice regardless of the type of SEND, for example:

  - Emphasising teachers' responsibility for every child in their class/setting.

  - Ensuring teachers understand and use the graduated response to meeting SEN.

  - Exploring how to deploy support staff effectively and outlining appropriate roles for teachers and support staff.

- Explaining how to find specialist support, such as speech and language therapy.

- Working with parents and carers as well as health and care professionals.

- Ensuring that all staff are aware of the research on the high levels of bullying experienced by children with SEND, are receive training on how to recognise and handle bullying when it occurs.

■ Schools cannot provide good SEND provision in isolation. SEND pupils living in any given locality need a carefully stitched together patchwork of support involving teachers, health care professionals and social workers and schools cannot be expected to coordinate this.

- Demand for support has increased without a concurrent increase in the supply of specialist services and this has taken place in the context of changing policy and diminished local authority capacity.

■ Professionals interacting with parents and young people must receive adequate training and be given the time and space to interact meaningfully. Resourcing and capacity must therefore be increased so that local authority caseworkers are no longer handling hundreds of cases.

■ Local Authorities attempt to balance a responsibility for determining eligibility for support with pressure to keep costs down. This causes a serious conflict of interest, and these two functions may therefore need to be separated in future.

■ Improving universal services such as the quality of teaching and pastoral care of pupils with SEND in mainstream schools should be seen as valuable way of reducing demand for specialist services.

Further reading

Don't Send Him in Tomorrow: O'Brien, J. (2016) Carmarthen: Independent Thinking Press.

Special Educational Needs and their Links to Poverty: Shaw, B., Bernades, E., Trethewey, A., and Menzies, L. (2016) London: Joseph Rowntree Foundation. Available online: https://cfey.org/wp-content/uploads/2016/02/Special-educational-needs-and-their-links-to-poverty.pdf

Joining the Dots: Have Recent Reforms Worked for those with SEND?: Bernardes, E., B. Shaw, L. Menzies, and S. Baars. (2015) London: Driver Youth Trust. Available online: https://www.cfey.org/wp-content/uploads/2015/10/DYT_JoinTheDotsReportOctober2015-2.pdf

The Special Educational Needs in Secondary Education (SENSE) Study: Final Report: Blatchford, P., and Webster, R. (2017) London: The Nuffield Foundation. Available online: http://maximisingtas.co.uk/assets/content/sense-final-report.pdf

Special or Unique: Young people's attitudes to disability: Odell, E. (2018) London: Disability Rights UK. Available online: https://www.disabilityrightsuk.org/sites/default/files/DR%20UK%20Special%20or%20Unique%20August%202019.pdf

References

1 Department for Education (2019) *Special Educational Needs in England*. London. Department for Education. Available online: https://assets.publishing.service.gov.uk/ government/uploads/system/uploads/attachment_data/file/814244/SEN_2019_Text. docx.pdf.

2 http://www.legislation.gov.uk/ukpga/2014/6/part/3/crossheading/special-educational-needs-etc/enacted?view=plain.

3 Mueller A. K., Fuermaier A. B., Koerts J., and Tucha L.. (2012) *Stigma in attention deficit hyperactivity disorder*. ADHD Attention Deficit and Hyperactivity Disorders, 4(3):101–114. https://www.ncbi.nlm.nih.gov/pmc/articles/PMC3430836/.

4 Elementary Education Act 1891. http://www.educationengland.org.uk/documents/ acts/1891-elementary-education-act.html.

5 Elementary Education (Deaf and Blind Children) Act 1893. http://www.educationeng land.org.uk/documents/acts/1893-elem-educ-blind-deaf-act.html.

6 Elementary Education (Defective and Epileptic Children) Act 1899. http://www. educationengland.org.uk/documents/acts/1899-el-ed-def-epi-children-act.html.

7 Mental Deficiency Act 1913. http://www.educationengland.org.uk/documents/acts/1913-mental-deficiency-act.html.

8 Hansard *Second Reading of the Education Bill 1944* https://api.parliament.uk/historic-hansard/commons/1944/jan/19/education-bill.

9 Oliver, M. (2004) *The social model in action: if I had a hammer.* In Colin Barnes and Geof Mercer (Eds) *Implementing the Social Model of Disability: Theory and Research.* Leeds: The Disability Press. pp. 18–31 https://disability-studies.leeds.ac.uk/wp-content/ uploads/sites/40/library/Barnes-implementing-the-social-model-chapter-2.pdf.

10 Education Act 1981 http://www.legislation.gov.uk/ukpga/1981/60/enacted.

11 Education Act 1993 http://www.legislation.gov.uk/ukpga/1993/35/pdfs/ukpga_ 19930035_en.pdf.

12 http://www.legislation.gov.uk/ukpga/2001/10/contents.

13 Special Needs and Disability Act 2001 http://www.legislation.gov.uk/ukpga/2001/10/ contents.

14 Department for Education, and Timpson, E. (2014) *Special Educational Needs and Disability: A Guide for Parents and Carers.* London: Department for Education. Available online: https://www.gov.uk/government/uploads/system/uploads/attachment_ data/ file/417435/Special_educational_needs_and_disabilites_guide_for_parents_and_ carers.pdf.

15 Chamberlain, T. George, N. Golden, S. Walker, F., and Benton, T. (2010) *Tellus4 National Report.* London: National Foundation for Educational Research.

16 Bossaert, G., Colpin, H., Pijl, S. J., and Petry, K. (2013) Truly included? A literature study focusing on the social dimension of inclusion in education. *International Journal of Inclusive Education,* 17(1), 60–79. https://doi.org/10.1080/13603116.2011.580464.

17 Chatzitheochari, Stella, Parsons, Samantha, and Platt, Lucinda (2016) Doubly disadvantaged?: bullying experiences among disabled children and young people in England. *Sociology,* online. pp. 1–19.

18 McLoughlin, C. Byers, R., and Peppin-Vaughan, R. (2010) *Responding to bullying amongst children with Special Educational Needs and/or Disabilities.* University of Cambridge for the Anti-Bullying Alliance. Available online: https://www.anti-bullyingalliance.org.uk/ sites/default/files/uploads/SEND_bullying_Literature_Review.pdf.

19 Webster, R (2018) *The Myth of Inclusion*. Times Educational Supplement. Available online. https://www.tes.com/news/toyoufromtes-myth-inclusion.

20 ibid.

21 Carroll, J., Bradley, L., Crawford, H., Hannant, P., Johnson, H., and Thompson, A. (2017) *SEN Support: A Rapid Evidence Assessment*. UK Government (Home Office).

22 Webster, R., Blatchford, P., Bassett, P., Brown, P., Martin, C., and Russell, A. (2010) 'Double standards and first principles: Framing teaching assistant support for pupils with special educational needs'. *European Journal of Special Educational Needs*, 25 (4): 319–336.

23 Ofsted (2017) *Ofsted Annual Report 2016/17: Education, Children's Services and Skills*. London: Ofsted. Available online:https://www.gov.uk/government/publications/ofsted-annual-report-201617-education-childrens-services-and-skills.

24 nasen (2014) *SEN Support and the Graduated Approach*. Available online: https://nasen.org.uk/uploads/assets/7f6a967f-adc3-4ea9-8668320016bc5595/SENsupportpress.pdf.

25 Scott, S., and McNeish, D. (2013) *Leadership of Special Schools: Issues and challenges*. London: Department for Education. http://www.ofsted.gov.uk/resources/inclusion-does-it-matter-where-pupils-are-taught https://assets.publishing.service.gov.uk/government/uploads/system/uploads/attachment_data/file/335724/Leadership-of-special-schools-issues-and-challenges.pdf.

26 Reed, P. Osborne, L., and Waddington, E. (2012) *A comparative study of the impact of mainstream and special school placement on the behaviour of children with Autism Spectrum Disorders. British Educational Research Journal*, 38(5): 749–763, October 2012.

27 Department for Education (2019) *Teacher Recruitment and Retention Strategy*. Available online: https://assets.publishing.service.gov.uk/government/uploads/system/uploads/attachment_data/file/786856/DFE_Teacher_Retention_Strategy_Report.pdf.

28 Earley, P., and Weindling, D. (2004) *Understanding School Leadership*. London: Paul Chapman Publishing.

29 O'Brien, J. (2016) *"Don't Send Him in Tomorrow"*. Carmarthen: Independent Thinking Press.

30 MacInnes, T., Aldridge, H., Bushe, S., Kenway, P., and Tinson, A. (2013) *Monitoring Poverty and Social Exclusion*. York: Joseph Rowntree Foundation. Available online: https://www.jrf.org.uk/report/monitoring-poverty-and-social-exclusion-2013.

31 Hansen, J., Codina, G., and Neary, S. (2017) *Transition Programmes for Young Adults with SEND*. Careers and Enterprise Company. Available online: https://www.careersan-denterprise.co.uk/sites/default/files/uploaded/careers-enterprise-what-works-report-transition-prog.pdf.pdf.

32 Ofsted (2016) *Moving Forward? How well the Further Education and Skills Sector is Preparing Young People with High Needs for Adult Life*. Available online: https://assets.publishing.service.gov.uk/government/uploads/system/uploads/attachment_data/file/509480/High_Need_Learners_FE_Skills.pdf.

33 Ibid.

34 Ofsted (2016) *The Annual Report of Her Majesty's Chief Inspector of Education, Children's Services and Skills 2016/17*. Available online: https://assets.publishing.service.gov.uk/government/uploads/system/uploads/attachment_data/file/666871/Ofsted_Annual_Report_2016-17_Accessible.pdf.

35 Ofsted (2006) *Inclusion: Does it Matter Where Pupils are Taught? Provision and Outcomes in Different Settings for Pupils with Learning Difficulties and Disabilities*. London: Ofsted. Available online: http://www.ofsted.gov.uk/resources/inclusion-does-it-matter-where-pupils-are-taught.

3 Mental health

Alix Robertson

3.1 Introduction

When I was at secondary school in the early 2000s, mental health was not a topic that we talked about, either in lessons with teachers or privately with peers. I knew I was not the only student in my year group with an eating disorder – but only through close observation and an awkward encounter with a girl from my English class in the foyer of the local health centre.

That health centre was the one location where people did want to discuss "what was wrong with me". It was a jack of all trades unit where they also sent vulnerable elderly people and teen pregnancy cases. I ended up there after being dragged to a couple of meetings with my GP by my mother, before being transferred to a specialist. He committed me to a weekly session at the health centre with a woman who wore giant, jangly earrings and looked like she might also run a local shop dealing in crystals and incense. Apart from my mother, she was the only person who spoke about my anorexia, reliably cocking her head sympathetically to one side and saying "so, how's it been?" week-in, week-out, but offering nothing else of any use.

My name and photo were on a bulletin board in the staffroom because of my diagnosis, and in the school was instructed that I must stuff down a high-calorie packed lunch every day in the presence of an adult witness who could tick off my consumption on a sheet. A teacher I did not know very well became my jailor; but she never really talked about what was going on. The only time we did not sit in silence through the embarrassing process was one occasion when she looked at me in frustration and said: "Why can't you just eat like a normal person?"

After being threatened with an inpatient placement at a London hospital that would mean forgoing the place I had been offered at university, I managed to put on enough weight to be signed off and released. But the treatment I received had mostly focused on what I was doing – starving myself – rather than why I was doing it, an altogether more complicated question. So, as soon as I was left to my own devices again as an undergraduate in a new city away from home, I was back at square one. This time it resulted in two years of weekly outpatient treatment at a specialist hospital, where I would sit in the waiting room and watch the really serious cases drift in and out of the dining hall or recreation room like ghosts.

The discussion around mental health has improved since the early 2000s. Celebrities now speak out about their struggles with anxiety and/or depression, and Instagram influencers walk their followers through daily struggles with eye-opening honesty. Overall, I think the public's understanding of mental health has changed for the better, with people now seeing it as something that everyone has, which needs to be nurtured in the same way as our physical health. However, alongside progress in the way we think and talk about mental health, have come new challenges that young people wrangle with every day. The intensity of social media, the pressures of a high stakes exam system, and the uncertainty created by political and environmental turmoil, are all threats to the positive mental health of "Gen Z".

Meanwhile, public services are stretched beyond belief. I did not think much of treatment I received at the time, but on reflection I was really very lucky to have had access to it. It is not enough for us to be able to talk more openly about mental health challenges if services are not sufficiently resourced to support an increasing number of referrals.

We still have a long way to go before young people facing mental health problems can feel assured that they will get the help they need. In this chapter, I argue that timely and personalised support for young people struggling with mental health challenges is vital in ensuring they do not go on to find themselves marginalised in society.

3.1 Defining mental health

3.1.1 What is mental health and what is wellbeing?

Mental health can be difficult to define, and mental ill-health can mean different things to different people. The World Health Organization (WHO) defines mental health as a state of wellbeing. Good mental health means every individual:

> ...realises his or her own potential, can cope with the normal stresses of life, can work productively and fruitfully, and is able to make a contribution to her or his community [1].

Alongside this, wellbeing is defined separately by the WHO, as something that is both subjective and objective. Wellbeing is made up of both a person's own experience of their life, as well as how their life circumstances compare with social norms and values.

> This definition says that wellbeing and health are interactive concepts with some common determinants, such as health and social systems [2].

Wellbeing is linked to a range of factors and circumstances including health, education, work, social relationships, built and natural environments, security, civic engagement and governance, housing and work-life balance. The state of a person's mental health "can change as circumstances change and as you move through different stages of your life" [3] and it is worth noting that during adolescence, it is developmentally appropriate to experience more difficult emotions and engage in more risky behaviour. This can affect a young person's sense of wellbeing.

There is increasing recognition that maintaining good mental health and wellbeing is as important as maintaining physical health, and activities such as seeing friends and getting enough sleep can act as consistent protective factors for positive psychological health across adolescence [4].

3.1.2 Links between mental and physical health

Our mental and physical health are closely linked. According to a 2014 study, the reduction in life expectancy from depression is 7–11 years. This is similar to the reduction from heavy smoking, which is 8–10 years [5]. Meanwhile, NHS figures suggest that those with "mental health issues have the same life expectancy as the general population did 50 years ago" [6]. Mental health struggles in childhood and adolescence are also strong predictors of poor health outcomes later in life, with Morgan et al. [7] noting that children who self-harm are approximately nine times more likely to die unnaturally during follow-up, and a US study suggesting that 75% of individuals experiencing depression during adolescence will make a suicide attempt in adulthood [8].

On top of this, mental health struggles can lead people to take less care of their physical health. Szatkowski and McNeill [9] found smoking rates among the English population with mental health conditions are twice as high compared to those without a mental health condition [10]. Similarly, physical disabilities can impact on mental health. A 2012 King's Fund and Centre for Mental Health report noted that: "Research evidence consistently demonstrates that people with long-term conditions are two to three times more likely to experience mental health problems than the general population" [11].

3.1.3 Young people's experiences of mental ill-health

One of the best ways of understanding how young people feel about mental health is to hear them describe their experiences or the challenges they face first-hand. Time to Change, a mental health campaign that aims to reduce mental health-related stigma and discrimination, runs a website where people are invited to share their experiences of mental ill-health. The contributions give a snapshot of the difficulties young people are facing and the places they go for support. They highlight the stress associated with balancing a mental health challenge and the routines of everyday life, the struggles with accepting that something is wrong, and their worries about asking for help.

One writer on the Time to Change website, 18-year-old Josh Davis, describes how support from family and friends helped him to speak openly about his experiences and get the help he needed to tackle his nine-year struggle with Obsessive Compulsive Disorder (OCD) [12]. He described how he had had to "ritualise breathing, hearing, smelling, blinking and talking" and had faced times when he felt he did "not wanted to continue" [13].

Other stories on the site include 21-year-old Chris, who experienced depression, self-harm and suicidal thoughts, but again had felt unable to talk about it. Like Josh, he felt that support from friends and family were key in helping him secure support to manage his mental health [13].

Posting in January 2020, Lucy described her experience of being diagnosed with anxiety at 15 and still coping with it into her twenties. She explained the need to respect that an individual can be an expert on their own mental health issues, even as a young person, and the importance of feeling that you are heard.

> You don't have to "get it", what matters is that you want to learn, and you can be mindful of what you say and do. These small changes in attitude can affect someone more than you realise [14].

> *Lucy*

I identify with a lot of the experiences shared on the platform. It took me around three years to accept that anything about my way of living might be problematic. There are a lot of feelings wrapped up in that process. Pride gets in the way of admitting you might need help, fear of losing control makes you reluctant to share your experiences with other people, shame makes you feel like you do not deserve support.

3.2 Trends in mental ill-health

In 2018, CfEY delved into the issue of mental health, publishing a joint report on "Schools and Youth Mental Health" with Minds Ahead, a social enterprise that is working to improve support in schools. Former Health Minister Norman Lamb, who is now Chair of the Children and Young People's Mental Health Coalition, and former Education Secretary Nicky Morgan (now Baroness Morgan of Cotes) both contributed forewords to the work, citing the importance of valuing and supporting the mental health and wellbeing of young people. Lamb said: "The mental health crisis facing our children and young people cannot be overstated", adding that schools are "an important part of the jigsaw" but must be "backed-up by properly resourced clinical mental health services".

Morgan's contribution highlighted that "young people are facing unacceptable delays in getting a diagnosis and receiving treatment" and said that early intervention is "key to minimising the impact of the problem on students' overall wellbeing and educational attainment". The report went on to examine these trends in considerable detail and in this chapter, I explore some of the themes that emerged, alongside additional data and research published after the report.

3.2.1 Trends over time

The NHS has only collected data on the prevalence of mental health problems among children and young people sporadically, which can make it difficult to follow trends. However, a study in 2017 found an increase in the proportion of 5 to 15-year olds that had at least one mental health condition,[1] from one in ten in 2004 to one in nine [16].

This research explored a range of mental health issues in young people, dividing them into "emotional", "behavioural", and "hyperactivity" disorders. Less common conditions were classified together, including autism spectrum disorder (also classed as a special educational need), eating disorders – like my own, and other conditions such as tics.

"Emotional disorders" in the survey include anxiety disorders, depressive disorders, and bipolar affective disorder. These were the most common amongst young people. This study found a rise in the prevalence of emotional disorders amongst five to 15-year-olds, from 4% in 2004 to nearly 6% in 2017. Some argue that these findings are evidence that increasing stresses during childhood are taking their toll on young people.

Behavioural (or "conduct") disorders were defined as those "characterised by repetitive and persistent patterns of disruptive and violent behaviour, in which the rights of others and social norms or rules are violated" [15]. Prevalence of both behavioural and hyperactivity disorders remained stable over time [16]. However, one of the challenges with disorders in this category is that they are diagnosed using observational methods, which can be problematic, for example in cases where the same behaviours or symptoms can be used twice to give two distinct diagnoses, such as conduct disorder and ADHD. This can call into question the accuracy of some figures.

3.2.2 Who is affected

Whilst all young people can be affected by poor mental health, certain groups are more at risk than others.

3.2.2.1 Teenage girls

Teenage girls tend to be particularly at risk of certain types of mental health problems, and especially between the ages of 17 and 19. The proportion of girls experiencing emotional disorders in this age group is double that found among those aged 11 to 16 years, and three times that of boys experiencing the same conditions at the same age. Young women with a mental health condition are also more likely to have self-harmed or made a suicide attempt than boys [17, 18].

In a "State of the Nation" report on the wellbeing of children and young people, the Department for Education specifically recognised the need to understand whether there are characteristics of teenage girls' experiences that drive increases in emotional problems as girls get older and whether anything can be done to mitigate this issue [19].

3.2.2.2 Income and ethnicity

Children from low-income families are four times more likely to experience mental health problems compared to children from higher-income families [20]. However, wellbeing among poorer young people is not uniformly low and links to poverty are not always clear cut.

Research has shown that while Black and minority ethnic (BME) communities are over-represented in adult mental health services, BME children and young people are under-represented in CAMHS (Child and Adolescent Mental Health Services). Although this could suggest that young people from these backgrounds experience lower rates of mental ill-health, it is more likely that they are disadvantaged in terms of their access to relevant support for mental health issues.

This could be due to underlying socioeconomic and health inequalities driving differences. Since poorer public services are available in low-income communities and BME groups are disproportionately concentrated in these communities, their access may be particularly hampered, and they may disproportionately suffer from funding shortfalls too [21].

It is also harder for young people from low-income communities to seek private specialist help. Memon et al. (2016) note that it is "not clear" whether disparities in access to mental health services are due to variation in actual BME mental health needs or are the product of "institutional, cultural and/or socioeconomic exclusion factors", which disadvantage those from a BME background [22].

On the other hand, it may also be due to social stigma surrounding mental health making young people from some minority backgrounds less likely to access services [23]. There is some evidence for this based in detailed qualitative studies which have reported that participants felt mental health was often perceived as a socially unacceptable topic for discussion within their community [24].

> Some cultures do not recognise concepts of stress or depression or may associate culturally unacceptable behaviours, such as aggression, with mental illness; consequently, symptoms may remain unrecognised [25].

There is therefore some debate about the impact of poverty and ethnicity on wellbeing and mental health.

3.2.2.3 SEND

The NHS Digital prevalence statistics on the Mental Health of Children and Young People in England in 2017 highlighted that children with recognised special educational needs were "significantly more likely" to have a mental health condition than those without special educational needs. This pattern was more marked in boys than girls [26].

However, it is important to recognise that the lines are somewhat blurred here. As the report goes on to clarify:

> It should be noted that the same condition might have been counted both as the special educational need and as the mental disorder present, potentially explaining much of the association [27].

Social, emotional and mental health (SEMH) is one of the four categories of need by which all special educational needs and disabilities are delineated. As noted by Whole School SEND, a consortium of organisations focused on special educational needs and disabilities, the SEND Code of Practice defines social, emotional and mental health needs in a broad manner, including "anxiety or depression, self-harming, substance misuse, eating disorders … attention deficit disorder, attention deficit hyperactive disorder or attachment disorder" [28].

3.2.2.4 Sexual orientation and gender identity

Young people who identify as lesbian, gay, bisexual, transgender or other categories of gender and sexuality (LGBT+) are also more at risk of depression or anxiety, suicidal behaviour or self-harm, than non-LGBT people [29].

The Stonewall School Report (2017) found that 45% of LGBT pupils (including 64% of trans pupils) had been bullied for being LGBT, and over half had heard homophobic language "frequently" or "often" at school. Nearly one in ten trans pupils reported being subjected to death threats at school.

45% of pupils who were bullied for being LGBT never told anyone about the bullying, while over half said that there was no adult at school that they could talk to about being LGBT. 40% of pupils who had been bullied for being LGBT had also skipped school because of this bullying, 84% had self-harmed, and 45% had attempted to take their own life. As bullying is a risk factor for mental health already, these young people effectively face a double challenge.

One 16-year-old pupil from a private single-sex secondary school in the South East told Stonewall about experiencing panic attacks and feeling sick whenever their class had a P.E. lesson, while a 19-year-old student who had moved to a university in Wales said the bullying they had experienced at school had precipitated depression, self-harm and suicidal thoughts. A 17-year-old student at an FE college in the North West said:

> The bullying went on for over five consecutive years. I ended up developing severe mental health issues and being sectioned twice [30].

In light of the findings, Stonewall makes a range of recommendations, including calling on schools to ensure all staff are equipped to tackle homophobic, biphobic and transphobic bullying and language. Teaching staff should also be trained in online safety, supporting LGBT pupils, and young people's mental health and wellbeing. Meanwhile they emphasise that an inclusive and open environment is the bedrock of a whole school approach to mental health.

3.3 Poor mental health and marginalisation

I found having mental ill-health created a lot of barriers in my life. With a serious eating disorder, nothing else can come first. Even if a best friend wants you to join them for an indulgent dinner on their 18th birthday, or your sibling needs to talk to you about a terrible day when you would normally be going to the gym, it feels like there can be no exceptions to your very strict daily routine. Having grown up loving swimming and competing for the county as part of a local team, I dropped out in my teens because I could no longer bear wearing only a swimsuit in front of other people. I once missed an afternoon of playing with friends in an amazing snowfall to go for a slippery run on my own in the freezing cold, because I couldn't allow myself a day off exercise. This kind of obsessive behaviour is hard to explain or justify to others, so I ended up hiding it, which led me to become more and more isolated.

I am not alone in having experienced this pattern. In 2016 the YMCA conducted research that involved over 2,000 interviews with young people aged between 11 and 24-years-old (over half of whom had experienced mental health difficulties), to investigate the stigma around mental health. The study found young people believed those experiencing difficulties with their mental health were treated negatively as a result of stigma. It also highlighted a link between stigma and prejudice, with young people reporting being left out of activities and verbally abused due to the state of their mental health. For the majority, school was the primary site of stigma that frequently emanated from their peers [31].

Within schools, there are important links between mental ill-health and school exclusion. Government guidance has explicitly encouraged schools to take into account mental health issues as potential contributing factors when considering excluding pupils. However, mental health problems can still contribute to school exclusion, according to research by Dr Tamsin Ford, Professor of Child and Adolescent Psychiatry at the University of Cambridge. This can in turn dramatically affect longer term outcomes, as noted in Chapter 1 [32].

Dr Ford's research involved two surveys of over 5,000 parents, one in 2004 and one in 2007. The study found "a bi-directional relationship" between exclusion from school and mental health problems in children, such that exclusion was both predicted by poor mental health, and a contributing factor to it. Dr Ford therefore recommended "early and rapid identification and intervention for children suffering psychological distress or demonstrating challenging behaviour", suggesting that doing so could "prevent both future exclusion and future psychiatric disorder" [33].

3.4 What influences mental health?

As part of our 2018 mental health roundtable we heard from Fiona Pienaar, Chief Clinical Officer of digital mental health charity Mental Health Innovations. She summed up the challenging environment around young people's mental health as follows:

> There are a lot of new stressors and more challenges that children and young people have to deal with: a lot more parent stress; time paucity... when I compare it to my own childhood there's a lot more that children and young people have to deal with and I think that impacts on mental health [34].

There are a range of hypotheses regarding these "new stressors" (such as social media, additional exam pressure and labour market uncertainty). However, it is hard to untangle these factors from difficulties with service provision. In reviewing the potential explanations below, I will therefore summarise the research whilst acknowledging that the patchy evidence base means that at present, no-one is certain what is driving the crisis.

3.4.1 Technology

The evidence base remains split over whether technology and screen time has an overall positive or negative effect on young people's wellbeing and mental health, or neither.

3.4.1.1 First generation of digital natives

The rise of the Internet has introduced new risks that have the potential to impact on young people's mental health as they grow up using it in so many areas of their lives. As a generation of "digital natives" [35], young people may find it tricky to explain to parents, carers or grandparents the difficulties they encounter online. For parents who have grown up without such sites, it might be hard to appreciate that "kids' online lives are an extension of their offline lives" [36] – a generational disconnect that may prevent young people from getting the help they need whilst causing tension in the home.

On the other hand, online interactions may help young people access support from charities or specialist organisations, as well as to feel connected to a community of like-minded peers.

3.4.1.2 Social media

Using the Internet and communicating via social media platforms has become an everyday staple for learning, working and playing for most young people. Children are watching YouTube videos before they have learned to speak, and many parents chart their children's progress through Facebook and Instagram updates. According to the OECD, a third of 3–4-year-olds in the UK go online, and as they grow up, they are more likely to go online via personal digital devices such as mobile phones and laptops, leading to less parental control over what they can access [37]. Furthermore, children are deliberately bypassing age restrictions for social media platforms, with one 2019 study, based on a combination of large-scale survey analysis and detailed qualitative research, suggesting that two thirds of children aged 11–18 have knowingly lied about their age when signing up to social media [38]. This is causing significant and growing concerns for parents [39] and as noted above, there appear to be close links between bullying, including online bullying, and psychological health or ill-health throughout mid to late adolescence [40].

These concerns are not restricted to secondary school level. Primary head teacher Samantha Jayasuriya argues that some of the issues associated with social media that were previously experienced by secondary schools are now extending into primary schools that are "not used to dealing with these things" [41].

3.4.1.3 Screen time

A 2017 report from the research organisation ChildWise found that around one in four young people find it difficult to go several hours without checking their devices, and that many say they have missed out on sleep because they have spent too long on gadgets. Given that many of these young people say they would like to spend more time away from their devices, we are not talking about young people necessarily making positive use of the technology that is increasingly in their hands and pockets and unfortunately, excessive screen time has been linked to lower happiness amongst adolescents [42].

On the other hand, while there is a "clear association" between social media usage and mental health problems [43], attempts to prove a causal link have as yet floundered and ultimately, evidence of concern is not the same as evidence of a problem.

One study that focused on teenagers' views on social media's impact found that although participants saw social media as problematic this tended to be because they had heard that it was, rather than because they had experienced it as such. Participants said they thought social media was addictive, that it directly caused mental ill-health, and that it exposed people to behaviours such as cyberbullying. However, they mostly generalised about the risks in a broad way, rather than reporting real life examples. The study's authors concluded that the young people were reflecting the dominant discourses surrounding social media use and that concerns seemed to "reify the moral panic that has become endemic to contemporary digital discourses" [44].

Questions about the true impact of social media have also been raised as a result of large-scale analysis of representative panel data. This has shown that social media use "is not, in and of itself, a strong predictor of life satisfaction across the adolescent population". This study concluded that the effects of social media use are thus "nuanced and small at best" [45].

3.4.1.4 Body image and unrealistic expectations

Problems with social media may be linked to issues with body image and may have a gendered dimension. Research has shown a stronger link between social media use and depressive symptoms among teenage girls than boys, with experiences of online harassment, poorer sleep quantity and quality, self-esteem and body image thought to explain the disparity [48]. However, this study resisted claiming causality as it was based on cross sectional rather than longitudinal or experimental data.

Potential causal mechanisms do exist though, since manipulated photos on social media sites may breed unrealistic expectations of body image, causing difficulties with self-esteem [46]. A "social ideal" may also lead young people to view their own lives unfavourably in comparison to those of others [47]. Whilst unrealistic portrayals have long plagued magazines, televisions and other media, sites and platforms like Facebook, Snapchat and Instagram are now so easily accessible on mobile phones that young people can compare themselves to others at regular intervals every day.

In his contribution to our 2018 roundtable, Julian Astle, Director of Education at the RSA, argued that as a society we need to think through the consequences of children and young people trying to fit in and developing their personalities under the constant lens of social, online scrutiny. As he put it, "it doesn't end when you walk out of the school gates it goes home with you" [48].

Efforts are being made to introduce a more positive online narrative around body image. A 2017 study from the University of the West of England explored the impact of different types of social media content by showing 160 women aged between 18 and 25 Instagram images containing one of the following:

a) Self-compassion quotes.

b) "Fitspiration" (a blending of the words "fitness" and "inspiration") images with messages aiming to motivate people to exercise more and eat healthily to achieve a specific body shape.

c) Neutral images of nature.

The research did not find that exposure to "fitspiration" images resulted in significantly poorer body image and negative mood compared to exposure to neutral Instagram images, though it did leave participants with some feelings of guilt. Meanwhile, women who viewed self-compassion quotes on Instagram reported greater body satisfaction, body appreciation, self-compassion, and lower negative mood [49].

3.4.1.5 Exposure to inappropriate material

Another risk introduced by technology is increased levels of exposure to inappropriate, or potentially disturbing, online content. For example, recent studies have shown that almost all young people have been exposed to pornography by the age of 14 [50], with over half of 11 to 13-year-olds reporting that they have seen pornography at some point [51]. Pornography may also exacerbate concerns about body image and create unrealistic expectations about sexual encounters. With much pornographic material centring on the male gaze [52], there is also a risk of aggressive behaviour and eroding norms around consent [53].

While a number of risks have been identified here, it remains difficult to determine or quantify impact and it seems that harm is often assumed rather than proven, with limited evidence of damage caused by exposure to pornographic material. One investigation into how children view pornography which was carried out by a panel of experts for the Department for Digital, Culture, Media & Sport, struggled to decisively state that viewing pornography at a young age was dangerous, despite being conducted with the aim of informing policy-makers on how to limit viewing. It concluded that, while the policy position underpinning the project was that pornography causes harm to children, it was also important to emphasise that:

> ... the relatively limited academic evidence of harm means that any policy interventions should proceed on the basis of a precautionary principle, namely seeking to avoid possible risks in the absence of certainty [54].

3.4.2 Increasing examination pressure

While exams have always been a stressful part of life, recent reforms to course structure mean pupils sitting GCSEs must now take approximately eight more hours of exams, and potentially even more if they have extra time due to special educational needs or disabilities. Meanwhile, changes to the structure of A-Levels have led to pupils only taking exams at the end of their two-year courses rather than accumulating marks through smaller modules throughout their courses.

Teachers' own anxiety about accountability pressures may result in them "passing on" the stress to their classes and putting additional pressure on pupils to succeed in this more challenging assessment environment. Therefore, whilst attainment is a "strong predictor of good mental health and wellbeing" [55], there is a danger that heightened pressure at school may be putting young people under increased stress, which might pose a threat to their mental health [56].

Young people in the UK are not unique among students in the developed world in having problematic and worsening levels of mental ill-health and poor wellbeing. However, the 2018 PISA report suggested that life satisfaction amongst UK students was lower than among their peers elsewhere in the world.

The study also found that 15-year-old UK students were more likely to feel anxious for tests, even if they felt well prepared, and to feel "very tense" when studying, relative to OECD averages [57]. The UK was also above average in terms of the proportion of students that said they worry about what others think of them when they fail.

3.4.3 Bullying

Sadly, 11 to 19-year olds with a mental health condition are nearly twice as likely to have been bullied than their peers with good mental health [58]. Studies have shown a causal link between exposure to bullying and mental health problems like anxiety, depression, hyperactivity and impulsivity, inattention, and conduct problems. These can persist for years after the bullying occurred, though tend to get gradually better over time [59]. One option for helping young people to cope with experiences such as bullying is teaching resilience skills. There is some evidence that developing soft skills such as optimism, tolerance, trust and the ability to regulate emotions can protect against depression, anxiety and the negative impact of bullying [60]. Some schools already deliver lessons in resilience skills, and increased uptake of such approaches could yield benefits. However, Brown and Dixon sound a note of caution, arguing that they found children to be critical when resilience was taught using a "push on through" narrative, which "was perceived as reflecting an individual attitude towards learning and academic achievement, with little focus on the wider environment" [61].

3.4.4 Life at home

NHS research has shown that young people dealing with trouble at home are more likely to have a mental health condition. This is especially true for children who have experienced certain types of adversity, such as parental separation or financial crisis at home. This problem also works the other way around, with challenges around mental health negatively affecting how well a family can function. Rates of mental disorder also tend to be highest in children living with a parent with poor mental health, or in children living with a parent who receives disability related income [62].

3.5 What are the problems with the current system?

Teachers, parents and young people all struggle to understand how to access mental health services. For example, only half of school leaders believe that staff are equipped to identify behaviour that may be linked to a mental health issue and only a quarter think that most staff know how to help students with mental health issues access specialist support outside school [63].

Parents also struggle to understand where they should go for help. In 2018 only around half said they were confident that they knew where to go for advice if they were concerned about their child's mental health [64], and the situation was similar amongst young people themselves in 2019 when two in five told the charity Mind that they did not know how to access mental health support services in schools [65].

Unfortunately, NHS guidance is not always clear either. 2019 guidance for example advised parents and carers to refer to:

- Other parts of the NHS website.

- "General advice and support ... online".

- The website and phoneline of the charity YoungMinds.

- The online e-portal MindEd.

- The Royal College of Psychiatrists.

- A teacher.

- A GP.

- Local "specialist child and adolescent mental health services" [66].

While it is important that different kinds of support are available given that they will be more or less relevant depending on the young person, the lack of a clear entry point for accessing mental health support, or a clear route through the system, is a significant problem. It is therefore no surprise that so many young people slip under the radar, as was the case with a child whose parent contributed to our 2018 roundtable:

> My daughter is 6 years old in a classroom with 30 children which has additional learning support in the classroom only in the mornings. To me, she seemed to be an invisible child as she's academic and didn't make a fuss once class started – teachers are so overstretched. After her bereavement and subsequent trauma, one teacher's response was "Come on, chin up" [67].

3.5.1 How does Child and Adolescent Mental Health Services (CAMHS) work?

CAMHS tackle a wide range of illnesses and operate locally in areas around the UK. Teams are made up of nurses, psychiatrists, psychologists, psychotherapists, support workers and social workers, as well as other professionals. Referrals can be made by a parent or any professional working with a child or young person, with consent from the child and their parent or carer where possible. Young people aged 16 or over can also refer themselves.

In the 1990s a tiered service model was developed involving four levels:

- Tier 1: non-specialists dealing with "common problems of childhood"

- Tier 2: CAMHS specialists focused on "assessment and treatment of problems in primary care". Educational psychologists also generally work in Tier 2, but are school-based

- Tier 3: a team, usually clinic-based, working on "problems too complicated to be dealt with at Tier 2"

- Tier 4: specialist services "where patients with more severe mental health problems can be assessed and treated" [68].

While this model was useful for highlighting the different services that young people might require, it has also been criticised for its "reification of service divisions" [72].

In an attempt to improve the tiered structure by placing the child or young person at the centre, the Anna Freud Centre and The Tavistock and Portman NHS Foundation Trust proposed a new system known as "THRIVE". This was set out in the "Future in Mind" report from the Children and Young People's Mental Health Taskforce in 2015. This model was designed to pay more attention to the services that young people might benefit from, rather than the severity of the problem. Targeting service provision in this way allows CAMHS to offer more tailored support and some regions have moved towards this structure, however it is not universal.

One example of a successful "THRIVE" approach is in Waltham Forest, where the local CAMHS have established a forum for discussions about whether a young person is ready to be discharged from treatment. Named the "THRIVE Clinic", it offers an opportunity for the young person, their family and professionals involved in their care to come together and discuss the best possible way forward. The clinic involves two senior clinicians from CAMHS and is held monthly. Through clinic meetings, a "THRIVE Plan" is developed collaboratively with the young person to address the following questions:

1. What is working well?

2. What is not going well?

3. What are their support needs?

4. What happens if there is a crisis?

Answering these questions enables the young person, their support network and the medical professionals to determine whether they are ready to be discharged from CAMHS [69].

Any developments that involve the young people themselves in decision-making are to be welcomed. I seldom felt in control of my own treatment until I decided to go private and pay for it myself as an adult – an option that for many simply is not possible. While receiving NHS treatment I felt like a clock was constantly ticking, putting pressure on me to make changes and improve before my allowance of help ran out. A system like the one introduced in Waltham Forest, which involves young people in the decision about whether they are ready to be discharged from mental health services is therefore a valuable step forward.

3.5.2 Fragmentation

Even when teachers and school leaders succeed in navigating mental health services, this does not mean they are successful in securing support. In 2017, The National Association of Head Teachers reported that more than half of Head Teachers had found it hard to find mental health services for their pupils [70]. In another survey by another union, the NASUWT, only a quarter of teachers and school leaders said they were very or fairly confident they would be able to get timely support from experts when needed [71]. As one respondent put it:

> The whole system seems woefully under-resourced and children wait far too long for effective intervention and it does not always seem to help them sufficiently to move on with their lives [72].

In many cases CAMHS have long waiting lists, and educational psychologists are called on to provide interim mental health support during this time. I spoke to one educational psychologist who described working with schools that were unable to provide the support children and young people needed because of budget constraints, while others say schools have enough money to identify needs but not to meet them.

In the past, local authorities provided support and expertise and commissioned services where necessary, but academies functioning independently can lack this infrastructure. While they are expected to commission support, Craig Thorley, of the NSPCC, explained that MATs frequently lack commissioning expertise:

> Academies are largely responsible for commissioning in their own support services and it's not always the case that academies will have the expertise in how to commission effectively [73].

In instances where referrals are accepted, there is no guarantee that a suitable service will be provided. Poor cooperation and information sharing amongst providers can also result in young people not receiving the support they need.

Overall, the different services available in the mental health support system rarely seem to work together coherently [78]. Inspections by the Care Quality Commission have revealed numerous examples of poor collaboration between different agencies, including inpatient provision that is largely cut off from any other teams or services [74]. Furthermore, mental health services provided in mainstreams schools such as counselling are not inspected at all, either by Ofsted or the CQC.

3.5.3 Under-resourced and ill-equipped services

A protracted period of austerity that began in 2008 has resulted in under-investment and increasing demand for mental health services. This in turn has left overstretched schools and CAMHS struggling to do more than fire-fight the most extreme cases.

One parent shared a heart-breaking account during our 2018 roundtable, telling us that when her teenage daughter took an overdose and ended up in hospital, she was told it was "not a serious enough attempt" to secure support. It was only when she took a second overdose that support arrived.

By 2017–18, between one fifth and one quarter of children referred to specialist services were being turned away when referred for specialist treatment, according to data gathered through freedom of information requests by the Education Policy Institute (EPI) [75]. EPI's study suggested that a conservative estimate of the number of rejected referrals in one year was 55,800 but added that the true number was likely to be higher because not all providers gave a response. There was also wide variation between providers, with some rejecting approximately half of all referrals and some reporting that they rejected less than 1% of young people referred in a year.

Whilst there is a general lack of capacity in mental health services, problems are particularly acute in youth services. The vast majority of mental health professionals (such as counsellors and psychologists, as well as other medical staff such as GPs and paramedics) receive no specialist training in children and adolescent's mental health. Maddie Burton, Senior Lecturer in Child and Adolescent Mental Health at the University of Worcester, argued that the situation had considerably worsened by 2018 compared to at the start of her career in CAMHS in 2013, with many young people now classed as "not meeting thresholds" for specialist support, despite desperately needing help [76].

One option to tackle the saturation of CAMHS would be to introduce a pre-CAMHS facility, run by local authorities. This could take the form of light-touch counselling, potentially within a school setting, to address young people's worries and causes of stress before they become unmanageable. Equipping local councils with the resources to introduce a network of support that addresses some of the factors known to put young people at risk of mental health challenges could ease the pressure on CAMHS and would go some of the way to replacing the support that was eroded as a result of government austerity.

3.5.4 Promises of change

When former Prime Minister Theresa May came to power in July 2016, she pledged to tackle the "burning injustice" of inadequate mental health provision. Her attention to the subject reflected society's growing concerns about mental health provision and she went on to announce that mental health training would be delivered in schools across the country by "Mental Health First Aid UK". While the aim was to make school staff better at spotting signs of mental health problems in pupils, the proposal did little to address how CAMHS would manage any subsequent increase in referrals from schools.

Later in 2017, the government announced plans to spend more than £300 million on new mental health leads in schools and to support teams linking education and health services. This funding was announced alongside a Green Paper promising funding for schools to appoint and train designated senior leads for mental health, as well as new mental health support teams to work with the NHS, offering support and treatments in schools. However, it has been difficult for staff on the ground to understand how to put the proposals into practice. For example, one educational psychologist explained that they had worked in a school which had access to a CAMHS worker for one day per week, but that this person was not allowed to work with a child if they had been seen by CAMHS directly. Logistical challenges like these create extra work for staff who are already overburdened. A joint Education and Health Committee therefore argued that the proposed changes would "put more pressure on the teaching workforce without sufficient resources" [82].

Further proposals cane in January 2019 and these aimed to address shortages in support and long waiting times. The NHS Long Term Plan pledged that an extra 345,000 children would be able to access mental health support by 2023–24 through local health services and new school-based mental health support teams. These teams would develop models of early intervention for mild to moderate issues, such as anxiety, behavioural difficulties or friendship issues, as well as providing help to staff within school and college settings. The Plan also announced a trial of four-week waiting times in some areas for children and young people who need expert support urgently. This would come alongside specialist care at A&E including crisis and liaison teams and intensive home treatment.

3.6 Conclusion

My recovery took ten years, and spanned childhood to adulthood. It included two rounds of cognitive behavioural therapy (CBT), a group course, visits to two different psychiatrists, and sessions with two private therapists which cost me hundreds of pounds. Many people do not have access to anything like this, and, even with it, getting through the day-to-day can be really difficult – just getting up and about, let alone taking exams or going to job interviews.

Treatment needs to be personalised, not generic, if it is going to work, and early identification is vital. A friend whose child was diagnosed with an eating disorder at just 11 once told me that they were trying to read everything about it to find out how to help their daughter, but they could not read fast enough. Every time they felt they had gained an understanding of it the condition had worsened and required a new approach. She was eventually withdrawn from school and hospitalised.

This should not happen: we need to be ahead of mental health challenges and ready to intercept and manage them as they arise, rather than treating them when things reach crisis point. CAMHS is overloaded because the current system is set up to fire-fight, rather than lead with preventative measures, information and support. Hopefully some of the changes proposed in The NHS Long Term Plan will help to address this problem, but this remains to be seen.

Without the right support and treatment young people will carry their mental health challenges into adulthood, continuing to seek support wherever it is offered. This should not be the outcome. While looking after our mental health is a lifelong commitment, children should be equipped with the tools they need as soon as possible so that they can move forward with their lives positively and feel empowered to tackle challenges in the future.

3.7 Taking action

Poor youth mental health plays out in a number of realms and has a range of causes. Policy-makers and practitioners therefore need to take a multi-pronged approach to tackle challenges.

3.7.1 Joined up thinking

All bodies involved in supporting young people's mental health need to open up lines of communication, so that support is more streamlined. This process should involve education and health professionals, along with parents and young people themselves. Clear communication needs to become the norm, whether in person, online or by phone and support should be well signposted by schools and health services so that families can get help easily and quickly. Concerns should be taken seriously straight away.

Regular safeguarding training for all school staff should make it clear that concerns about mental health constitute safeguarding concerns and that these should be passed on to the senior leader responsible for safeguarding who can make a referral to CAMHS where necessary.

When working with a family, staff in all agencies should share regular updates with each other whilst observing data protection rules. Where possible, budgets should be pooled to make sure the right help is available at the right time.

3.7.2 Early intervention

Expert support is needed within schools to ensure that pupils with clinical needs are adequately supported day-to-day. Schools should be resourced and staffed to provide in-house mental-health experts, potentially shared between a number of schools to make support more affordable.

Depending on their operating model, MATs should either advise their schools on mental health commissioning or commission support centrally across their schools. Schools should share information about mental health support with parents as well as pupils, reinforcing the concept of wellbeing and a holistic approach to health.

3.7.3 Improved support in schools

School leaders should be true to their moral purpose and prioritise pupil needs in the face of perceived accountability pressures, so that decisions are taken with due consideration for their impact on pupil and teacher wellbeing. Schools should review potential risk factors for pupil wellbeing within their school community. Such factors might include stressed teachers, pared back PSHE provision, unhealthy demands on pupils and teachers and inappropriate forms of behaviour management.

PSHE teaching in relation to pupil wellbeing should be delivered solely by teachers with the skills and expertise to skilfully handle sensitive issues. PSHE teaching should include issues such as learning to deal with stress or learning about healthy use of social media as per the PSHE Association Curriculum [77]. Teaching about such issues should happen alongside communication with parents so that they can play a full role in reinforcing healthy routines, such as talking about feelings openly or limiting screen time.

3.7.4 Oversight

The Education and Health Committees should continue to monitor the government's progress in rolling out reforms promised in the Transforming Children and Young People's Mental Health Provision Green Paper and push for delivery to take place as rapidly as possible without compromising quality.

Since 2015, Ofsted has been monitoring school performance in the category of "personal development, behaviour and welfare". This includes areas such as pupils' self-confidence and self-awareness, their management of their own feelings and behaviour, and their understanding of how to keep themselves safe from risks such as abuse, sexual exploitation and extremism – including when using the internet and social media. This was reinforced in the new 2019 framework, which stated that Inspectors will:

> Make a judgement on the personal development of learners by evaluating the extent to which … the curriculum and the provider's wider work support learners to develop their character – including their resilience, confidence and independence – and help them know how to keep physically and mentally healthy [78].

Ofsted should continue this assessment, including monitoring in-school provision such as counselling and mentoring and should report on progress, especially in large MATs. It should also gather and present evidence about how the new framework is working when it comes to pupil wellbeing.

3.7.5 More specialists

There is a dramatic shortage of mental health specialists within the NHS and this shortage is even more pronounced when it comes to youth mental health. Alongside developing the role of mental health leads in school, a new school-based mental health development programme should be established, building on the success of programmes like Teach First, Think Ahead, Unlocked Grads and FrontLine. This could create new pre-clinical mental health specialists who would work in schools.

Campaigns and careers outreach programmes for school-aged pupils should be developed to encourage more young people to consider careers in youth mental health. This work could be enhanced and supported by educational psychologists already working in school, who are well placed to offer guidance.

Further reading

State of the Nation 2019: Children and Young People's Wellbeing: Department of Education. (2019). Retrieved from https://assets.publishing.service.gov.uk/government/uploads/system/uploads/attachment_data/file/838022/State_of_the_Nation_2019_young_people_children_wellbeing.pdf

Schools and Youth Mental Health: A briefing on current challenges and ways forward: Menzies, L., Bernardes, E., & Huband-Thompson, B. (2018). Retrieved from https://www.lkmco.org/wp-content/uploads/2018/06/Schools-and-Youth-Mental-Health.-Menzies-et-al.-2018.pdf

Good Childhood Report 2019: The Children's Society. (2019). Retrieved July 4, 2020, from https://www.childrenssociety.org.uk/sites/default/files/the_good_childhood_report_2019.pdf

Note

1 It should be noted that although the study used clinically diagnosable definitions of disorders, these children had not all previously been diagnosed as having these conditions. Instead, a sampling methodology was combined with clinical testing to see who would have received a clinical diagnosis, whether or not they had one before.

References

1 World Health Organization. (2014, August). Mental health: a state of well-being. Retrieved from http://origin.who.int/features/factfiles/mental_health/en/.
2 The WHO Regional Office for Europe. (2013). Measurement of and target-setting for well-being: an initiative by the WHO Regional Office for Europe. Retrieved from http://www.euro.who.int/__data/assets/pdf_file/0009/181449/e96732.pdf?ua=1.

3 Mental Health Foundation. (2020). What is mental health? Retrieved from https://www.mentalhealth.org.uk/your-mental-health/about-mental-health/what-mental-health.

4 Department of Education. (2019). State of the Nation 2019: Children and Young People's Wellbeing. Retrieved from https://assets.publishing.service.gov.uk/government/uploads/system/uploads/attachment_data/file/838022/State_of_the_Nation_2019_young_people_children_wellbeing.pdf.

5 University of Oxford. (2014, May 23). Many mental illnesses reduce life expectancy more than heavy smoking. Retrieved from http://www.ox.ac.uk/news/2014-05-23-many-mental-illnesses-reduce-life-expectancy-more-heavy-smoking.

6 McShane, M. (2013, November 18). Parity of Esteem. [Blog post]. Retrieved from https://www.england.nhs.uk/blog/parity-of-esteem/.

7 Morgan, C., Webb, R. T., Carr, M. J., Kontopantelis, E., Chew-graham, C. A., Kapur, N., & Ashcroft, D. M. (2017). Incidence, clinical management, and mortality risk following self harm among children and adolescents: cohort study in primary care. *BMJ*, https://doi.org/10.1136/bmj.j4351.

8 Auerbach. (2015). Depression in adolescents: Causes, correlates and consequences. Retrieved from http://www.apa.org/science/about/psa/2015/11/depression-adolescents.aspx.

9 Szatkowski, L., & McNeill, A. (2015). Diverging trends in smoking behaviors according to mental health status. *Nicotine and Tobacco Research*, *17*(3), 356–360. https://doi.org/10.1093/ntr/ntu173.

10 Ohrnberger, J., Fichera, E., & Sutton, M. (2017). The relationship between physical and mental health: A mediation analysis. *Social Science and Medicine*, *195*, 42–49. https://doi.org/10.1016/j.socscimed.2017.11.008.

11 Naylor, C., Parsonage, M., McDaid, D., Knapp, M., Fossey, M., & Galea, A. (2012). Long-term conditions and mental health: The cost of co-morbidities. Retrieved from https://www.kingsfund.org.uk/sites/default/files/field/field_publication_file/long-term-conditions-mental-health-cost-comorbidities-naylor-feb12.pdf.

12 Time to change (2016, June 11). When I talk about my OCD I hope people will listen. Retrieved from https://www.time-to-change.org.uk/blog/when-i-talk-about-my-ocd-i-hope-people-will-listen.

13 Ibid.

14 Time to change (2017, April 19). True friends are there for a mate going through depression. Retrieved from https://www.time-to-change.org.uk/blog/true-friends-are-there-mate-going-through-depression.

15 It's hard to understand anxiety, but you can still support someone. (2020, January 27). Retrieved from https://www.time-to-change.org.uk/blog/its-hard-to-understand-anxiety-you-can-still-support-someone.

16 Mandalia, D., Ford, T., Hill, S., Sadler, K., Vizard, T., Goodman, A., Mcmanus, S. (2018). *MHCYP - Professional services, informal support, and education.* (November). Retrieved from https://files.digital.nhs.uk/8E/AAB376/MHCYP2017 Service Use.pdf.

17 Pisano, S., Muratori, P., Gorga, C., Levantini, V., Iuliano, R., Catone, G., Masi, G. (2017). *Conduct disorders and psychopathy in children and adolescents: aetiology, clinical presentation and treatment strategies of callous-unemotional traits. Italian Journal of Pediatrics*, 1–11. https://doi.org/10.1186/s13052-017-0404-6.

18 Ibid.

19 NHS Digital. (2018). Summary of Key Findings. *Community*, (November 2018), 233–244. https://doi.org/10.2307/j.ctv39x8m4.19 Received from https://files.digital.nhs.uk/A6/EA7D58/MHCYP%202017%20Summary.pdf.

20 Marcheselli, F. (2018). *MHCYP – Behaviours, lifestyles and identities.* (November 2018), 1–48. Retrieved from https://files.digital.nhs.uk/81/542548/MHCYP2017 Behaviours Lifestyles Identities.pdf.

21 Department of Education. (2019). State of the Nation 2019: Children and Young People's Wellbeing. Retrieved from https://assets.publishing.service.gov.uk/government/uploads/system/uploads/attachment_data/file/838022/State_of_the_Nation_2019_young_people_children_wellbeing.pdf.

22 Morrison Gutman, L., Joshi, H., Parsonage, M. & Schoon, I. (2015) *Children of the new century: mental health findings from the Millenium Cohort Study,* London: Centre for Mental Health. Retrieved from https://www.centreformentalhealth.org.uk/sites/default/files/2018-11/Children%20of%20the%20Millennium.pdf.

23 Care Quality Commission. (2017). *Review of children and young people's mental health services: Phase one report | Care Quality Commission.* (October). Retrieved from https://www.cqc.org.uk/sites/default/files/20171103_cypmhphase1_report.pdf.

24 Memon, A., Taylor, K., Mohebati, L. M., Sundin, J., Cooper, M., Scanlon, T., & Visser, R. De. (2016). Perceived barriers to accessing mental health services among black and minority ethnic (BME) communities: a qualitative study in Southeast England. *BMJ Journals,* 1–10. https://doi.org/10.1136/bmjopen-2016-012337.

25 Ibid.

26 Ibid.

27 Ibid.

28 NHS Digital, NHS, Sadler, K., Vizard, T., Ford, T., … NHS. (2018). Mental Health of Children and Young People in England, 2017: Trends and characteristics. *Health and Social Care Information Centre.,* (November), 1–45. https://doi.org/10.7748/paed2009.06.21.5.28.c7079.

29 Ibid.

30 Department of Health, D. of E. (2015). Special educational needs and disability code of practice: 0 to 25 years. Government Policies: Education and Health, (January), 292. Retrieved from https://assets.publishing.service.gov.uk/government/uploads/system/uploads/attachment_data/file/398815/SEND_Code_of_Practice_January_2015.pdf.

31 Rethink Mental Illness. (2017). LGBT+ mental health. Retrieved from https://www.rethink.org/advice-and-information/living-with-mental-illness/wellbeing-physical-health/lgbtplus-mental-health/.

32 Bradlow, J., Bartram, F., Guasp, A., & Jadva, D. V. (2017). *School report.* Retrieved from https://www.stonewall.org.uk/system/files/the_school_report_2017.pdf.

33 YMCA. (2016). A report investigating the stigma faced by young people experiencing mental health difficulties. Retrieved from https://www.stonewall.org.uk/system/files/the_school_report_2017.pdf.

34 Department for Education. (2017). *Exclusion from maintained schools, academies and pupil referral units in England.* Retrieved from https://assets.publishing.service.gov.uk/government/uploads/system/uploads/attachment_data/file/641418/20170831_Exclusion_Stat_guidance_Web_version.pdf.

35 Ford, T., Parker, C., Salim, J., Goodman, R., Logan, S., & Henley, W. (2018). The relationship between exclusion from school and mental health: A secondary analysis of the British Child and Adolescent Mental Health Surveys 2004 and 2007. *Psychological Medicine,* 48(4), 629–641. https://doi.org/10.1017/S003329171700215X.

36 Menzies, L., Bernardes, E., & Huband-Thompson, B. (2018). *Schools and Youth Mental Health: A briefing on current challenges and ways forward.* Retrieved from https://www.lkmco.org/wp-content/uploads/2018/06/Schools-and-Youth-Mental-Health.-Menzies-et-al.-2018.pdf.

37 Department of Health, 2015.

38 O'Keeffe, G., & Clarke-Pearson, K. (2011). *Clinical Report – The Impact of Social Media on Children, Adolescents, and Families.* https://doi.org/10.1542/peds.2011-0054.

39 Graafland, J. H. (2018). DIRECTORATE FOR EDUCATION AND SKILLS New technologies and 21st century children: Recent trends and outcomes OECD Education Working Paper No. 179. Retrieved from www.oecd.org/edu/workingpapers.

40 Childwise, (2019). New research into underage use of social media sites. Retrieved from http://www.childwise.co.uk/uploads/3/1/6/5/31656353/childwise_press_release.pdf.

41 OfCom. (2019). Children and Parents: Media Use and Attitudes. In *Ofcom.* Retrieved from https://www.ofcom.org.uk/__data/assets/pdf_file/0023/190616/children-media-use-attitudes-2019-report.pdf.

42 Department of Education. (2019). *State of the Nation 2019: Children and Young People's Wellbeing.* Retrieved from https://assets.publishing.service.gov.uk/government/uploads/system/uploads/attachment_data/file/838022/State_of_the_Nation_2019_young_people_children_wellbeing.pdf.

43 Menzies, L., Bernardes, E., & Huband-Thompson, B. (2018). *Schools and Youth Mental Health: A briefing on current challenges and ways forward.* Retrieved from https://www.lkmco.org/wp-content/uploads/2018/06/Schools-and-Youth-Mental-Health.-Menzies-et-al.-2018.pdf.

44 Twenge, J. M., Martin, G. N., & Campbell, W. K. (2018). Decreases in psychological well-being among American adolescents after 2012 and links to screen time during the rise of smartphone technology. *Emotion, 18*(6), 765–780. https://doi.org/10.1037/emo0000403.

45 Beardsmore, R. (2015). Measuring National Well-being: Insights into children's mental health and well-being. Retrieved from https://www.ons.gov.uk/peoplepopulationand-community/wellbeing/articles/measuringnationalwellbeing/2015-10-20.

46 O'Reilly, M., Dogra, N., Whiteman, N., Hughes, J., Eruyar, S., & Reilly, P. (2018). Is social media bad for mental health and wellbeing? Exploring the perspectives of adolescents. *Clinical Child Psychology and Psychiatry, 23*(4), 601–613. https://doi.org/10.1177/1359104518775154.

47 Orben, A., Dienlin, T., & Przybylski, A. K. (2019). Social media's enduring effect on adolescent life satisfaction. *Proceedings of the National Academy of Sciences, 116*(21), 10226–10228. https://doi.org/10.1073/pnas.1902058116.

48 Kelly, Y., Zilanawala, A., Booker, C., & Sacker, A. (2018). EClinicalMedicine Social Media Use and Adolescent Mental Health: Findings from the UK Millennium Cohort Study. *EClinicalMedicine, 6,* 59–68. https://doi.org/10.1016/j.eclinm.2018.12.005.

49 Frith, E. (2017). *Social media and children's mental health: a review of the evidence.* Retrieved from https://epi.org.uk/wp-content/uploads/2018/01/Social-Media_Mental-Health_EPI-Report.pdf.

50 De Lenne, O., Vandenbosch, L., Trekels, J., Karsay, K., & Eggermont, S. (2018). *Living the Ideal Life on Social Media.* Retrieved from https://osf.io/sqj5v/.

51 Menzies, L., Bernardes, E., & Huband-Thompson, B. (2018). *Schools and Youth Mental Health: A briefing on current challenges and ways forward.* Retrieved from https://www.lkmco.org/wp-content/uploads/2018/06/Schools-and-Youth-Mental-Health.-Menzies-et-al.-2018.pdf.

52 Slater, A., Varsani, N., & Diedrichs, P. C. (2017). #fitspo or #loveyourself? The impact of fitspiration and self-compassion Instagram images on women's body image, self-compassion, and mood. *Body Image, 22,* 87–96. https://doi.org/10.1016/j.bodyim.2017.06.004.

53 Martellozzo, B. E., Monaghan, A., Adler, J. R., Davidson, J., Leyva, R., & Horvath, M. A. H. (2017). "… I wasn't sure it was normal to watch it …" A quantitative and qualitative examination of the impact of online pornography on the values, attitudes, beliefs and behaviours of children and young people. Retrieved from https://learning.nspcc.org.uk/media/1187/mdx-nspcc-occ-pornography-report.pdf.

54 bbfc. (n.d.). *Young people, Pornography & Age-verification. The following research contains graphic sexual content and pornographic language.* Retrieved from https://www.revealingreality.co.uk/wp-content/uploads/2020/01/BBFC-Young-people-and-pornography-Final-report-2401.pdf.

55 Fesnak, M. (2016). Organizing Pornography, Organizing Desire. *The IJournal: Graduate Student Journal of the Faculty of Information, 1*(2). Retrieved from https://theijournal.ca/index.php/ijournal/article/view/27079.

56 House of Lords (2015). *Library Note: Impact of Pornography on Society [Online].* Retrieved from http://researchbriefings.files.parliament.uk/documents/LLN-2015-0041/LLN-2015-0041.pdf.

57 Adler, J. R., & Livingstone, S. (2015). *Identifying the Routes by which Children View Pornography Online: Implications for Future Policy-makers Seeking to Limit Viewing Report of Expert Panel for DCMS*, (November), 1–34.

58 Care Quality Commission. (2017). *Review of children and young people's mental health services: Phase one report I Care Quality Commission.* (October). Retrieved from https://www.cqc.org.uk/sites/default/files/20171103_cypmhphase1_report.pdf.

59 Young Minds. (2018). *Your Voices Amplified.* Retrieved from https://youngminds.org.uk/media/2152/amplified-insights-survey-2018.pdf.

60 Ibid.

61 NHS Digital. (2018). Summary of Key Findings. *Community*, (November 2018), 233–244. https://doi.org/10.2307/j.ctv39x8m4.19. Retrieved from https://files.digital.nhs.uk/A6/EA7D58/MHCYP%202017%20Summary.pdf.

62 Singham, T., Viding, E., Schoeler, T., Arseneault, L., Ronald, A., Cecil, C. M., … Pingault, J. B. (2017). Concurrent and Longitudinal Contribution of Exposure to Bullying in Childhood to Mental Health: The Role of Vulnerability and Resilience. *JAMA Psychiatry, 74*(11), 1112–1119. https://doi.org/10.1001/jamapsychiatry.2017.2678.

63 Moore, B., & Woodcock, S. (2017). Resilience, Bullying, and Mental Health: Factors Associated with Improved Outcomes. *Psychology in the Schools, 54*(7), 689–702. https://doi.org/10.1002/pits.22028.

64 Brown, C. and Dixon, J., 2020. 'Push on Through': Children's Perspectives on the Narratives of Resilience in Schools Identified for Intensive Mental Health Promotion. *British Educational Research Journal, 46*(2), 379–398.

65 NHS Digital. (2018). Summary of Key Findings. *Community*, (November 2018), 233–244. https://doi.org/10.2307/j.ctv39x8m4.19. Retrieved from https://files.digital.nhs.uk/A6/EA7D58/MHCYP%202017%20Summary.pdf.

66 NFER. (2017). *Teacher Voice Omnibus survey.* (March). Retrieved from https://www.nfer.ac.uk/what-we-do/omnibus-surveys/

67 Young Minds. (2018). *Your Voices Amplified.* Retrieved from https://youngminds.org.uk/media/2152/amplified-insights-survey-2018.pdf.

68 Mind. (2019). Three in five young people have experienced a mental health problem or are close to someone who has. Retrieved from https://www.mind.org.uk/news-campaigns/news/three-in-five-young-people-have-experienced-a-mental-health-problem-or-are-close-to-someone-who-has/.

69 NHS. (n.d.). Children and young people's mental health services (CYPMHS) information for parents and carers. Retrieved June 9, 2020, from https://www.nhs.uk/using-the-nhs/nhs-services/mental-health-services/camhs-information-for-parents-and-carers/.

70 Menzies, L., Bernardes, E., & Huband-Thompson, B. (2018). *Schools and Youth Mental Health: A briefing on current challenges and ways forward*. Retrieved from https://www.lkmco.org/wp-content/uploads/2018/06/Schools-and-Youth-Mental-Health.-Menzies-et-al.-2018.pdf.

71 Wolpert, M., Harris, R., Jones, M., Hodges, S., Fuggle, P., James, R., ... Fonagy, P. (2014). *The AFC–Tavistock Model for CAMHS*. Retrieved from http://repository.tavistockand-portman.ac.uk/941/1/Thrive model for CAMHS.pdf.

72 Ibid.

73 i-THRIVE. (n.d.). How the Waltham Forest THRIVE Clinic helps support children and young people considered to be at risk. Retrieved June 6, 2020, from http://implementingthrive.org/case-studies-2/getting-risk-support-case-studies/case-study-10/.

74 NAHT/Place2Be. (2017). *Half of schools struggle to get mental health support for pupils*. Retrieved from https://www.naht.org.uk/news-and-opinion/news/pupil-well-being-news/struggling-to-get-mental-health-support/.

75 NASUWT. (2019). *The Big Question 2017 - An opinion survey of teachers and head-teachers*. Retrieved from https://www.nasuwt.org.uk/uploads/assets/uploaded/7649b810-30c7-4e93-986b363487926b1d.pdf.

76 Robertson, A. (2017, April 17). Three in four unable to access mental health support for pupils. *Schools Week*. Retrieved from https://schoolsweek.co.uk/three-in-four-unable-to-access-mental-health-support-for-pupils/.

77 Menzies, L., Bernardes, E., & Huband-Thompson, B. (2018). *Schools and Youth Mental Health: A briefing on current challenges and ways forward*. Retrieved from https://www.lkmco.org/wp-content/uploads/2018/06/Schools-and-Youth-Mental-Health.-Menzies-et-al.-2018.pdf.

78 Care Quality Commission. (2017). *Review of children and young people's mental health services: Phase one report | Care Quality Commission*. (October). Retrieved from https://www.cqc.org.uk/sites/default/files/20171103_cypmhphase1_report.pdf.

79 Ibid.

80 Crenna-Jennings, W., & Hutchinson, J. (2018). *Access to children and young people's mental health services 2018*. https://doi.org/10.1002/bs.3830080318.

81 Menzies, L., Bernardes, E., & Huband-Thompson, B. (2018). *Schools and Youth Mental Health: A briefing on current challenges and ways forward*. Retrieved from https://www.lkmco.org/wp-content/uploads/2018/06/Schools-and-Youth-Mental-Health.-Menzies-et-al.-2018.pdf.

82 Education and Health and Social Care Committees. (2018). *The Government's Green Paper on mental health: failing a generation*. (May), 1–3. Retrieved from https://publications.parliament.uk/pa/cm201719/cmselect/cmhealth/642/64204.htm%0Ahttps://publications.parliament.uk/pa/cm201719/cmselect/cmhealth/642/642.pdf Retrieved from https://www.parliament.uk/business/committees/committees-a-z/commons-select/health-and-social-care-committee/news/green-paper-on-mental-health-report-published-17-19/.

83 PSHE Association. (2020). Programme of Study for PSHE Education (Key stages 1–5). Retrieved from https://www.pshe-association.org.uk/curriculum-and-resources/resources/programme-study-pshe-education-key-stages-1%E2%80%935.

84 Ofsted. (2019). *The education inspection framework* (Vol. *190015*). Retrieved from https://www.gov.uk/government/publications/education-inspection-framework.

4 Area-based inequalities and the new frontiers in education policy

Sam Baars

4.1 Introduction

A decade ago, in the depths of winter, I started two years of fieldwork in a neighbourhood on the southern tip of Manchester with a group of boys on the edge of the mainstream school system. Last week, as the autumn term finally gave way to the Christmas break, I visited a school right on the outskirts of south London. As the school gate clanked shut behind me and I headed back to the station, I reflected on the startling similarity between these two experiences, separated by ten years and two hundred miles. The demographics of these two places are closely aligned: predominantly white, socially renting communities – living in semis and terraces rather than flats – with relatively high rates of unemployment, low levels of qualification and car ownership, and few people working in highly-skilled jobs. Both places occupy the same outer-urban hinterland: vast expanses of solid and spacious interwar housing, designed around garden city principles and linked by the slender thread of a tramline to the rest of their respective cities but, in reality, largely detached from their economy and opportunities. And two schools struggling in similar ways; pupils not doing as well as they could, few going on to higher education and parents wary of engaging.

These two schools, and the neighbourhoods they serve, have unmistakeable similarities which are apparent as soon as you set foot in them. You do not need the Office for National Statistics' Census-based area classification to tell you they belong to the same "type" of neighbourhood: your senses tell you that the streets outside these two schools could flow seamlessly together. The history of how they were planned, built and settled; their specific, peripheral location in relation to the city, and the way in which they are connected to transport, jobs and amenities gives them a shared lineage which goes so much further than simply being "deprived" or "disadvantaged". And we know that of all the neighbourhoods that young people grow up in, it is these types of area in which young people's outcomes and prospects are often most limited.

Together, these schools in south Manchester and south London shed light on a crucial frontier in youth and education research: the link between particular "types" of area and the outcomes of the young people who live in them. We tend to talk about places where young people struggle to make fulfilling transitions to adulthood in one of two ways. Either we use broad categories like "deprived" or "disadvantaged", or we pick out particular locations such as "the North" or "the inner city". Often we combine both narratives, identifying a specific location of concern because we deem it to be "disadvantaged" or "deprived".

Both elements of this approach have their strengths and weaknesses. Broad descriptors such as "deprived" or "disadvantaged" capture crucial aspects of the underlying conditions that can impact negatively on young people's life chances, such as material poverty and a limited local labour market. But these broad descriptors lack nuance: "deprived" areas come in multiple guises, and in the capital – home to many of England's most deprived boroughs – young people achieve some of the best educational outcomes in the country. Meanwhile, a location-based approach addresses the fact that every place has its own unique constellation of assets and constraints, and that there are indeed some specific parts of the country where young people struggle most, such as the twelve "Opportunity Areas" identified by the Secretary of State for Education between 2016 and 2017. But targeting discrete locations takes emphasis away from the shared challenges these areas have in common. This in turn makes it harder to recognise the coordinated national policies that would be most effective in tackling them.

In this chapter I make the case for a different approach to identifying, and talking about, the areas where young people fare worst; the places which put young people on the margins. In doing so I am indebted to decades of research on area-based initiatives in education [1–4] neighbourhood effects [5–8] and the role of area classifications in social policy [9–11]. The approach I advocate involves talking about "types" of area, rather than identifying particular locations or defining them as simply being more or less "deprived" or "disadvantaged" than others. I argue that while Opportunity Areas – the current basis of area-based education policy in England – are a robust means of identifying specific areas to target interventions, they leave us none the wiser about "types" of area where young people struggle to do well, and the structural causes that lie behind these poor outcomes. The long tradition of area-based policymaking in education offers few pointers here: most previous policies have lacked specificity and tend to fall back on well-worn notions of "deprived" and "disadvantaged" areas. Drawing on new analysis, I suggest specific new frontiers that require greater policy attention. In the process, I demonstrate that area types may be a far more powerful predictor of young people's outcomes than deprivation alone. They also offer a way of formally codifying "that feeling" I got in the outskirts of both London and Manchester. Moreover, by maintaining a focus on broader types of area, we make it easier to identify wider issues and common causes which we need to tackle as a society. If some types of area systematically let young people down, coordinated national policy is an essential part of the solution.

4.2 Opportunity Areas

In October 2016 Justine Greening, then Education Secretary, announced plans to tackle social mobility "cold spots" which would give pupils "the best start in life, no matter what their background." These twelve "cold spots" (six announced initially with a further six following in 2017) were named "Opportunity Areas" (OAs), and built on the Achieving Excellence Areas announced by the previous Secretary of State in a 2016 white paper which promised "a sharp new focus on areas of the country where standards are unacceptably low." Alongside an area-based focus, and a desire to raise school standards, the Opportunity Areas policy also reflected a newly-resurgent social mobility discourse under Theresa May's premiership, which aimed to recast Britain as a "great meritocracy", combined with a focus on schools' capacity to improve by means of system leaders, teacher recruitment and the support of multi-academy trusts.

The current set of 12 Opportunity Areas is designed to target local authority districts where social mobility is lowest and where schools have the least capacity to improve. The areas were selected on the basis of their scores on two separate measures: the Social Mobility Index and the Achieving Excellence Areas Index. The Social Mobility Index is based on the educational attainment of those from poorer backgrounds, from the early years, through primary and secondary school, to post-16 outcomes and higher education participation, alongside outcomes achieved by adults locally, such as average income, prevalence of low paid work, availability of professional jobs, home ownership and the affordability of housing. Meanwhile the Achieving Excellence Areas Index focuses on school performance – essentially a basket of attainment and progress measures – and capacity to improve, assessed for instance through local density of Teaching Schools and National Leaders of Education.

The final set of 12 OAs were places that scored lowest on both indices, offered regional spread, and belonged to a variety of area "types" (coastal, urban and rural). The OAs span from West Somerset and Hastings in the south of England, as far north as Blackpool and the North Yorkshire Coast. Although each area has a distinct set of strategic priorities, most focus on three common goals:

1. Raising poorer pupils' attainment and progress at school.

2. Strengthening teaching and school leadership.

3. Supporting young people's progression into the labour market.

4.3 Area-based approaches: nothing new under the sun

Despite the fanfare, Opportunity Areas are not a significant departure from several decades of area-based education policymaking in England. Policies that set out to tackle youth- and education-related outcomes by taking an area-, place- or neighbourhood-based approach stretch back at least half a century and involve a veritable alphabet soup of acronyms, including Education Priority Areas (EPAs), Education Action Zones (EAZs), Excellence in Cities (EiC), EiC Action Zones and Excellence Clusters, and Inspiring Communities.

There is much to be learned from these previous attempts to tackle area-based inequalities. Past policies involved a range of approaches to tackling underachievement including targeted additional funding, new forms of governance and partnership working, or bringing together local services spanning education, health, and regeneration. These policies raised the profile of young people's neighbourhood context as a determinant of outcomes and, in some cases, appeared to have a positive impact on these outcomes. However, there is also a sobering reminder in this lengthy back-catalogue of area-based policymaking: despite decades of attention, we are still grappling with stubborn inequalities in young people's outcomes that appear to be firmly rooted in the areas they grow up in.

Part of the explanation lies in the identification of target locations (Table 4.1) that was based on a weak understanding of the causes of the social problems the policies set out to solve. Policies such as EiC were targeted based on nothing

Table 4.1 Geographical targeting of previous area-based education policies in England

Policy	Areas targeted
Education Priority Areas (1968)	Initially rolled out in parts of London, Birmingham, Liverpool and the West Riding of Yorkshire. Authorities used different indices to identify their most disadvantaged communities. The most sophisticated "Education Priority Indices" were developed by the Inner London Education Authority (ILEA) and were based on pupil-level measures of disadvantage, such as the proportion of pupils on roll eligible for free meals, and area-level measures of disadvantage, such as social class composition and overcrowding [3]. These measures were rolled together into a composite index of educational disadvantage, producing a unidimensional score, much like the current Achieving Excellence Areas Index.
Education Action Zones (1998)	Targeted at areas with a combination of underperforming schools and "seriously disadvantaged" contexts [2].
Excellence in Cities (1998), EiC Action Zones and Excellence Clusters (1999)	EiC was targeted at "inner city" schools. Excellence Clusters took a broader focus on schools in "deprived areas", both urban and rural. EiC Action Zones took on the formers EAZs.
Inspiring Communities (2009)	Supported 15 neighbourhoods, covering a population of around 10,000 people and containing at least one area of "high deprivation".

more than the geographical shorthand of the "inner city". Meanwhile EAZs, EiC Action Zones, Excellence Clusters and Inspiring Communities appealed to notions of "deprivation" or "disadvantage" that were only weakly specified. In neither case were these policies' target areas identified based on detailed analysis of the causal conditions that produced poor educational outcomes in particular areas. As Lupton argues:

> One could argue that these are genuinely only area-based initiatives, that is they take place in particular areas, rather than being motivated by any concern with spatial processes per se [1].

Area-based policies such as Education Priority Areas and the current Opportunity Areas have far more data-rich underpinnings. However, their targeting is based on a methodology that focuses on pupil outcomes. Thus, they focus on effect rather than cause. As a result, these policies follow in their counterparts' mould by forgoing the necessary grounding in the area-level causal conditions that they set out to tackle. Moreover, as analysis by Education Datalab shows, targeting local authority areas with low average pupil attainment only captures a relatively small proportion of the lowest performing pupils nationally – many of whom live in areas where attainment is, on average, strong [11]. As a result, any area-based approach which targets areas, fully or in part, based on average pupil outcomes risks missing a large proportion of the young people who would benefit most from targeted support. Most area-based initiatives in education fall foul of this "ecological fallacy", where we wrongly assume that the characteristics of individuals can be inferred from the characteristics of the areas they live in [1].

In summary, area-based policymaking in education tends to either:

a) be too vague about the kinds of area where young people struggle, using descriptors such as "deprived" which capture a wide variety of contexts, many of which do not harbour poor outcomes; or,

b) home in on specific areas where we know outcomes are poor, but without demonstrating much understanding of the features of these areas that might be involved in producing these outcomes.

The first approach leads us to cast the net too wide, while the second approach encourages us to focus on effects rather than causes. In the remainder of this Chapter, I make the case for a third approach to area-based targeting (see Table 4.2). This has the potential to open up an era of more effective area-based policymaking in education. In making this case I draw on existing distinctions between different approaches to talking about, describing and classifying places, in particular the work of Lupton et al. [12].

4.4 Where next?

There is an alternative approach to identifying the type of places in which young people are most likely to be marginalised, and it involves "types" of area. This

Table 4.2 Relative merits of different approaches to targeting area-based education policies

Approach	Outcomes targeting	Understanding of area-level causes
1) Deprivation-led	Index of Multiple Deprivation scores are moderately linked to educational outcomes, but with many key exceptions. For instance, in some deprived areas, such as inner London, educational outcomes are strong.	IMD provides a rich understanding of area-level context on a range of domains. However, the Index provides a rank ordering of areas rather than a sense of different "types" of area, and deprived areas comes in various different forms. For example, Blackpool and Hackney are both in the top ten most deprived local authorities but have stark differences in their ethnic composition, urban/rural location and characteristics of their local economies.
2) Opportunity Areas	Opportunity Areas are strongly linked to educational outcomes, with OAs targeted according to a range of outcome measures.	While very specific geographical locations are targeted, little is understood about the area-level causes at play in each location. OAs are based on far fewer area-level characteristics than IMD; they provide a limited picture of area-level context which is mainly based on features of the local education system.
3) Area types	The "type" of area a neighbourhood belongs to is a better predictor of young people's outcomes than its degree of deprivation.	Area types are based on a wide range of characteristics, and clustered into meaningful "types", allowing us to draw qualitative distinctions between areas accompanied with tangible descriptions of their common features.

approach begins with a range of data on the characteristics of every small area of the country, from the average qualification levels of their residents, to the type of housing they live in, their ethnic composition, whether or not they own a car and how many children they have, alongside dozens of other indicators. To this extent, a focus on area "types" is based on similar foundations to approaches focusing on "deprivation" or "disadvantage". However, area-based approaches built on the Index of Multiple Deprivation or Achieving Excellence Areas Index combine this wide pool of indicators into a single, unidimensional score or rank, which does not allow for meaningful distinctions between different "types" of area [4]. An approach built on area "types", on the other hand, looks for distinct groups of areas, defined by clusters of one or more characteristics that particularly stand out.

Two types of area might emerge which have similar levels of deprivation but entirely different mixes of housing and quite distinct ethnic compositions. This approach yields qualitatively distinct clusters of area rather than simply more or less "deprived" or "disadvantaged" ones. One type of deprived area might generally be found in inner cities; another might generally be found on the urban periphery and the coast. Taking the average of young people's outcomes in each area type, we can then target those area types in which average outcomes are relatively poor. This approach also means that young people's outcomes are treated, as they should be, as an outcome – rather than as the main component of the description of the area they live in, as is the case with Opportunity Areas. Because area types are constructed on the basis of characteristics of the areas themselves, we can talk more meaningfully about how these structural conditions shape young people's outcomes.

By grouping areas into types, we acknowledge that places like the ones I visited in London and Manchester might be separated by distance but nonetheless share common features. These features might, in turn, be determined by wider national forces, such as the differential effect that particular social and economic policies have on areas with particular histories of industry and employment [5].

As Lupton (drawing on the foundational work of Doreen Massey) argues, "the characteristics of poor neighbourhoods... are the spatial consequence of the wider dynamics of the post-industrial economic order" [13]. By grouping areas into types, and acknowledging that their similarities are often due to a shared exposure to wider political and economic forces, there is an inherent risk of overlooking the nuances of specific places (see Table 4.4 on p.87); the sense in which all areas are unique and have localised features, such as amenities, transport links and local norms which need to be understood in order to make "sense" of a place [14]. In putting forward a case for focusing on "types" of area in education policymaking, I acknowledge that there are different layers of causes that marginalise young people in particular areas; some neighbourhood-level causes might be properly local, while others really have a basis in wider features of our national economy.

Despite this balancing act, all in all, an area type-based approach instantly opens up a more meaningful conversation about the richly diverse contexts in which young people grow up, and overcomes the weaknesses inherent in the two main existing approaches to targeting area-based policies in education (see Table 4.2).

4.5 The power of "area type"

A range of research sets out to explore the relative importance of the individual, school, family and neighbourhood when it comes to impact on young people's educational outcomes when they leave school. Despite the range of estimates emerging from this research base, the overall pattern is clear: the characteristics of individual pupils and their families account for the vast majority (around 80%) of the differences in young people's attainment, with secondary schools accounting for around 10%, and primary school and area effects making up the remaining 10% [15].

The most sophisticated studies of the relative importance of neighbourhood effects are multilevel models which take into account the fact that pupils are not individual islands of characteristics, but share things in common such as the school they attend, the class they sit in for maths, or the street they live in, and that these shared characteristics have an impact on how they do. When it comes to the effect of school and neighbourhood, some of the most rigorous studies also take into account the fact that young people's contexts are not static; they change schools, or move house, and so these models provide a truer picture of the sometimes piece-meal spatial and institutional contexts that young people move through during their time in compulsory education. A study of this type from the University of Bristol found a small but significant area effect on young people's GCSE results [16], p.547.

Contemporary studies of the relative effect of the individual, family, school and neighbourhood may have sophisticated designs, taking into account young people's shared characteristics and the upheavals they experience. However, they tend to look at areas through the lens of deprivation scores, in the tradition of area-based policymaking in education, and this provides only a limited picture of the role that neighbourhoods play. This is not a new critique of the literature on area effects. As Lupton [13], p.10 argues, most neighbourhoods research is based on quantitative methods that are restricted to the datasets available. This leads to three main weaknesses in the literature:

> It tends... to focus on temporally current features of neighbourhoods rather than their historical evolution, on neighbourhoods in isolation rather than in relation to others, and on characteristics of neighbourhood residents (such as poverty or employment status) rather than broader economic and social processes.

In 2007, two geographers brought a different angle to the matter and looked at how young people's outcomes at school vary between different types of area, using market research data that groups postcodes according to hundreds of area-level variables, from Census-based statistics on health and employment, to survey-based measures relating to expenditure and social attitudes. Their analysis was simple, but it suggested that area type could be as powerful a predictor of a young person's attainment at the end of secondary school as any other data we hold about them [16]. More recently, my own analysis using the Office for National Statistics' Output Area Classification suggests much the same: on the face of it, area type appears to be a more powerful predictor of GCSE attainment than area-level deprivation [17].

Without applying more sophisticated modelling techniques, however, we cannot accurately estimate the effect of the type of area in which a young person lives, compared to the role of individual, family and school characteristics. Using a quantitative approach, the effect of area type is likely to be relatively small compared to these other characteristics, partly because many of the most powerful determinants of educational outcomes, such as class and ethnicity, tend to be understood in statistical analyses as purely properties of individuals and families: when we consider them as features of an area, their effect has already been accounted for by these individual-level variables. Qualitative research, on the other hand, tends to adopt a more interconnected view of individuals and areas, where people shape places and places shape people. For instance, the presence of a high proportion of unemployed people in an area (a fact about individuals) may give rise to certain forms of local identity and institutional provision (a fact about an area as "a place with high unemployment"), which in turn influences local people's ability to engage with the labour market [18]. For this reason, as van Ham et al. argue, "studies using qualitative methods, which focus on the experiences and perceptions of residents, have tended to report stronger and more consistent evidence of neighbourhood effects than those that use quantitative methodologies" [5].

For the time being, quantitative studies of area effects are unlikely to find that neighbourhood type has a sizeable impact on young people's outcomes. However, this arguably reflects the difficulty of capturing what we mean by "place" and "neighbourhood" in existing datasets, rather than the insignificance of place itself.

4.6 The new frontiers

To date, researchers have yet to unlock the full potential of area typologies, such as the Output Area Classification, to explore and explain how young people's lives are shaped by the spatial contexts they inhabit. However, we do have early indications of the types of area in which young people's outcomes fall short, and to a large extent these are areas that sit on the margins – away from the highly deprived urban centres that have traditionally formed the focus of education policies and interventions.

My own research suggests that there are stark differences in aspirations [19], school effectiveness [20], and pupil attainment [21] between ethnically mixed, inner city area types, and ethnically homogenous neighbourhoods that we tend to find on the outskirts of urban areas – like the ones I know in south London and south Manchester. For instance, pupils attending schools in "cosmopolitan" inner city areas outperform those in "hard-pressed" outer-urban areas by almost a grade and a half in every GCSE they sit – even though both of these contexts are similarly deprived (see Table 4.3). Although educational disadvantage, in terms of free school meal eligibility, is becoming less and less concentrated in urban centres [19], inner-urban areas continue to rank highest on broad measures of deprivation. Such measures of deprivation, then, do not offer the best compass for identifying areas of educational disadvantage. Meanwhile, my own analysis of relatively less deprived areas where young people's educational outcomes are relatively poor identifies a "belt" of marginalised young people across the heart of the country – away from the main urban centres which still attract such a large proportion of policy focus [22]. These are areas that would not necessarily be highlighted on a map of the most deprived parts of the country, and yet they are the types of area where young people can be most marginalised.

Table 4.3 Descriptions of the two OAC area types with the most divergent outcomes for young people [23]

OAC supergroup	Characteristics
Cosmopolitans	The majority of the population in this supergroup live in densely populated urban areas. They are more likely to live in flats and communal establishments, and private renting is more prevalent than nationally. The group has a high ethnic integration, with an above average number of residents from EU accession countries coinciding with a below average proportion of persons stating their country of birth as the UK or Ireland. A result of this is that households are less likely to speak English or Welsh as their main language. The population of the group is characterised by young adults, with a higher proportion of single adults and households without children than nationally. There are also higher proportions of full-time students. Workers are more likely to be employed in the accommodation, information and communication, and financial related industries, and using public transport, or walking or cycling to get to work.
Hard-pressed communities	The population of this group is most likely to be found in urban surroundings, predominately in northern England and southern Wales. There is less non-White ethnic group representation than elsewhere in the UK, and a higher than average proportion of residents born in the UK and Ireland. Rates of divorce and separation are above the national average. Households are more likely to have non-dependent children and are more likely to live in semi-detached or terraced properties, and to socially rent. There is a smaller proportion of people with higher level qualifications, with rates of unemployment above the national average. Those in employment are more likely to be employed in the mining, manufacturing, energy, wholesale and retail, and transport related industries.

4.7 Area effects and the role of "place"

Identifying area-level associations with particular education- and youth-related outcomes is not the same as explaining how these effects operate. Existing academic research, particularly quantitative work, tends to focus its attention on identifying area-level differences in outcomes, whilst spending relatively little time explaining the causal mechanisms which bring about these spatial patterns (p.3 [5]). Policy discourse proceeds in much the same vein. The effort expended on identifying target areas for intervention outweighs the time spent getting under the skin of exactly how young people respond to spatial environments. As I propose elsewhere [24], the literature on area-based effects identifies six broad ways in which areas shape young people's outcomes (see Table 4.4). My typology draws

Table 4.4 Types of mechanism through which area effects are realised

Mechanism	Examples
Institutional resources	The presence of local amenities, their quality and capacity, e.g. leisure facilities, libraries, parks and open spaces, youth clubs.
Norms and collective socialisation	Ways of looking at the world and patterns of behaviour that are locally-rooted, e.g. traditions and customs, a sense of belonging to a regional or urban centre, class identities linked to local industries.
Relative perceptions	People's sense of how their area is seen and defined by others, e.g. territorial identities, awareness of living somewhere with a "reputation".
Social capital	The ties, trust and knowledge that come from social interactions with family, friends, neighbours and other community members.
Routine activities	The way in which geography and elements of the planned environment, such as transport networks, organise and constrain how and when people come into contact with each other, e.g. the presence of busy roads, proximity of transport connections, availability of safe public spaces for gathering with friends.
The dynamics of local labour and housing markets	The quality and density of local housing, stability of private vs. social rental arrangements, proximity and diversity of job opportunities.

heavily on the work of Sampson et al. [7] and sits alongside others, most notably the work of Galster [5] who puts forward four types of mechanisms through which neighbourhood context shapes individual behavioural outcomes.

Many of these mechanisms demonstrate the importance of "place" – young people's subjective perceptions and understandings of the objective, officially labelled aspects of the world around them. The idea of place is central to a rounded understanding of area effects, because it captures how the features and characteristics of an area translate into the beliefs and actions that shape young people's outcomes at school and beyond.

For instance, my research in a "hard-pressed" outer-urban area of Manchester [25] revealed how boys could be aware of, and engaged by, the opportunities available in their neighbouring city, but simultaneously attached to family, friends and the familiarity of their community, which was planned and built as a post-war garden city and tightly bounded by countryside, motorways and an airport. One boy, despite wanting to pursue a university degree and a professional career, struggled with the idea of leaving this place which was "like the world... I've never been anywhere else."

Even when outer-urban, hard-pressed communities have good transport links to further and higher education and employment prospects, a sense of place can increase the perceived risk of pursuing these opportunities and leaving behind what is familiar. Ultimately this process of converting spatial surroundings into a sense of place is highly individualised: a group of young people can produce myriad ideas of place from the same outer-urban deprived context [18]. The process can also be highly nuanced, and powerful. I found that boys from the same isolated, outer-urban neighbourhood might be equally aware of the shortcomings and reputation of their neighbourhood, but some would translate this into a territorial sense of place which drove them to stay whilst others would develop an outward-looking sense of place which motivated them to leave. Ultimately, a young person's sense of place is rooted in an idea of living in a "type" of area; a discussion that goes far beyond whether their neighbourhood is more or less deprived.

Taken together, these insights suggest that area-based policymaking in education should pay more consideration to types of area, young people's understandings of their area, and the concrete ways in which areas shape young people's lives, rather than simply identifying associations between areas and outcomes.

A good start would be to focus systematically on the types of area where young people's outcomes seem to be most precarious. These are areas that the government's own typologies variously refer to as hard-pressed communities, and areas with a services and industrial legacy.

In England, the largest clusters of these area types are in the urban areas on the periphery of Birmingham, in a line between Nottingham and Leeds, and between Manchester and Liverpool. However, smaller pockets can be found in housing estates on the edges of most cities and towns, including many urban fringes with little or no connection to large urban conurbations, or the ex-mining or manufacturing context that tends to receive much attention in education research.

We should pay more attention to the features that appear to make these areas distinctive, and the ways in which they work together to shape daily life.

To illustrate one example, families in hard-pressed or manufacturing legacy areas are more likely to have a family member with low qualifications, without a job and with poor health and, therefore, to have younger family members with caring or earning responsibilities. This translates into an increased likelihood of adult children living at home – an arrangement that is facilitated by the nature of the housing stock in these areas which is often large, socially rented and, therefore, accompanied by some degree of stability despite families' precarious financial situations. Conducting my fieldwork on the edge of Manchester I saw how this web of factors that is often hidden under the surface of headline statistics became clear on the ground. I also watched how it shaped the lives of many of the young people I spoke to, in many cases limiting their horizons.

Crucially, I also saw how "hard-pressed" neighbourhoods contained countless assets, from dynamic and committed forms of third-sector provision, to a strong sense of historical connectedness, and a commitment to fight against the sense of fatalism that can take root in an area's reputation. We know in broad terms that community-level resources and structures can be relatively strong in deprived inner-urban areas, but that they can be weaker in more peripheral hard-pressed areas. Where present, these assets can all be directly channelled into improving young people's outcomes. They are genuinely area-level characteristics, which can't be captured by simply aggregating individual- and household-level features. The Community Needs Index [22] offers a useful way forward in capturing these assets and needs, or "opportunity structures" as they are often termed in the literature [26]. The Index draws together multiple measures of local social infrastructure, connectedness, and community activity and engagement. Community needs appear to be strongly linked to area type, and are highest in hard-pressed communities. This paves the way for a better understanding of how young people's home lives are overlaid with area-level characteristics such as access to community, civic and cultural assets, services and digital infrastructure, the extent of democratic participation and the vitality of the local community and voluntary sector.

4.8 Conclusion

In England today, young people's educational outcomes continue to vary significantly between different parts of the country, despite decades of area-based education policymaking. While previous and current policies have tackled this problem using a range of different policy levers, and chosen their target areas with increasingly sophisticated datasets, they have largely failed to make headway because of two common shortcomings.

Firstly, area-based policies have tended to target areas based on a broad notion of deprivation, which does not always provide a clear or useful compass for locating educational disadvantage. This approach does not distinguish between different "types" of deprived area, despite evidence suggesting that the largest area-level differences are between different types of area rather than more and less deprived ones. In many deprived areas, including a considerable chunk of London, young people's educational outcomes in the aggregate offer no particular cause for concern. As a result, by focusing on deprivation, we overlook many of the places, and young people, who are truly marginalised.

Secondly, area-based policies have tended to gloss over the causal mechanisms that link young people's neighbourhoods to their individual outcomes (see Table 4.4), leading Lupton to point out that *how* an area contributes to educational disadvantage is often "weakly articulated" in policy texts (p.15 [1]).

Policies such as "Opportunity Areas" are often heavily focused on outcomes – defining their target areas primarily, or entirely, in terms of those outcomes. At the same time, they are often light on their descriptions of the areas they focus on, and their hypotheses of how area-level features shape young people's outcomes. This weakness is bound up with the use of sliding quantitative scales of deprivation, rather than more qualitative distinctions between types of area, drawing on the particular clusters of characteristics they house. It is also bound up with the general practice of defining areas according to aggregated features of the people who live in them (such as unemployment, qualification levels, and poor health), rather than genuinely area-level features (such as the presence of particular amenities, and the shape of the labour market).

Another important part of the causal story that policy tends to overlook is the role of "place" – that is, how young people interpret their surroundings, and how these interpretations frame and shape their actions. My research demonstrates that young people's sense of place can provide the key to understanding important elements of their school-to-work transitions, such as their aspirations.

Adopting an approach to area-based policymaking that sees the world through the lens of area types, and develops better causal stories of how neighbourhood contexts shape young people's outcomes, would put efforts to tackle area-based inequalities in education on a stronger footing. It would also reduce the risk of overlooking young people on the margins by helping us spot common issues, whilst making it easier to understand the causes that link young people's outcomes with the neighbourhoods they live in.

Specifically, we need to focus more attention on the hard-pressed, "left behind", outer-urban neighbourhoods that can be found on the edge of almost all metropolitan areas in England, like those I visited on the fringes of Manchester and London. While many of these neighbourhoods sit in parts of the country that are accustomed to the policymaker's magnifying glass, such as the former industrial towns and cities of the North and Midlands, we should pay equal attention to the hard-pressed neighbourhoods that lie elsewhere in England and face similar struggles, such as the peripheries of smaller cities and towns. There are hundreds of such neighbourhoods across England, from Penzance to Berwick, but adopting the lens of area types allows us to take two important steps. Firstly, it allows us to see the similarities between the individual predicaments of these places. Secondly, we can identify common policies and approaches which, if successful in one hard-pressed outer-urban area, stand a good chance of working in another.

4.9 Taking action

In this chapter I have proposed an approach to area-based education policymaking that has the potential to significantly improve our chances of effectively supporting young people on the margins. Despite decades of policy attention, area-based inequalities in young people's outcomes persist, and a new approach is needed.

■ School improvement, leadership development, and teacher recruitment programmes should be geographically targeted based on the area types in which outcomes are poor, rather than on the basis of deprivation alone. For example, the Department for Education should support experienced governors and senior leaders to take up roles in areas with limited infrastructure for system leadership (for example few teaching schools or National Leaders of Education). Schools in these areas are likely to face similar challenges but have access to more limited resources for school improvement.

■ The Department for Education should establish a "Challenge" for schools in hard-pressed areas, similar to the London, Manchester and Black Country Challenges that ran between 2003 and 2011. This could involve forming families of schools which serve similar communities in different parts of the country, to share expertise between geographically distant areas and provide opportunities for professional development.

■ As part of their preparation for a school inspection, Ofsted should provide inspectors with pen portraits of the main area types from which a school draws its pupils, to help them quickly but accurately begin to understand a school's context.

Meanwhile, school leaders should:

■ Draw on students' understandings of "place" (for example through student councils). This could support efforts to engage with parents and employers and shape an effective careers education offer. This approach would ensure employer engagement is more responsive to students' concerns or misconceptions about the local labour market.

■ Work with academics to create opportunities for teachers to engage in research that deepens their knowledge of the local context in which they work, and how their efforts to raise attainment for "disadvantaged" pupils can be honed to their specific areas context. Research opportunities could form the basis of long-term partnerships between schools and universities, leading to ongoing, accredited professional development that feed into schools' improvement plans [24, 27].

■ MATs should use area typologies to build hubs of schools with common contextual challenges, even when the schools within them may be a considerable distance apart. This approach would allow MATs to build meaningful clusters of schools, with a common approach to responding to neighbourhood context, such as supporting young people's aspirations and expectations in areas lacking diverse labour market opportunities.

Further reading

Place, space and imagined futures: how young people's occupational aspirations are shaped by the areas they live in: Baars, S. (2014). University of Manchester.

Educational failure and working class white children in Britain: Evans, G. (2006). London: Palgrave Macmillan UK.

2011 OAC: Geodemographics derived from the UK's 2011 census: Gale, C. and O'Brien, O. (2020). Available at: https://oac.datashine.org.uk/ [Accessed June 5, 2020].

The Mechanism(s) of Neighbourhood Effects: Theory, Evidence, and Policy Implications: Galster, G. (2012). in M. van Ham, D. Manley, N. Bailey, L. Simpson, and D. Maclennan (eds) *Neighbourhood effects research: new perspectivese*, London: Springer.

Using and developing place typologies for policy purposes: Lupton, R., Tunstall, R., Fenton, A. and Harris, R. (2011). London: DCLG.

References

1 Lupton, R. (2010). Area-based initiatives in English education: what place for place and space? In C. Raffo, A. Dyson, H. Gunter, D. Hall, L. Jones, & A. Kalambouka (Eds.), *Poverty and education in affluent countries*. London: Routledge, 111–123.

2 National Audit Office. (2001). *Education action zones: Meeting the Challenge – the lessons identified from auditing the first 25 zones*. London: National Audit Office.

3 Sammons, P., Kysel, F., & Mortimore, P. (1983). Educational Priority Indices: A New Perspective. *British Educational Research Journal*, 9(1), 27–40.

4 Smith, G.. (1987). Whatever Happened to Educational Priority Areas? *Oxford Review of Education*, 13(1), 23–38.

5 George Galster. (2012). The mechanism(s) of neighbourhood effects: theory, evidence, and policy implications. In M. van Ham, D. Manley, N. Bailey, L. Simpson, & D. Maclennan (Eds.), *Neighbourhood effects research: new perspectives*. London: Springer, 23–56.

6 Leckie, G. (2009). The Complexity of School and Neighbourhood Effects and Movements of Pupils on School Differences in Models of Educational Achievement. *Journal of the Royal Statistical Society. Series A: Statistics in Society*, 172(3), 537–554.

7 Sampson, R. J., Morenoff, J. D., & Gannon-Rowley, T. (2002). Assessing "Neighbourhood Effects": Social Processes and New Directions in Research. *Annual Review of Sociology*, 28(1), 443–478.

8 van Ham, M., Manley, D., Bailey, N., Simpson, L., & Maclennan, D. (2012). *Neighbourhood effects research: new perspectives*. London: Springer.

9 Lupton, R., Tunstall, R., Fenton, A., & Harris, R. (3). *Using and developing place typologies for policy purposes*. London: DCLG.

10 Office for National Statistics. (2015). 2011 residential-based area classifications – Pen portraits and radial plots. Retrieved January 21, 2020, from https://www.ons.gov.uk/methodology/geography/geographicalproducts/areaclassifications/2011areaclassifications/penportraitsandradialplots.

11 FFT Education Datalab. (2016). Social mobility opportunity areas: déjà-vu, again? Retrieved June 5, 2020, from https://ffteducationdatalab.org.uk/2016/10/social-mobility-opportunity-areas-deja-vu-again/.

12 Lupton, R., Tunstall, R., Fenton, A., & Harris, R. (3). *Using and developing place typologies for policy purposes.* London: DCLG.

13 Lupton, R. (2016). Re-thinking values and schooling in white working class neighbourhoods. In C. Timmerman, N. Clycq, M. McAndrew, B. Alhassane, L. Braeckmans, & S. Mels (Eds.), *Youth in education: the necessity of valuing ethnocultural diversity.* Abingdon; New York: Routledge, 233-248.

14 Thomson, P. (2002). *Schooling the rustbelt kids: making the difference in changing times.* London: Trentham.

15 Cook, W. (2013). *How intake and other external factors affect school performance.* London: RISE.

16 Webber, R., & Butler, T. (2007). Classifying Pupils by Where They Live: How Well Does This Predict Variations in Their GCSE Results? *Urban Studies,* 44(7), 1229–1254.

17 Baars, S. (2015). *Inner city schools do better than ones in less deprived rural and suburban areas.* New Statesman. [Online]. 13th March 2015. Retrieved November 20, 2020, from:http://may2015.com/ideas/inner-city-schools-do-better-than-ones-in-less-deprived-rural-and-suburban-areas/.

18 Baars, S. (2014). Place, space and imagined futures: how young people's occupational aspirations are shaped by the areas they live in. University of Manchester, Manchester.

19 FFT Education Datalab. (2017). Explore England's changing free school meals rates. Retrieved January 21, 2020, from https://ffteducationdatalab.org.uk/2017/12/explore-englands-changing-free-school-meals-rates/.

20 Baars, S. (2014). The coastal question: ofsted and the new frontiers in education research. Retrieved January 21, 2020, from https://cfey.org/2014/11/the-coastal-question-ofsted-and-the-new-frontiers-in-education-research/.

21 Baars, S. (2015). Inner city schools do better than ones in less deprived rural and suburban areas. New Statesman.

22 Baars, S. (2013). Counter-deprivational outcomes. Retrieved January 21, 2020, from http://sambaars.com/counter-deprivational-outcomes/.

23 OCSI. (2019). *Developing a measure of 'Left-behind' areas Phase 2.* Brighton: OCSI.

24 University of Manchester. (2020). *Local matters.* Retrieved June 5, 2020, from https://www.research.manchester.ac.uk/portal/en/projects/local-matters(d9cb0336–6364-4c20-8af0-868a40e1d63c).html.

25 Baars, S. (2017). White working-class boys in the neoliberal meritocracy: the pitfalls of the "Aspiration-Raising" agenda. In G. Stahl, J. Nelson, & D. Wallace (Eds.), *Masculinity and aspiration in an era of neoliberal education.* London: Routledge, 53-68.

26 Roberts, K. (2009). Opportunity Structures Then and Now. *Journal of Education and Work,* 22(5), 355–368.

27 Beckett, L. (2012). "Trust the Teachers, Mother!": The Leading Learning Project in Leeds. *Improving Schools,* 15(1), 10–22.

5 Gypsy, Roma and Traveller young people

Ellie Mulcahy and Abi Angus

5.1 Introduction

In spring of 2017, I began a research project about one of the most marginalised groups of people in the UK: Gypsies, Roma and Travellers (GRT). Days spent reading literature on the poor educational achievement and plethora of other disadvantages experienced by these communities ignited a sense of déjà vu. The research stretched back decades and yet reports written a couple of years ago were strikingly similar to those written in the 60s and 70s. It seemed the issue had been long publicised and yet very little had changed.

However, it was not until I started engaging with members of GRT communities and those that work with them, that I truly began to appreciate both the pervasiveness of their marginalisation in society and the frustration brought about by a systematic failure to address issues affecting this community.

On a windy May day, in a basement seminar room of King's College London, we gathered together a group of experts and practitioners, many from GRT backgrounds, for a roundtable discussion on GRT pupils' educational outcomes. It was the first roundtable I had ever chaired and I was excited about the opportunity to speak to such a diverse range of experts. However, it quickly became one of the most difficult conversations I have been involved in, let alone managed, and still remains the most challenging research activity I have conducted.

What made the experience so different to similar roundtables I have chaired since, was the rawness of attendees' emotions. I remember one person explaining the extent to which mainstream media, including television programmes like *My Big Fat Gypsy Wedding*, had exacerbated the racism and bullying her children suffered at school. She said that the bullying they experienced was "merciless" and the racist slurs directed at her children were not addressed by teachers. This built a tension that was palpable, and I left feeling that although many participants had brought clear insights and practical solutions to the discussion, the road to a fair education for this group of young people remained a long one.

This chapter explores what I learnt conducting this research and speaking with people from GRT communities. Firstly, we look at who these groups actually are; how they are defined and how many young people from GRT backgrounds there are. Next, we highlight data on the group's educational outcomes to show why these young people's experiences in education warrant a chapter in this book. We explore the range of challenges and barriers to education that many GRT families face, while dispelling misconceptions. Finally, we set out what can be done to ensure GRT children and young people are included in education and achieve positive outcomes.

Throughout, we seek to avoid a deficit discourse, instead recognising the value of cultural practices that may sit uneasily alongside mainstream systems, whilst also highlighting the severity of the issues and outcomes experienced by GRT pupils and communities. This is not always an easy balance and perhaps contributes to so few people in the sector being willing to participate in an open discussion about the persistent racism experienced by GRT communities. We also emphasise the need to acknowledge the diversity and variation within the communities that fall under the GRT umbrella term, while recognising the commonalities that can point the way towards strategies that might improve outcomes and contribute to greater social justice.

5.2 Who are these young people?

5.2.1 Different groups

GRT is an umbrella term. No individual identifies as a *"Gypsy, Roma and Traveller"* as each of the three groups is distinct and comprised of multiple sub-groups. Table 5.1 describes the main groups but is not an exhaustive list of communities that could be included under the term "GRT".

Knowing these groups and categorisations can be useful, but it is important to understand that, as Brian Belton, an academic, author and English Gypsy, puts it, "hard edged and simplistic categorisations" are problematic. For example, while British Gypsy and Roma people are grouped under "Romany Gypsies" based on shared ancestry, nowadays, individuals may consider themselves to be from distinct groups and may face different circumstances and challenges. Furthermore, many Roma people view the term "Gypsy" as a slur due to its derogatory use in Europe.

Nevertheless, these groups share some cultural similarities as well as multiple disadvantages and some of the poorest outcomes of all ethnic groups in the UK, including [2]:

- the poorest health outcomes in the UK;

- lower than average life expectancy;

- poor educational attainment and low levels of qualifications; and

- considerable prejudice, racism and discrimination.

Table 5.1 Summary of GRT groups [1]

Summary of GRT groups

Ethnic Travellers	Romany — English or Welsh "Romany" Gypsies (or Welsh Kale)	Sometimes referred to as "Romanichal", these people have a long history of living and travelling in the UK. It is suggested that they originated in India, although their ancestry has been disputed in the literature (see Okley, 1997). Many speak one of seven distinct languages, primarily Anglo-Romanes and Romani, as well as English.
	European Roma	Though descended from the same ancestry as British Romany Gypsies this group arrived only recently in the UK from central and Eastern Europe, following the expansion of the EU to include Eastern European countries such as Romania, Hungary, Poland, Slovakia and the Czech Republic. Roma includes a great variety of groups, distinct in their language, culture and values. This group often rejects the term "Gypsy", preferring "Roma". This creates a problem of low ascription rates when they are asked to identify in a group under a term which includes "Gypsy" such as in the school census category "Gypsy/Roma". Generally, the European Roma have only limited interaction with other Romany Gypsies.
	"Travellers" — Irish Travellers	Also called "Pavee" and "Mincéiri", these Travellers often move between the UK and Ireland and are of Celtic descent. The term "Traveller of Irish Heritage" is used in the census and on other official forms. They speak "Cant" or "Gammon", termed "Shelta" by some linguists, as well as English.
	Scottish Gypsy Travellers	This subgroup consists of further subgroups and was only recently recognised as a separate ethnic group. They may also refer to themselves as "Nachins" and "Nawkins".
Cultural Travellers	Occupational Travellers — Showmen: fairground and circus people	Showmen have a long history in the UK where fairgrounds have been popular for many centuries. Showmen own and work on fairgrounds and circuses and travel to different sites for seasonal work.
	Bargees and boat dwellers	Those who live on boats, primarily narrowboats, on canals and waterways. Historically, barges and boat dwellers travelled for employment.
	New Travellers	Though the term "new" is seen as offensive to some, it is used to differentiate Travellers who adopted the travelling lifestyle since the 1970s by choice. Often this group simply call themselves "Travellers".

5.2.2 Population and demographics

It is difficult to pin point exactly how many GRT people there are in the UK and how many GRT pupils there are in school, or indeed, out of school. Official census statistics underestimate the size of the population significantly due to low literacy rates, the failure to distribute the census to those in mobile housing and a reluctance to publicly identify as a Gypsy, Roma or Traveller for fear of discrimination.

A category for "Gypsy, Traveller or Irish Traveller" was included on the census for the first time in 2011[1]. 63,000 people in the UK ascribed their identity as such, making them the smallest ethnic group in the UK (0.1% of the population). However, researchers estimate the true population to be around 250,000 to 300,000 [3].

In 2011, there was no opportunity for Roma to ascribe their ethnicity on the census. However, the 2021 census is due to include it [4]. In 2013, it was estimated that there are approximately 200,000 Roma in the UK and the population is heavily skewed to younger age groups. Taking these figures together puts the total GRT population at half a million, 0.8% of the population, or 1 in every 125 people in the UK.

School census counts do not give us an accurate impression of the number of school aged GRT young people in the UK either. Table 5.2 shows the official count of Gypsy, Traveller and Roma young people in primary and secondary schools. The school census uses different categorisations to the national census, including the highly problematic combination of Gypsy and Roma despite it being widely known that Roma people are understandably unwilling to identify themselves under the term "Gypsy". Therefore, studies estimating the true size of the Roma population may be more useful.

The proportion of GRT pupils in secondary school is much lower than the proportion at primary school and this drop is due to the large proportion of GRT pupils who attend primary school but either do not progress to secondary school

Table 5.2 GRT population estimates

Source	School Phase	Subgroup	Number
		Gypsy/Roma	18,000
	Primary School	Traveller of Irish Heritage	4,600
School Census Statistics		Gypsy/Roma	8,000
	Secondary School	Traveller of Irish Heritage	1,000
Brown, Martin and Scullion (2013) and Penfold (2015)	All phases	Roma	124,000

or do so, but leave in Key Stage 3 or early in Key Stage 4. A higher proportion of GRT children are home schooled or not in registered in any school compared to the rest of the population.

This "under-ascription" is an issue with far reaching consequences which is why I feel so passionately about the need to encourage ascription and to change ethnicity categories in the census whilst creating welcoming school cultures. At the moment, under-ascription makes it easier for policymakers to underestimate the number of people affected by issues, weakening the impetus to take action. It also means that practitioners may not know who their GRT pupils are, which makes it hard to ensure they get the right support.

Mark Penfold, EAL lead at a high performing school in Leicester and an expert in Roma education, told me how at Babington Academy, an institution often held up by the DfE as a beacon of excellent practice with Roma pupils, they "encourage pupils to say, "I'm Roma, I'm proud of being Roma"". Mark emphasised that getting pupils to identify as Roma is "the first step and a key step" in helping the school connect with families.

5.3 What is the cause for concern?

GRT pupils have the worst educational outcomes in the UK, from the Early Years to higher education, on all measures including attainment, attendance, exclusions and higher education participation. The trends are stark.

Far fewer pupils ascribing as "Traveller of Irish Heritage" and "Gypsy/Roma" achieve "a good level of development" at the end of their reception year, compared to the national average, for example in 2018–19 only a third of Gypsy/ Roma children and 4 in 10 Irish Traveller children achieved "a good level of development" compared to nearly three-quarters of children nationally. The situation only worsens as children progress through the Key Stages. At GCSE only 14% of Gypsy/Roma young people and 28% Irish Traveller pupils achieve grades 4–9 in GCSE English and Maths compared to 64% nationally, less than 10% of pupils from these groups achieve strong passes (grade 5–9) at GCSE English and Maths.

GRT pupil groups also achieve a progress 8 score of between −0.8 and −1.05 at secondary school and have an average attainment 8 score less than half the national average (Figure 5.1).

GRT pupils also have the highest exclusion rate of any ethnic group. For example, in 2017–18 the rate of temporary exclusion for Black Caribbean pupils was 10% but for Gypsy/Roma pupils and pupils of Irish Traveller Heritage it was around 17%. As shown in Chapter 1, the consequences of exclusion are far reaching for both the young person and society (Figure 5.2).

"This is not a new problem". We are not suddenly unearthing this shocking data and scratching our heads trying to come up with solutions. Over 50 years ago, the Plowden report said that Gypsy children were "probably the most severely

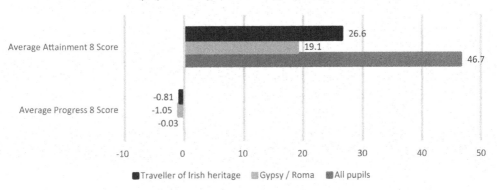

Figure 5.1 Attainment of Gypsy/Roma and Irish Traveller pupils (2019).

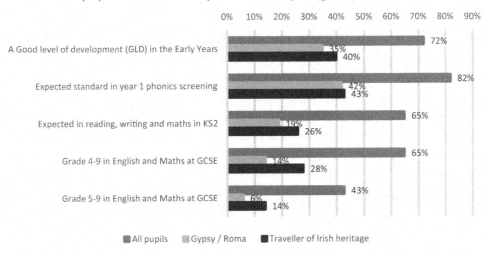

Figure 5.2 Outcomes of Gypsy/Roma and Irish Traveller pupils from Early Years to Key Stage 4 (2019).

deprived children in the country" and that their educational needs were "extreme and largely unmet" (p.59 [5]). The report also predicted what would happen to future generations of Gypsies:

> Unless action is taken to arrest the cycle, their children will in turn suffer educational deprivations which will become increasingly severe in their effects as general standards of education rise. (p.59 [6])

Unfortunately, action was not taken and this educational disadvantage has become "increasingly severe". Countless reports in the intervening decades identified similar issues and made almost identical calls for action. In April 2019, 52 years on from the Plowden report another government report reached eerily similar conclusions:

> Gypsies, Travellers and Roma are among the most disadvantaged people in the country and have poor outcomes in key areas such as health and education. (p.7 [7])

Once again, a high-profile government report was calling for action while acknowledging "there has been a persistent failure by both national and local policymakers" (p.3) to tackle long-understood disadvantage in these communities "in any sustained way". However, this report did not fully acknowledge the context of the past two decades in which retrenchment followed hot on the heels of promising progress.

Between 1990 and that late 2000s, there were a number of initiatives aimed at GRT pupils' underachievement, including centrally funded Traveller Education Service (TES), the National Strategies Programme and Ofsted's reviews and research on education outcomes for GRT pupils. Academics and practitioners that were involved at the time note that these activities were having a positive impact. However, in 2010 the political landscape changed.

The economic recession of 2009, followed by austerity, combined with the dramatic reduction of LA control, the growth of academies and what some describe as a narrowing of Ofsted's focus ultimately resulted in a considerable reduction in the support available to GRT pupils and families, perhaps most notably, the "savage" [8] reduction of the TES [9].

Given that the TESs were frequently cited as being at the core of good practice [10], their decimation was particularly discouraging. A 2019 report [11] by The Traveller Movement notes that "positive steps taken between the years of 2003–2008 have largely been reversed" (p.9), while a House of Commons report [12], published in the same year, notes that good practice and potential solutions were not novel solutions but instead felt like a return to the previous practice of TESs.

The fact that cuts have thwarted positive steps, is beyond frustrating; generations of young people have been failed and have not fulfilled their potential and it is this frustration that was expressed so fervently at our roundtable back in 2017.

It is easy to feel that without system change nothing will change, but individual practitioners can still take action in the face of policy inertia, and understanding the issues GRT young people and their communities face is an important first step in doing so.

5.4 Why are these young people marginalised?

GRT pupils can face a range of ethnic or culture-specific barriers to making the most of educational opportunities. On top of community specific issues, GRT children and young people are more likely to experience issues like poverty that hamper all affected young people's achievement.

On the other hand, it is important not to assume all GRT young people face these barriers – for example not all GRT young people grow up in poverty. During our research we worked with numerous families who were keen to emphasise that many GRT people have professional careers and are well off. Furthermore, issues that are frequently discussed, such as the impact of a nomadic lifestyle on education, do not apply to all, since many GRT families live in "bricks and mortar". It is therefore important not to assume that GRT young people are a homogeneous group or that they all come from poor or disadvantaged backgrounds.

Below, we outline the main issues which negatively impact on GRT pupils' educational progress. These potential barriers can be grouped under three headings:

1. **Prejudice and discrimination**.

2. **Cultural barriers** including: mobility and a nomadic lifestyle, difficulty navigating official systems, and, cultural norms and values that may be incompatible with an inflexible mainstream system.

3. **Material barriers** including housing issues and poverty.

5.4.1 Prejudice and discrimination: "The last respectable form of racism"

What shocked me most when I started studying the experiences of GRT communities were the statistics regarding attitudes towards them. Previous research has found that 50% of British people admitted having an "unfavourable view" of Roma people [13] and one in three held prejudice against Gypsies and Travellers [14]. When writing this chapter, I hoped to find updated statistics to indicate that things have improved, but I was disappointed.

A national poll in late 2017 found that around 40% of British people would be unhappy with a close relative having a serious relationship with a Gypsy or Traveller or their child having a playdate with a Gypsy or Traveller child [15]. 13% thought that Gypsies and Travellers should be refused entry to shops, restaurants and businesses because of their ethnicity. Thus, it appears that more than 1 in 10 British people consider overt discrimination against Gypsies and Travellers acceptable while a further 3 in 10 believe Gypsy and Travellers should be treated the same as others by businesses but would not extend them this respect in their own families. 15 years ago, Sir Trevor Phillips said that prejudice and discrimination towards GRT people was "the last respectable form of racism". It seems little has changed.

Fear of discrimination is the primary reason for GRT parents removing their children from school [16]. At times, this could be masked as disinterest in education or a reluctance to integrate with the non-GRT, "*gaujo*" or "buffer"[2], community. But given that as many as 80% of Gypsy and Traveller young people report suffering discrimination during their education, and a third believe teachers are prejudiced against them, it is not hard to see why this would be a chief concern of many GRT parents [17–19].

It is stories like Cassie's below that highlight the insidious and normalised nature of discrimination against these groups. It also serves to remind us that it is not just individuals who "cause trouble", "commit crimes" or "disrupt communities" by living on illegal sites (see section 5.4.3.2), that suffer the effects of this racism – not that those on illegal sites deserve to be subject to discrimination either. When children and young people endure "jokes" or taunts at school this unsurprisingly impacts their education.

Cassie's story

Cassie is a bright, twenty-something law graduate and a Romany Gypsy. I interviewed her because she was a young person who had "bucked the trend" by entering and completing higher education, something very few Romany Gypsy young people do.

Cassie called me from her offices at a law firm, during her break. She was friendly, interested in the research and clearly passionate about discussing her background and the challenges her peers might face.

I was expecting Cassie to tell me a story of how she overcame the barriers I had been reading about in the literature: insecure housing, a transient lifestyle, poverty and parents with little experience of education themselves. If I am honest, I was keen to hear about these barriers so that I could see how they had been tackled. However, Cassie's story was nothing like this. Her parents were educated professionals and she had grown up in a fairly affluent suburb in the home-counties, attending school regularly. For her, there were not "barriers to overcome", just a "normal" childhood, a talent for academia and a natural progression to higher education.

Nevertheless, her journey to university was punctuated by "small instances" of discrimination such as name calling from school peers following the release of *My Big Fat Gypsy Wedding* and occasions when she was pressured to hide her identity:

> I was drafting my personal statement and I put in a passage about how I wanted to go into law because of the discrimination that the community faced and I wanted to do something about it. But my tutor at college... said, "If I'm honest, I think you should take this passage out". It wasn't her prejudice, but she said "people are prejudiced".

The story she told me after telling me about her background and path to university brought home to me how inescapable this prejudice can be for many GRT young people.

In her first term reading law at one of the UK's highest-ranking universities she was sitting in a lecture next to her newly made friends when her lecturer made a joke about "pikeys". Everyone laughed. Cassie described how she remembered her face burning with embarrassment and with anger, but she did not feel she could do anything about it. She tried to avoid attending that lecturer's sessions from then on.

Here was a young person who- having avoided many of the disadvantages that others with the same ethnicity face - sat in her place of education feeling uncomfortable and out of place, enduring casual racist jokes made by people in positions of authority and influence. This exemplifies many GRT families' fears. As Cassie explained:

> To have a lecturer make a joke about "pikeys" and for 200 people around me to be actually belly-laughing while I sat there knowing I'm from that community and actually "pikey" is a derogatory term… It's the fear of things like that, it's one of the reasons that people pull kids out of school and why they are scared of university… so if universities are seriously committed to helping to raise aspiration and attainment, they've got to also be making sure that when the kids get there, things like that aren't happening. He probably didn't even know it was derogatory…it's just that ignorance, but the flipside of that is maybe he didn't think that in a million years anyone from that community would be sat in his lecture theatre.

5.4.2 Cultural Barriers: incompatible with mainstream systems

A range of cultural factors can act as barriers to GRT children and young people's education:

- exclusion from and difficulty navigating official systems;

- mobility and a nomadic lifestyle;

- differing cultural norms and values including differing employment aspirations, gender-based expectations and early onset adulthood; and

- a fear of cultural dilution or corruption.

5.4.2.1 Exclusion from official systems

Navigating various aspects of the education system, from school admissions to parents' evenings, can be difficult where families remain "culturally isolated" from mainstream systems and communities. Many GRT parents have limited or negative experiences of education and thus, can have limited knowledge regarding how to support their children through mainstream education. Meanwhile, for Roma parents, experiences of extreme institutionalised discrimination and state sanctioned segregation in their country of origin frequently leave them with a limited understanding of school systems or a fear of schools and staff.

Additionally, GRT adults are more likely than the general population to lack basic literacy skills, often as a direct result of historic failures to address GRT pupils' needs. Therefore, where accessing services and navigating systems requires filling in forms or writing letters this can be a barrier to engagement with education as well as other services such as welfare benefits or healthcare.

5.4.2.2 Mobility and a nomadic lifestyle

Traditionally, the fact that many GRT, particularly Gypsy and Traveller families, lived a nomadic lifestyle for part or all of the year was a major barrier to GRT children accessing a consistent education. However, living in "bricks and mortar", does not preclude people from being Gypsies or Travellers and in fact, only around a quarter of them live in mobile housing such as caravans. Even amongst these families, many do not travel, or only travel for part of the year [20]. Mobility is therefore not a barrier for the majority of GRT pupils. However, there are many issues relating to the decline in nomadism including "culture shock" caused by "forced settlement" – as many Gypsy and Traveller families who are "settled" still express a strong preference for travelling [21].

For the minority of pupils that do still travel regularly, this can indeed be disruptive to education. In such cases, schools need to take a flexible and supportive approach and we discuss this further below.

5.4.2.3 Differing cultural norms and values

Cultural norms in GRT communities may differ from mainstream norms, and given that the education system is built around mainstream culture, these communities' norms and values may sit at odds, resulting in a lack of engagement.

Research shows there is no lack of aspiration amongst parents and young people in GRT communities [22]; however, their aspirations may not align with the aims of mainstream education. Many GRT families are keen for children to continue a family business or take on traditional employment. The knowledge and skills that take priority in order to achieve these aspirations may conflict with those that are prioritised in formal schooling, especially once basic reading, writing and maths are mastered. This can mean that once children have finished primary school, the more advanced skills and subjects taught in secondary school are seen as less valuable for fulfilling aspirations related to traditional employment. This partly explains the tendency for some GRT children to be withdrawn from education after primary school.

Again, it is crucial to bear in mind that this does not apply to all GRT families. Given that in Eastern Europe, Roma pupils are often segregated into "special schools", Roma families in particular often highly value the mainstream, conventional education that is on offer in the UK since this was not available to them in their countries of origin.

Additionally, recent research suggests that GRT parents are becoming less likely to view formal, mainstream education as valueless or at odds with their aspirations. This is primarily due to increased mechanisation and difficulty making a living from traditional trades [23], as well as improved relationships with schools in some areas [20].

Caroline, a parent I interviewed for our research exemplifies this shift in attitudes. Caroline is a Showman. She grew up travelling with her family's fair and left school aged twelve to focus on learning the family trade, she explained: "we had what we needed and the rest you are going to learn just by doing it". Caroline now has two teenage children and her attitudes are very different to her parents'. She feels that making a living as a Showman is now too difficult and furthermore, does not want to restrain her children's aspirations and options. Crucially, she has a good relationship with her children's schools and teachers have also held high expectations of the children. Caroline's daughter has gone to university while her son is studying for his A levels.

However, in other families non-mainstream attitudes continue to take priority. At the roundtable I chaired on that May morning Chris Derrington highlighted that, in her five-year longitudinal study of GRT pupils [24] she observed that schools might find that pupils' initially broad aspirations narrow as they get older [1]. One Gypsy pupil who my colleague spoke to described a range of careers and educational pathways they could pursue while writing a "life timeline". However, he then titled this timeline "This wouldn't be so easy because Travellers normally work with their dad... most of the Travellers don't care about school". This highlights the conflict between a desire to pursue a wide range of options and the traditional expectations in some GRT communities (Figure 5.3).

This narrowing of aspirations as children enter adolescence is linked to a culture of "early onset adulthood" and specific gender roles.

In certain GRT cultures, some families consider young people to have reached adulthood at the age of 12 to 13 [23]. At this point they may be expected to contribute to their family economically and may also find it difficult to navigate their different roles between home, where they are treated as an adult, and school, where they are treated as a child. Additionally, cultural norms can dictate different expectations for girls and boys. While young men are expected to enter employment early, young women may be expected to become homemakers and therefore from this point families may perceive greater value in what can be taught at home compared to what is learnt in school.

It is undoubtedly challenging for teachers and leaders to understand cultural differences among GRT groups and to ensure that their practice is flexible enough to avoid a situation where mainstream norms "push out" families and communities

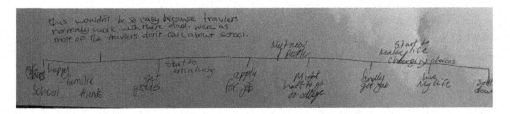

Figure 5.3 Pupil's life timeline

with different views or a contrasting way of life. However, as Laura's story (shared by Mark Penfold) demonstrates, when schools work closely with families to understand these competing priorities, solutions can be found to ensure a young person is able to flourish.

Laura's story

Laura was a Roma pupil attending Babington Academy in Leicester, a school with a high proportion of Roma pupils and a history of excellent practice working with their communities. Mark Penfold is a teacher, EAL lead and expert on Roma education. His role involves working closely with Roma pupils and families.

In January of Laura's time in Year 11, Mark found her "in floods of tears" after receiving her GCSE mock exam results. Laura was a bright and ambitious young person who had good attendance and loved most of her subjects. She had failed her French exam, her maths exam and her art exam. Mark's first step in addressing this issue was to talk to Laura's parents.

> I went round to the house and I said to mum "Laura is the oldest in the family, isn't she?", "Yes.", "She's coming home, she's doing chores and she's looking after the little ones isn't she?" "Yes". I said "That's a problem".

The school's existing relationship with the family and understanding of her home life meant that these issues could be confronted and Mark was able to persuade Laura's family to find her a space to study at home and give her time to prioritise her exams. Six months later, Laura passed all her GCSEs. Mark emphasises the need to recognise that parents are unlikely to disregard their child's educational needs but may not understand how to support them. Through his years of working with Roma families, he has often found that helping parents to understand what a child needs to succeed is all that is necessary to change a situation.

5.4.2.4 A fear of cultural dilution or corruption

Many GRT communities feel that operating within mainstream systems and spaces will result in cultural traditions and values being worn away. However, we could also view this as mainstream culture's failure to "make room for" and promote the diversity of GRT cultures despite their being part of the UK's heritage.

Removing children from school early or home educating them is often part of an effort to protect GRT cultures. Families may fear that if a young person is not educated and immersed primarily in their culture it will lead to the erosion of culture and tradition. Concerns about "cultural corruption", where mainstream culture and values are seen as harmful and negative, can also lead to disengagement with education. Sex and relationship education could be "a particular sticking point for families". GRT cultures value chastity highly, especially for girls, and they can be concerned that mainstream culture will 'corrupt' this cultural identity.

Two stories exemplify how this concern can play out differently depending on a school's understanding of GRT cultures and practitioners' flexibility in seeking a solution in collaboration with a family. The first story was told to me by Maria, a young woman from a Romany Gypsy background and concerns a Gypsy family with a thirteen-year-old daughter who attended the same school as Maria. At a parents' evening, a staff member speaking to the girl and her father tells the young person: "we know you've been hanging around with boys because other girls have told us" [1]. Although the teacher did not wish to harm the pupil's education, the consequences of such an exchange can be serious. Our interviewee explained:

> I don't think it's coincidence that a couple of weeks later, she never came back to school. So it's things like that not to say to people, especially the Gypsy girls, one of the things not to say to those girls if you want them to stay in school is 'you've been going around with boys', especially with gaujo boys... the way I was brought up, hanging out with boys was not a thing. (p.35 [25])

In contrast, the second story, taken from the government's most recent report on GRT education, shows that solutions can be brokered between schools and families.

In one school, a Gypsy pupil and her family felt it was not appropriate for her to learn about sex and relationships in a mixed classroom environment. The school allowed the pupil to study alone in the library during sex and relationships education. This special dispensation removed a barrier to her learning and her engagement with school more widely.

Whilst this approach may not be widespread, it shows that working with families and communities can allow solutions to be brokered, avoiding a young person's education being cut short.

Of course, it is tricky for all teachers to gain a good understanding of GRT cultures and to avoid making mistakes like those discussed above, especially alongside the myriad of different challenges teachers and schools face. When I was teaching, I knew little to nothing about these different communities. However, a small amount of knowledge and a trusting relationship with parents can go a long way.

5.4.3 Material barriers: a bleak picture but a skewed picture

5.4.3.1 Poverty

There is relatively little research pinning down the extent to which GRT children and young people live in poverty. However, poverty's corrosive impact on children's educational outcomes is documented throughout this book and GRT families who experience poverty are similarly disadvantaged.

Poverty among Roma people in Europe is widespread and UK research tends to find high levels of unemployment in GRT communities. Research also suggests that GRT people face difficulties with housing, health and accessing welfare benefits, all of which are consistent with higher prevalence of poverty.

However, the limited data and research that is available may skew the picture. One Romany Gypsy who took part in my 2017 research highlighted that people are "counted" as GRT when they come into contact with support services, whereas affluent members of the community may remain "under the radar".

> The academically successful and the "middle class" (in the gaujo sense, not in our sense, because we don't have true distinction in our community)... I don't think that the literature attempts in any way to understand that picture. It's a skewed picture. (p.37 [1])

5.4.3.2 Housing

Around a fifth of the mobile GRT population is legally homeless and insecure or unsuitable housing, particularly on so-called "illegal sites", perhaps better termed "unauthorised roadside encampments". This is often cited as a key reason behind GRT young people's underachievement.

The terms unauthorised or illegal sites might be used to describe temporary roadside encampments or more permanent settlings where a community does not have permission to settle or build. In many cases, sites that are described as illegal are on land that is owned by Gypsies or Travellers but they are unable to get planning permission [26]. Experts and advocates for GRT rights have highlighted the importance of recognising that the term "illegal sites" is stigmatising and the term "roadside encampments" is more meaningful to GRT communities [23, 27]. However, it is also important to understand that these sites *are* unauthorised and therefore the families that live on them face severe challenges accessing basic living necessities as well as constant uncertainty and the threat of eviction.

The 3,000 to 4,000 families living on unauthorised sites face a constant threat of eviction and poor living conditions. Meanwhile some legal sites have inadequate living conditions, including vermin and sewage and waste disposal issues. This doubtless has a detrimental effect on the education of these children and young people.

However, it is important not generalise these issues to the whole population and assume underachievement is entirely due to housing status since this is not the norm across GRT communities, given that only around a quarter of Gypsies and Travellers lived in mobile accommodation at the last census count. Additionally, only 16% of Traveller caravans are on unauthorised sites.

Housing issues should therefore not dominate the debate. Yet, the provision of sites frequently dominates the policy discourse about issues affecting GRT communities. Furthermore, challenges associated with unauthorised sites are often used as a justification for prejudiced attitudes and dislike of GRT communities as a whole [28].

Disturbingly, intensive focus on Gypsy and Traveller sites, to the exclusion of other issues, has made it even harder for people to gain "Gypsy or Traveller status".

[29] People with this status are generally more likely to be allowed to build on land not previously approved for development. However, new rules mean Local Authorities can refuse to recognise a person's Gypsy or Traveller ethnicity on the grounds that they do not travel frequently. This can then be used as grounds for refusing planning permission. In turn, this can become a barrier for children's access to education. For example, some families may have chosen to settle on a permanent site in order to facilitate their children's education while preserving the tradition of living in mobile accommodation. However, these rules mean that the very act of staying in one place, means forfeiting the right to settle legally on land they own. 90% of GRT planning permission applicants are turned down, compared to 20% of applications overall [30], despite the government having encouraged GRT people to buy the land they wish to settle on. In fact, 6 out of 10 of the aforementioned "unauthorised sites", which cause such controversy and have been used so frequently as political propaganda, are owned by the Gypsies and Travellers that reside on them [16] but have been refused planning permission.

5.5 What can be done?

GRT pupils' poor educational outcomes should provide a call to action. However, as we have seen, numerous reports over the last half a century have argued that GRT pupils' educational prospects need to be improved, but little has changed.

Some argue that the data on educational outcomes is skewed, and GRT pupils whose families do not ascribe their identity are attaining much more highly. Recent positive changes such as the inclusion of "Roma" on the census may shed more light on whether this is the case. Regardless, this group of young people clearly experience significant disadvantage and this must be addressed irrespective of whether a proportion of their un-ascribed peers are more successful (Figure 5.4).

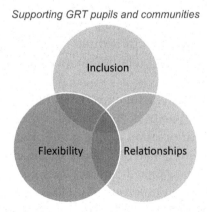

Figure 5.4 Actions that would support improvements for GRT pupils.

There are three key themes underpinning the action that needs to be taken to improve GRT young people's educational outcomes:

1. Eliminating discrimination and replacing it with value and inclusion.

2. Building relationships between schools and families and communities.

3. Taking a flexible approach to enrolment, timetabling and distance learning.

These approaches would be strengthened by system change but organisations and individuals working with GRT young people can nevertheless take action at a smaller scale. The three approaches are also interlinked. For instance, building relationships between families and schools would contribute to inclusion.

5.5.1 Eliminating discrimination and replacing it with value and inclusion

To eliminate discrimination against GRT pupils, schools need to address bullying and this should sit alongside an overarching inclusive and culturally sensitive approach. Schools and other organisations working with young people should therefore take a three-pronged approach to eliminating discrimination and fostering inclusion:

1. A rapid and robust response to discrimination, bullying and name calling.

2. Provision that explicitly includes and values GRT communities, for example through ethos and curriculum.

3. A workforce that understands GRT communities and cultural sensitivities.

Discrimination and prejudice against GRT pupils or families must be "recognised, acknowledged and deemed unacceptable" [1]. It should quite clearly be treated with the same severity as other forms of racism. Case studies of schools with good practice highlight the importance of a quick response which includes parents, informs all relevant staff and involves speaking with both the bully and the bullied to explain how the behaviour is unacceptable and facilitate reconciliation [31]. A headteacher at a primary school recognised for excellent practice explained the need to work with both the bully and bullying victim supporting pupils to better understand one another [32].

GRT pupils' reports of bullying often go hand-in-hand with accounts of teachers not taking bullying seriously or displaying prejudiced attitudes themselves. Therefore, addressing discrimination among pupils, starts with staff. Leaders must ensure that all staff are committed to GRT pupils' inclusion and achievement as well as the elimination of racism against them. Staff may need to training to understand of GRT communities better but unfortunately, INSET training previously provided by TESs is no longer widely available. Schools therefore often have to develop their own approach, for example through research in staff peer groups. Case studies of best practice [11] show the benefits of ensuring that teachers and other staff are aware of the discrimination these groups experience so they can incorporate their understanding of historical and community context in their responses.

Of course, racism is most effectively addressed and avoided when the overall ethos of a school values diversity and the curriculum teaches pupils about different cultures. For a curriculum to be inclusive of GRT culture it needs to avoid tokenism. GRT history month (in June) is a good opportunity to encourage the inclusion of GRT culture in the curriculum but I have heard many unfortunate stories about "colouring-in caravans" where pupils engage in relatively meaningless activities which touch on GRT culture but which are not embedded in the curriculum. This can even serve to entrench stereotypes.

June also should not be the only time GRT culture is taught and celebrated. Good practice means year-round inclusion, for example through books and resources which reflect GRT culture. In one case a school had a Gypsy and Traveller display board in the entrance and this allowed pupils to share their communities' way of life, for example photos of their experiences at Appleby Horse Fair. The headteacher explained that this was needed in order to send the message that GRT cultures and history are "legitimate, relevant and worthy of celebration" (p.45 [31]).

Valuing and celebrating GRT culture also includes valuing a nomadic way of life, despite the difficulties this may cause for continuity in education. The below recommendation addresses how flexibility can mediate the effects of a mobile lifestyle. Staff should also recognise that GRT children's experience of travelling can provide learning for that child and for the whole class.

5.5.2 Building relationship between families and educational institutions

Parental engagement is a key facilitating factor for all children's education [33]. However, many of the barriers to GRT pupils' education including, fear of cultural dilution and corruption, fear of discrimination, and aspirations and expectations that are incompatible with mainstream education, stem from parents and families. This means that parental engagement can be even more important when it comes to GRT pupils' education.

Parents' mistrust of official institutions, including schools, can only be reduced by inviting them into those spaces and ensuring they feel comfortable. Research has found common practices among schools that have good relationships with GRT communities, including:

- An acknowledgement that the onus is on the school to build trust.

- A designated member of staff to work with GRT families.

- An involved and welcoming head teacher and senior leadership team.

Given that government and education institutions have known about GRT underachievement for over 50 years but have failed to effectively address it, and given that widespread discrimination continues, it is easy to understand why some GRT families are reluctant to engage with schools. Research with schools demonstrating excellent practice with GRT communities highlight how the onus is on schools and leaders to build trust with families [31].

A school's head teacher and senior leadership team should be part of efforts to welcome GRT families. In successful schools the head teacher welcomes GRT families to the school and offers private welcome tours to those not comfortable attending events or tours with non-GRT parents. The head teacher of one primary school regularly visited the site that their GRT pupils lived on, to talk to parents about their children's education and to hear parents' concerns.

Bhopal's research also highlights schools' success where a member of staff has been given a specific role to work with the GRT community. Previously, this key person could work with the TES to broker relationships with families, however, given that this support is no longer available in most areas, schools now have little choice but to build these relationships themselves. One way to do this where resources allow, is to employ a member of the local GRT community to fulfil this role. In her previous role as an Education Advocate at The Traveller Movement, Abi Angus, co-author of this chapter, saw first-hand the impressive impact that a dedicated staff member can make on the relationship between a school and local GRT communities as she recounts below.

> ### Employing a dedicated staff member as a GRT community link
>
> While working for a GRT non-profit organisation as an education advocate, I worked with a secondary school that took a proactive approach to engaging with their local Gypsy community.
>
> Among the high proportion of Gypsy pupils, the school had on role, many had low attendance and were arriving very late in the morning. The school took several approaches to addressing the attendance issue, including providing a school minibus to and from the site each day. They were also making a concerted effort to make their school a welcoming place for the Gypsy families. However, fear and anger about racism was undermining their efforts.
>
> On top of this, while the school had made efforts to tackle racism, when I spoke to pupils some told me they were facing abuse from other pupils which was not being addressed. Often, staff members' lack of understanding of what constitutes racism seemed to be at the root of the issue. Ultimately this had led to instances where pupils on the receiving end of racist comments had been punished for their reactions to the abuse, while the racism went unchallenged. This had lowered families' trust in the school as they felt their children were not being protected. Additionally, the school knew that many Gypsy parents had previously had negative experiences in the education system: some feared discrimination from staff.
>
> School leaders and staff recognised that their lack of understanding of GRT cultures made it difficult for families to trust them and that they were therefore struggling to

involve the community in developing solutions to pupils' low attendance and engagement with school.

To support staff to better understand the community and to ensure all families felt welcomed, the school recruited a dedicated GRT liaison member of staff, employing Ruby, a Gypsy parent who lived on one of the local sites and had experience working with young people. The role was designed to provide a visible point of contact for Gypsy pupils and families. It was important that this work was paid, valuing this Ruby's skills and experience and recognising her as a vital resource.

Employing Ruby was a vital step in creating a more inclusive school culture and ensured that pupils and families could access support from someone that understood them. Families were able to approach Ruby for support and could request that she attended school meetings with them. Pupils could visit her office during the school day if they were in need of an encouraging conversation or extra help.

Having an in-school trusted point of contact brought families into the school community and teachers learnt more about families' cultures and traditions, as well as the systematic racism GRT people are subject to. This contributed to ensuring that any racism was dealt with effectively.

5.5.3 Taking a flexible approach

Although we have acknowledged that not all GRT families maintain the traditional nomadic lifestyle, many do travel for all or part of the year to attend cultural events or family occasions. This can cause significant disruption to a pupil's education. However, travelling is not inherently bad – our school system is just not currently set up to accommodate it. Yet sticking to rigid structures can, in effect, mean that the system, and some schools, punish children by further jeopardising their education in response to their communities' non-mainstream lifestyles. Every effort should therefore be made to allow children to access as much education as they can.

Given that most schools are not currently set up to provide flexibility, it can be difficult for individual teachers to adapt provision for travelling pupils. This is even harder in the context of resourcing pressures and reduced funding for support staff. However, pockets of good practice exist and many schools are willing to support other schools in adopting new ways of working [34].

Flexible practice across three areas characterises many successful schools' approaches:

1. enrolment;

2. time tabling; and

3. home education including distance learning.

5.5.3.1 Enrolment

A flexible and supportive approach to GRT pupils' enrolment supports GRT families and avoids a negative impact on schools' attendance data. If families are travelling and a school has not worked with the family to prepare, they will have to mark that pupil as having an unauthorised absence, which is highly problematic for attendance metrics. It can also result in action being taken against parents, not to mention the fact that the child is missing out on their education. However, if schools work closely with families this does not have to happen:

- Firstly, if a family informs a school of their intention to travel for work, then pupils can be marked "T", rather than as an unauthorised absence [35].

- Secondly, all pupils are able to register at more than one school, this is known as "dual registration". A pupil that is dual registered will have a "base school" which is the school they most recently attended in the past 18 months when the family was not travelling. A base school cannot remove a child from their roll because the child is registered at another school while travelling, but a non-base school can do so. If a child is attending a non-base school, their base school can simply mark them as "present at another school at which they are registered" rather than as absent.

When a GRT family (or indeed any family) registers a child at a non-base school, parents should be encouraged to share details of the base school so that the two schools can coordinate and provide continuity for the pupil. If a base school ensures they have good relationships with families, parents are more likely to do this which will make it easier for the base school to fulfil their responsibilities. Flexibility and a commitment to working with families is needed from both the base school and the non-base schools so that families are aware of and access their entitlement and of course, non-base schools need to be willing to enrol a child for short time, which can be challenging.

Undoubtedly, this arrangement may require a considerable investment of time from teachers and leaders. However, each arrangement will be different and some will be relatively simple. For example, a family that attends the base school for terms one to five, but due to travelling elsewhere for work in summer months attends a non-base school for Term 6, will require only two handovers between the base and non-base school each year. Furthermore, while these flexible arrangements take time to organise, post-hoc interventions to tackle issues with attendance and academic progress where a pupil has missed out are also resource-intensive and, in all likelihood, less effective. The load can be lightened if schools have a specific staff member dedicated to supporting GRT families, although this is more feasible for schools with a high proportion of travelling pupils on their role.

5.5.3.2 Time tabling

When pupils return from travelling, if they have not been in school, they may have trouble adjusting to being in school full-time. Additionally, many GRT pupils joining a school bring with them a history of negative experiences in education. This may lead to behavioural issues and consequently the child being removed by their parents or excluded. Schools demonstrating good practice and good results for GRT pupils allow for specialist attendance arrangements and adjusted timetables for Gypsy and Traveller pupils to "ease them into the school curriculum". A senior leader at one such school reasoned that it was more beneficial for pupils to be in school "for an hour and achieve than have them here for a day and fail". (p.49 [31])

In some cases, pupils were allowed to attend only the lessons they enjoy or to spend time with siblings until they became comfortable in the school. This flexibility might seem extreme but when leaders recognise that the alternative of this flexible provision is pupils not attending altogether, the choice seems simple. It is also a key element of ensuring that pupils and families are able to build up more positive experiences of education. One headteacher in a school working with Gypsy and Traveller communities explained that they allow for flexible arrangements including children attending school for a few hours a day or pupils spending time with their siblings in other year groups. This flexibility was tailored to the families' needs and arranged in collaboration with them, the headteacher explained:

> It's a way of gaining the confidence of people who may have no confidence in the education system. (p.49 [36])

Many will argue that this flexibility and differing expectations is both logistically difficult to achieve and problematic in terms of fairness. Recent years have seen greater efforts to stop parents taking children on term time holidays and thus many will rightly point out that these policies for GRT families sit at odds with that and could result in non-GRT parents requesting term time holidays. However, it is clear that decades of applying the same expectations for GRT pupils, and a lack of flexibility and inclusion have led to extremely poor outcomes for this group and an alternative approach is not only warranted, it is urgently needed.

5.5.3.3 Home education and distance learning

All parents have a legal right to educate their child at home and GRT families that exercise this right should not be assumed to be less able to do so than other families. However, we must recognise that some GRT families choose to home educate due to discrimination or cultural considerations (discussed in Section 5.4) rather than because they feel well equipped to provide an education equivalent to a school. It is difficult to balance competing narratives here. On one hand, some will assert that GRT parents are among those least qualified to provide a suitable home education due to generations of low qualification levels, low literacy levels and negative experiences with education. However, on the other, we must recognise that in some cases these assertions might be borne of prejudiced attitudes and GRT parents have the same rights as other parents.

Firstly, it is crucial that schools do not encourage parents to home educate as a solution to issues such as bullying which are the schools' responsibility to resolve. Secondly, if families choose to home educate because they are travelling or because they want to, the school should ensure they provide support and resources and the opportunity to re-engage with the school at a later date.

Some families home educate temporarily, and pupils can remain on a school's roll. To avoid pupils falling behind, schools must support the pupil with distance learning. Schools that have done this successfully provide a range of resources, alongside the school work, in distance learning packs. One school explained the need to include practical resources that facilitate communication with the school in the learning packs, such as stamped envelopes and postcards, as well as other resources such as pens and paper [37].

Many schools find that such provision is highly valued by parents and is seen as "reflective of the high expectations surrounding their levels of achievement". (p.51 [38])

Again, some may argue that this level of flexibility for GRT pupils represents an excessive allowance that other families may not receive and is therefore unfair to other pupils. However, GRT pupils, especially those that travel, face a unique set of barriers to their education. Just as other pupils who face additional barriers, such as those with special educational needs (SEN), deserve flexible support, GRT pupils do also. Of course, having a SEN is not a choice whereas travelling is not enforced, but children and young people do not get to decide on this lifestyle. Furthermore, from a pragmatic point of view, the current educational outcomes of GRT groups paint a stark picture of what happens for pupils who do not receive this support, so if schools and practitioners want to affect change, working within the constraints of pupils' different lifestyles is necessary.

5.6 Conclusion

At the time of the roundtable I recalled at the beginning of this chapter, I was only just beginning to learn about the challenges, poor outcomes and injustice that people from GRT communities often face. Since then, I have connected with many more community members alongside activists and practitioners working with GRT communities. In doing so I have heard countless examples of prejudice, discrimination and pupils struggling in their education. However, I have also heard many examples of good practice, and seen advocacy and support organisations fighting hard to support the communities they work with, despite the fact that they are often facing intense funding pressures.

What has become eminently clear to me is that, despite persisting narratives that GRT communities are responsible for their own isolation or exclusion from mainstream society, most families from GRT communities, just like families from non-GRT communities, value education and want their children to have broad and rich opportunities. However, in order to engage with mainstream systems, they need to feel safe, included and understood.

This is the key message I would like leaders, teachers and other practitioners to hear. While communities can be mistrustful of schools and other authorities, for the reasons we have explored throughout this chapter, they are not unreachable. If a school, in particular the school leaders, demonstrate a culture of inclusion they will be able to recruit staff from the community or ensure that an existing staff member become a trusted bridge between the school and GRT families. Through this type of committed practice, they will be able to engage with the communities they serve.

Talking to my colleague and co-author Abi about the families she worked with in her previous role as an education advocate has made this ever clearer. She has shared countless stories with me about families facing a multitude of barriers to engagement with education who were well able to overcome these challenges with the right support.

The Coopers are one such example. The family's story – told here by Abi, exemplifies not only the barriers faced by many Gypsy, Roma and Traveller families, but also the gaps in support left by cuts to services.

The Cooper Family, as told by Abi Angus

I first spoke to Rosaleen when she phoned to find out about grants to help her cover the cost of uniforms for her children. There had previously been a Traveller Education Worker in their area who had helped families with this kind of issue, but the service had been cut and Rosaleen was not sure who she could ask for help. While she was a smart and capable woman, dyslexia and an interrupted education meant that she found reading and writing difficult. Money was tight for this single parent family and school uniforms costs add up. I brought the paperwork and we completed an application over a cup of tea while chatting about how she and her kids were finding school.

The family lived on a site on the outskirts of a lovely village, bordered by train tracks on one side and beautiful countryside on the other. The family's pitch contained a large trailer next to a small outhouse building. It was home to Rosaleen and her five children, ranging in age from two to ten years old. The families on the site were a close-knit community, but the rest of the village kept their distance. The village primary school had a great reputation, but the family did not feel welcome as part of the school community.

The youngest of the school age children was Josie, a bright little girl who had been diagnosed with Autism before starting reception. After the summer, Josie found the transition back to school very difficult, she struggled to follow the school rules and to stick to a routine that differed hugely from the one she was used to at home. She also found it hard to make friends with other children. These difficulties were expressed through behaviour that the school found difficult to manage. For a while the school trialled keeping her in a separate room to the other children but Rosaleen was not comfortable with what she felt was punishment for behaviour that was not deliberate. However, she worried the school would not listen to her suggestions for alternative strategies.

Shortly after starting Year 1, Josie was permanently excluded. The local authority suggested she should attend a special school in the county. At this time, Rosaleen got back in touch with me to ask for help, she was worried about splitting up her children and felt that, with the right support, mainstream was right for Josie. After a series of assessments, meetings, letters and phone calls from the family, myself and eventually a solicitor, the local authority finally provided Josie with a place in a local Catholic primary school. Arranging this placement took around six months.

As Josie settled back into education, Rosaleen decided to transfer her other two school age children to the same school. The school had worked with Traveller families before and were more understanding of cultural differences as well as barriers faced by some GRT families. They ensured that communication was regular, that updates on her children's progress were given verbally and that the school was a welcoming environment for parents and children. Attending a school outside of the village also allowed the children to make friends with children from families that were not hostile to the local Traveller community. While Josie's behaviour continued to throw up occasional challenges, strategies were planned and evaluated with Rosaleen's input and Josie thrived.

As the school year progressed, there were new challenges for the family. The second-youngest child, James, was due to start reception after the summer and the oldest was ready for secondary. Rosaleen had not been sure which forms would be necessary, or how to complete them, so the paperwork had not been completed.

We worked together to complete the necessary forms; however, there was no space for James at the same school his siblings attended. Rosaleen decided that if there was no place for him, she would keep him at home rather than send him to the village school on his own. We ensured he was on the waiting list, sent a supporting letter explaining why it was important for him to attend the school that had adequately supported his family and not the one geographically closest to their home and crossed our fingers.

Rosaleen was also concerned about her eldest attending secondary school. She had heard stories about other Traveller girls who had been bullied, had learnt about sex or who had spent time with "gaujo" boys, and she was very concerned about how she could best keep her daughter safe. We talked through the support available at the school and about the SRE curriculum. We made sure that the family had a point of contact within the new school. While she did not feel comfortable arranging a visit, looking through information about the school with me and the reassurance that if things did not go well there would be support, put her mind at ease.

In September, a year after Rosaleen had first contacted us, four of the children went to school, and the youngest started nursery. James had been allocated a place in reception at the same primary school as his two siblings, and the oldest daughter went to the local secondary school with a friend who also lived on the same site.

Despite her worries, the support she had received in response to her valid concerns, meant Rosaleen was able to work with the schools to ensure all her children were supported and accessed appropriate education in environments that understood their needs and respected their culture.

Had she been unable to access this support, it is easy to see how things could have played out very differently.

5.7 Taking action

This chapter has shown that decades of inadequate action have been compounded in the last decade by a retrenchment of efforts to help young people from GRT families succeed in education.

Action is therefore needed (and long overdue) on the part of policymakers, whilst schools themselves can also take action that would directly improve young people's day-to-day experience in school.

5.7.1 Policymakers

■ Politicians should lead by example, making it clear that prejudice, discrimination and racist remarks are unacceptable. This includes refraining from suggestions that the behaviour of a small subset of the GRT population explains and excuses mainstream prejudice against the whole population.

■ Policymakers should continue to push for change in official data collection forms so that GRT are each given the opportunity to ascribe their identity. This will need to include a separate "tick-box" for each of the three main groupings as a minimum on both census and school census forms.

■ The government must recognise that reducing (and in many cases eliminating), funding for services such as the TES makes it more difficult to achieve the professed goal of improving GRT educational outcomes. Cuts to such services should therefore be reversed.

5.7.2 Institutions and organisations

■ Organisations serving young people must not tolerate discrimination. Teachers and school leaders should eliminate discrimination against GRT pupils and their families and replace it with value and inclusion. Where discrimination and bullying occur, this should be dealt with rapidly, and the response should include the bully, the bullied and parents.

■ Schools and youth organisations should establish an inclusive ethos by including GRT culture in the curriculum in a non-tokenistic way. This involves making explicit declarations that they welcome GRT communities and pupils and ensuring that all staff are knowledgeable about and sensitive to GRT culture.

- Schools must build positive relationships with GRT families by:

  - Acknowledging that the onus is on the school to build trust.

  - Designating a member of staff to work with GRT families.

  - Ensuring the head teacher and senior leadership team are outward facing and welcoming.

Schools must realise that if they do not do this, some GRT families are likely to struggle to trust and engage with them.

- A flexible approach by schools is also needed, especially when working with GRT pupils whose families travel. Flexibility in enrolment practices, attendance and timetabling are crucial, as is support with home education and distance learning.

5.7.3 Individual practitioners

- Practitioners should ensure they understand GRT groups, cultures and issues. This will enable them to be more culturally sensitive in their interactions with GRT families and avoid stereotyping.

- Practitioners should look for ways to include GRT culture within their curriculum, drawing on and recognising the value of this diversity of experience, culture and language.

- Teachers and support staff should create resources which support pupils' distance learning where necessary.

- Practitioners should also be prepared to take a flexible approach to including pupils who travel including allowing them to have a part time timetable or spend time with siblings.

Further reading

For a thorough review of the barriers to education faced by GRT pupils:*Inequalities experienced by Gypsy and Traveller communities: A review*: Cemlyn, S. (2009). For recommendations and examples of good practice with Gypsy and Traveller pupils and families: *Working towards inclusive education: Aspects of good practice for gypsy traveller children*: Bhopal, K., Gundara, J., Jones, C., & Owen, C. (2000). Norwich: HMSO.

Gypsy, Roma and Traveller pupils in schools in the UK: Inclusion and "good practice": Bhopal, K., & Myers, M. (2009). *International Journal of Inclusive Education, 13*(3), 299–314. For a review of GRT underrepresentation in higher education and recommendations to facilitate access for GRT young people *The underrepresentation of Gypsy, Roma and Traveller pupils in higher education: A report on barriers from early years to secondary and beyond*: Mulcahy, E., Baars, S., Bowen-Viner, K., & Menzies, L. n.d.

Notes

1 "Gypsy, Traveller or Irish Traveller" was used on the England and Wales census form, "Gypsy/Traveller" was used in Scotland and "Irish Traveller" was used in Northern Ireland.
2 "Gaujo" or "gorger" is the Romany Gypsy word for non-Gypsy people, while "buffer" or "country people" are terms used by Irish Travellers to describe non-Traveller people.

References

1 Mulcahy, E., Baars, S., Bowen-Viner, K., & Menzies, L. (2017). *The Underrepresentation of Gypsy, Roma and Traveller Pupils in Higher Education*, King's College London: LKMco. Available at: https://www.cfey.org/wp-content/uploads/2017/07/KINGWIDE_28494_proof3.pdf.
2 *ibid.*
3 Brown, P., Scullion, L., & Martin, P. (2013). *Migrant Roma in the United Kingdom: Population size and Experiences of Local Authorities and Partners*, Salford: University of Salford.
4 2021 Census topic research update (2018). Available at: https://www.ons.gov.uk/census/censustransformationprogramme/questiondevelopment/2021censustopicresearchupdatedecember2018.
5 Department of Education and Science, & Plowden, L. (1967). *Children and Their Primary Schools: Vol I: the Report: A Report of the Central Advisory Council for Education*, HM Stationery Office. Available at: http://www.educationengland.org.uk/documents/plowden/plowden1967-1.html.
6 *ibid.*
7 As cited in House of Commons Women and Equalities Committee (2019). *Tackling Inequalities Faced by Gypsy, Roma and Traveller communities*. Available at: https://publications.parliament.uk/pa/cm201719/cmselect/cmwomeq/360/full-report.html.
8 Boyle, A., Flynn, M., & Hanafin, J. (2018). Optimism despite disappointment: Irish traveller parents' reports of their own school experiences and their views on education. *International Journal of Inclusive Education, 24*(13), 1389–1409.
9 Ryder, A. (2017). *Sites of Resistance: Gypsies, Roma and Travellers in School, Community and the Academy*, London: Trenthan Books Limited.
10 Bhopal, K., & Myers, M. (2009). Gypsy, Roma and Traveller pupils in schools in the UK: Inclusion and 'good practice'. *International Journal of Inclusive Education, 13*(3), 299–314.
11 The Traveller Movement, (2019). *A Good Practice Guide for improving outcomes for Gypsy, Roma and Traveller Children in education*, Available at: https://travellermovement.org.uk/phocadownload/TTM%20Good%20Practice%20Guide%20Education_web.pdf.
12 House of Commons Women and Equalities Committee, (2019). *Tackling Inequalities Faced by Gypsy, Roma and Traveller Communities*, Available at: https://publications.parliament.uk/pa/cm201719/cmselect/cmwomeq/360/full-report.html.
13 Pew Research Center (2014) *Global Attitudes and Trends*, Available at: http://www.pewglobal.org/2014/05/12/chapter-4-views-of-roma-muslims-jews/.
14 Valentine, G., & McDonald, I. (2004). *Understanding Prejudice: Attitudes Towards Minorities, Stonewall*. London: Citizenship 21.

15 YouGov and The Traveller Movement (2017). *Survey results* available at: https://d25d2506sfb94s.cloudfront.net/cumulus_uploads/document/f7je2vut1g/YG-Archive-060917-TravellerMovement.pdf.

16 Bhopal, K. (2004) Gypsy travellers and education: changing needs and changing perceptions. *British Journal of Educational Studies, 52* (1), 47–64

17 Derrington, C., & Kendall, S. (2004). *Gypsy Traveller Students in Secondary Schools: Culture, Identity and Achievement.* Stoke-on-Trent: Trentham Books.

18 Ureche, H., & Franks, M. (2007). This is who we are, *A Study of the Views and Identities of Roma, Gypsy and Traveller Young People in England.* Children's Society.

19 The Traveller Movement (2017). *The Last Acceptable form of Racism? The Pervasive Discrimination and Prejudice Experienced by Gypsy.* London: Roma and Traveller communities.

20 Cromarty, H. (2019). Gypsies and Travellers, *House of Commons Library.* Available at: https://commonslibrary.parliament.uk/research-briefings/cbp-8083/.

21 Smith, D. M., & Greenfields, M. (2013). *Gypsies and Travellers in Housing: The Decline of Nomadism.* Policy Press.

22 Levinson, M. P. (2015). 'What's the plan?' 'What plan?' Changing aspirations among Gypsy youngsters, and implications for future cultural identities and group membership. *British Journal of Sociology of Education, 36*(8), 1149–1169.

23 Myers, M., McGhee, D., & Bhopal, K. (2010). At the crossroads: Gypsy and Traveller parents' perceptions of education, protection and social change. *Race Ethnicity and Education, 13*(4), 533–548.

24 Derrington, C. and Kendall, S. (2008) Challenges and Barriers to Secondary Education: The experiences of young Gypsy Traveller students in English secondary schools. *Social Policy and Society 7*(1), 1–10.

25 *ibid.*

26 Balogh, B. and Clark, C. (2019) The persecution of Britain's Gypsy and traveller communities continues. *The Traveller Times,* Available at: https://www.travellerstimes.org.uk/features/persecution-britains-gypsy-and-traveller-community-continues.

27 Clark, C. (2017). How the youth of Britain's Roma, Gypsy, and Traveller communities fight the injustices they face. *LSE British Politics and Policy,* Available at: https://blogs.lse.ac.uk/politicsandpolicy/roma-gypsy-traveller-youth/.

28 Mulcahy, E. (2020) "Traveller crime" documentary was racist – Now it's up to schools to pick up the pieces.' *CfEY,* Available at: https://cfey.org/news-and-events/2020/05/traveller-crime-documentary-was-racist-now-its-up-to-schools-to-pick-up-the-pieces/.

29 The Economist (2018). *Who is a gypsy? Britain's new definition is causing problems,* Available at: https://www.economist.com/britain/2018/01/11/who-is-a-gypsy-britains-new-definition-is-causing-problems.

30 ACERT and Wilson, M. (1997) *Directory of Planning Policies for Gypsy Site Provision,* Bristol: Policy Press.

31 Bhopal, K. (2000). *Working towards Inclusive Education: Aspects of Good Practice for Gypsy Traveller pupils.* DfEE. Research Report No 238, Department for Education and Employment, 2000.

32 *ibid.*

33 Department of Education and Early Childhood Development (DEECD) (2008). *Blueprint for Early Childhood Development and School Reform: A School Reform Discussion Paper.* Melbourne: DEECD.

34 *ibid.*

35 Department for Education (2019). *School Attendance Guidance for Maintained Schools, Academies, Independent Schools and Local Authorities*, Available at: https://assets.publishing.service.gov.uk/government/uploads/system/uploads/attachment_data/file/818204/School_attendance_July_2019.pdf.

36 *ibid.*

37 *ibid.*

38 *ibid.*

Children who come into contact with social services

Will Millard

6.1 Introduction

I met Annie on a crisp, sunny November morning at a café in Victoria Station. Cup of tea in hand, Annie told me about her time managing two children's care homes, one in South London, and one in Kent. Annie has since moved into the world of policy research, determined to improve children's experiences of care across the system as a whole. However, it was clear that the young people she had worked with had left an indelible impression on her.

Annie told me about Karl, who was 16 when he moved into a care home in Kent. When she talked about Karl, Annie smiled a lot, describing him as an "utter sweetheart". Charismatic, funny and caring, Karl had a loving relationship with his mother and siblings. Annie's face grew pensive as she described why Karl was living at the care home. Karl was dealt a difficult hand in life, and his story helps illustrate some of the reasons why young people come into contact with social services and the care system.

Karl grew up in a house where the threat of domestic violence from his father was ever-present. Carrying feelings of anxiety, confusion and anger, Karl himself became prone to volatile and aggressive behaviour. At age 15, he was sent to a young offenders' institution for assaulting his girlfriend.

It was on his release aged 16 that Karl entered the care system. Despite a strong bond with his mother and siblings, Karl's conviction meant he was sent to live in a care home in Kent, where he shared the space with two other young people living there. Karl and his girlfriend maintained their relationship, and it was not long before she gave birth to their first child. Karl began a vocational mechanics course at college and enjoyed having an outlet for his curiosity. While his ADHD and conduct disorder sometimes made it difficult for him to remain focused, Karl spoke openly and enthusiastically to Annie about the course.

"This sounds like a story with a happy ending", I said to Annie. Annie shook her head. Needing money, Karl became involved in petty crime. Despite raising her concerns with Karl's social workers, Annie was upset when Karl's attendance dropped so low that the college kicked him off the course. Furthermore, significant staff pressures (including high staff turnover and underqualified and inexperienced personnel) meant that Karl was not consistently receiving the support he needed at the home. More alarmingly still, Karl soon turned 18 and transitioned out of the care system altogether. Annie had not seen or spoken to Karl since he moved out of the care home.

Karl's story is just one of many thousands about children who interact with social services or experience the care system every year, but it reveals themes that are all too familiar to those who work with this marginalised group of young people, and which emerge throughout this chapter.

Firstly, in a society that is at least to some extent founded on an idea of what a "normal" family looks like, children like Karl whose care is entrusted to the state for some of their childhood (and who are classified as "children looked after"[1]) are often seen as "other" [1–3]. Some are assumed to be "trouble" with their lives pre-determined by their difficult pasts [4].

Secondly, Karl's story shows that children interact with public provision in many guises during their young lives, including education, health, police, justice and social services. This can be especially true for children in need of support from social services. Annie believed that Karl's local authority considered him "dealt with" because he was in her care home, even though his needs remained manifestly unmet. Different services work to different sets of performance and accountability targets, but all face significant pressures in terms of funding and capacity. Agencies are therefore often keen to process cases quickly, and staff sometimes prioritise "doing things right" over "doing the right thing".

Thirdly, trusting relationships are fundamentally important for these children. Karl's bond with his mother meant an absence of parental love was not the reason for his entering care. However, his faith in relationships was disrupted by his father's violence, and further compounded by high staff turnover at the care home. Yet the growing pressure on children's social care services makes it harder for practitioners to develop strong relationships with the children in their care.

On average, "children in need" – those coming into contact with social services including the care system – experience considerably worse outcomes than their peers. I taught some young people like Karl, but did not really understand the world of children's social care even though it affects a large number of families. This chapter therefore serves an introduction to the world of children's social care, for those who, like me, could do with knowing a bit more about lives like Karl's.

6.2 Who are "children in need"?

6.2.1 Terminology

The term "children in need" was introduced in the 1989 Children Act, and refers to children who come into contact with social services including those taken into care. The term therefore refers to a sizeable group of young people, with social workers starting new cases for over 1,000 children a day on average [5]. In 2018, 1 in 10 children had been in need at some point over the previous six years [6], meaning the vast majority of schools will serve pupils who have needed a social worker at some point [7]. However, the proportion of children classified as in need is not evenly distributed across England.

Of nearly 400,000 children in need in early 2019[2]:

- Over two thirds (around 270,000 children) had "Child in Need Plans": These plans set out the statutory input these children need from the local authority in order for them to achieve a reasonable level of health or development.

- A little over 1 in 10 (around 50,000) had a Child Protection Plan: These plans are created following reviews involving a range of professionals, and set out how children will be protected (for example by regular visits from social workers). These children were judged to be at risk of or experiencing significant harm.

- Nearly 2 in 10 (around 80,000) were classified as looked after: They were therefore in the care of the local authority, for example by a foster carer, or in a children's home [8].

In addition, many children and families receive "early help", a locally-defined offer for children not meeting the threshold for a Child in Need Plan. Families' involvement in early help is voluntary, although adherence to Child Protection Plans is statutory.

Disabled children are also considered to be children in need, recognising that these families need support. Disabled children account for a little over 1 in 10 of all children in need (some of whom may also require an additional care plan).

The level of support associated with these different categories varies but, overall, the law states that without support, children in need are unlikely to maintain a reasonable standard of health or development and risk impaired health or development [9].

6.2.2 Demographics

6.2.2.1 Age

A third of all children in need are aged between 10 and 15 years old, and around a fifth are aged 16 or 17 [8]. The proportion of children in need aged 10 and over (and 16 and 17 in particular) has grown over the last decade, and correspondingly the proportion of young children aged nine and younger has shrunk.

There are several possible explanations for the "ageing" of children in need. One is that because children's services in health and education have been cut and are less readily available, intervention is needed more often once these children become teenagers [10]. Another explanation is that risk factors facing teenagers are becoming more prevalent and, in comparison with children aged 12 and under, teenagers are more likely to have experienced child sexual exploitation (six times as likely as children under 12) or trafficking (12 times as likely), gone missing from home (seven times as likely), or been involved in gangs (five times as likely) [11]. Additionally, some argue that teenagers' needs are more profound and complex. For example, the Children's Commissioner estimates that teenagers aged 13 or older are 50% more likely to have special educational needs or disabilities than younger children, and ten times as likely to attend a Pupil Referral Unit [12].

6.2.2.2 Ethnicity

In line with the country's wider population, children in need predominantly come from white backgrounds (reflecting this group's majority ethnic status). However, the proportion coming from minority ethnic backgrounds has been growing slowly to around 3 in 10. Similar trends are apparent among children looked after [13]. Children and young people of black ethnicity are slightly over-represented, although this may be because minority ethnic families are more likely to live in poverty, and poverty is a key driver of children needing support from social services [14].

6.2.2.3 Poverty and geography

Children living in the most deprived 10% of neighbourhoods in England are over ten times more likely to be looked after or on a Child Protection Plan compared to children in the least deprived 10% [15]. Local authorities with higher levels of deprivation also have higher rates of child social care issues on average [10, 16]. This affects the North East in particular, which has the highest rates of children entering care in the country. Comparing Blackpool's rate of 0–18-year olds in need with that of Hertfordshire in 2018 is particularly striking: 1,323 per 100,000 in Blackpool compared to 301 in Hertfordshire [15].

On top of the effect of local area deprivation, it is important to note that local authorities set their own protocols for assessing and responding to children in need, although these processes must be in line with the government's statutory guidance [17], and Ofsted judges the extent to which they are appropriate. Variations in protocols may therefore also play a role in disparities.

6.2.3 What happens when a child is referred to social services?

The first step in supporting a child in need is referral; this is a request for children's social care to provide support to a child not yet judged to be in need. Once referred, social workers must decide within one working day on the appropriate next steps, including whether a full assessment of the child's needs is required.

At a full assessment, a child's needs are reviewed and further support identified as appropriate (which may include initiating child protection or care proceedings). In recent years there have also been an increasing number of "re-referrals", where a young person is referred again within 12 months of a previous referral [8].

There are four decisions a local authority might take following an assessment, and these represent differing levels of severity [18]:

1. Taking no further action, or supporting the child and family through the provision of universal services.

2. Creating a "Child in Need Plan" to meet the child's and family's needs.

3. Initiating child protection proceedings.

4. In the most severe cases, initiating care proceedings (including court proceedings) and, depending on the outcome of this, taking a child into care (which is done through a court order).

Each local authority has its own protocol for deciding which children to support, and on the thresholds for this support. Protocols are written and thresholds set in accordance with the government's statutory guidance for safeguarding and, in theory, assessments and decisions are based upon a three-part model in which professionals investigate [17]:

1. the child's developmental needs;

2. parents' or carers' capacity to respond to these needs; and

3. the impact and influence of other adults, the community or environmental factors.

However, in practice, decision-making about the appropriate course of action for a child can vary hugely both within and between local authorities. In 2018, the All-Party Parliamentary Group (APPG) for Children raised concerns about a "postcode lottery", showing that children with similar needs receive differing levels of support and intervention from their local authority depending on where they live [19].

Outcomes differ due to several interwoven factors. Some are structural: the sheer number of cases, availability of funding, and staffing pressures can make supporting children harder in some areas than in others. However, there are also reasons relating to how individuals and groups of people make decisions, which Ward et al. summarise in their 2014 review for the Department for Education [20]:

■ The information that social workers and other professionals contribute to assessments and decisions about children's needs is complex and often messy. It can be incomplete and miscommunication can take place between families and professionals, as well as between professionals themselves. Parents may feel understandable pressure to shape the information they provide in particular ways, and children may sometimes conceal abuse to protect adults towards whom they may have conflicting feelings.

- Social workers' and other professionals' interpretation of information is affected by their own personal viewpoints and experiences, and also by cultural and organisational expectations, and political agendas.

- Social work rightly relies heavily on relationships, but this can mean decisions are taken on the basis of intuition over observed information. In practice, this can mean disproportionate weight is sometimes placed on first impressions, single dramatic events, and more recent evidence. There can also be a risk of "groupthink" (indicated by high levels of consensus in child protection conferences) perhaps indicating practitioners' desires to avoid conflict or save time.

- Different types of evidence are taken more and less seriously, with verbal evidence and evidence from professionals prized above written submissions and testimony from family and community members. This can mean certain "types" of parents (those who are more articulate or plausible) are more likely to be believed. Furthermore, a resistance to standardised tools such as validated scales and psychometric instruments can reduce opportunities for gathering other forms of evidence.

- Pressure in terms of the inherently emotional and stressful nature of social work (dealing with families who often have significant needs), compounded by a lack of financial and human resource, can impede decision-making.

The Association of Directors of Children's Services (ADCS) has emphasised that it is difficult to overstate the influence of structural challenges on local provision, arguing that decisions about whether or not children and families need support (and what support is appropriate) can sometimes be driven by resources not by need. In particular the ADCS notes that budget cutbacks, social worker recruitment and retention challenges, the availability of appropriate and affordable accommodation, and arrival of unaccompanied asylum-seeking children have all shaped decision-making in recent years [10]. Furthermore, reduced availability of early help and "wraparound" support (intended to keep families together while providing support with parenting) is another reason children may need to become looked after [18].

This affects initial decisions and assessments about what support children and families require, as well as what happens in courts, with profound consequences for children and families whose fates are at stake. In their research Trowler et al. note that over the last decade a growing number of families have been subject to court proceedings that "could have gone either way" [21]. They argue that fewer cases should reach court to begin with, and that decisions reached in court should be clearer about whether or not entering care would be beneficial for a child. The researchers note the challenges for social workers in cases when families do not communicate or cooperate and argue that this is compounded by a lack of other options such as whole-family support, and care options such as shared care between family and state. It is worth noting the other countries including Denmark,

France and Germany make more use of part-time, shared-care (for whole families) and respite care (to give families a break), making the decision to take a child into care less seismic [22].

Variation in the numbers of children entering care per head of population in different areas could also be a reflection of disparities in how judges respond to cases. Increases in the number of applications for Supervision and Care Orders could suggest social workers' intuitions are generally accurate, with their concerns leading to applications that go on to reach court.

However, at their heart, these issues all relate to fundamental questions about the state's right to intervene in parenting. The courts' role is therefore to act as a check and balance, stress-testing the evidence about the best course of action for a child. While social workers face the pressures mentioned above and a tendency towards risk aversion which can drive a predilection for more drastic support such as Care Orders [23], judges must dispassionately apply the law. This can mean disagreeing with social services about the appropriate course of action. For example, judges have declined applications to take children into care on the basis of their parents' ideological beliefs, mental and physical health, and past behaviours [24]. One judge famously remarked that social services are not "guardians of morality" [25].

Thus, by its nature, state intervention in children's and families' lives (through social services) is inherently contested and contestable. It is not just that it *is* open to debate, but that it *requires* debate in order for the best decisions to be made.

6.2.4 Why are children referred to social services?

During our coffee together, Annie told me about another boy in one of her two homes, and why he had entered care. David had lived in London with his mum, and suffered from chronic and significant physical health issues. He had developed anxiety about his health, and a drug addiction which Annie believed to be a form of self-medication. David's mother was controlling, and her intense anxieties about his physical and mental welfare exacerbated David's own worries. David's mental health deteriorated, and he was sectioned and put into care after making a suicide attempt. It was at this point he was sent to live with Annie.

David's story helps capture some of the key themes behind children's entry into the care system. He suffered abuse from his mother, who loved him dearly but whose own mental health impeded her parenting to the point where it actively harmed David. While David did not have a physical disability, his long-term physical and mental health problems made it difficult for him to defend himself against his mother's controlling and abusive parenting (children with forms of SEND are especially vulnerable to abuse) [26]. Consequently, David entered care to improve his day-to-day welfare and so that he could learn the skills he needed to live independently at the age of 18. Upon arrival at Annie's home David demonstrated some of the warning signs for emotional abuse: withdrawn and anxious, he was fearful of doing things wrong. He seemed relieved when he entered care, and quickly grew in confidence once beyond his mother's control.

Nationally speaking, the police are responsible for the largest proportion of referrals and this is unsurprising given that the police are likely to interact with families during acute crises. Meanwhile, teachers and other education services make 1 in 5 referrals [8], perhaps partly because of their sustained interactions with children and their parents.

During initial assessment social workers identify a child's needs and the most commonly identified need is abuse or neglect. This accounts for over half of all cases. When it comes to children in the looked after category, abuse and neglect is the primary identified need for an even higher proportion of young people, equating to nearly two thirds of all cases [13]. The next most frequently cited primary need is family dysfunction (although this is well under 1 in 5 cases) whilst illness and disability (of the child or their parents or carers) accounts for less than 1 in 10 children's primary need.

Another important element of initial assessment is to identify the *cause* of the need. Here, the most common factor is domestic violence (including that directed at children, a parent or carer, or another adult in the household). This is followed by mental health (again, of the child, or an adult in the household). Together, these two factors account for more than a third of all factors identified. Drug and alcohol abuse also feature in a high number of cases.

While some safeguarding concerns come from within children's families and homes, "contextual safeguarding concerns" represent risks from the community. For example, gangs are prevalent in a small but growing number of cases, as is trafficking, sexual exploitation and abuse linked to faith.

Despite the wide variety of circumstances in which abuse or neglect can take place, there are some general signs that professionals working with children can look out for and these are presented in the table, below [26, 27]. This is important because, as the government's statutory guidance highlights, safeguarding is the responsibility of all professionals working with children [17]. Learning about these signs is a key aspect of any safeguarding training, making strong safeguarding training the first frontline in spotting and responding to abuse.

6.2.5 What options are available for children taken into care?

6.2.5.1 Placement purpose

The majority of children looked after are placed in foster care (over 70% in 2019) [13]. Most of these placements are with people a child does not know, as opposed to "kinship care" provided by another family member or friend. Some argue that entering care offers children the chance of a clean break, and vital distance from parents or home environments that threaten their physical and mental wellbeing [4, 28].

Table 6.1 Spotting and responding to abuse

Issue	Possible warning signs	Notes
Physical abuse: the deliberate physical harm of a child	• The child has frequent injuries, especially fractures and broken bones, or burn marks, bite marks or cuts. • The child often feels sick (which can be a sign of poisoning).	• Children can be more at risk if their parents struggle with substance abuse, mental health issues, or have a history of domestic violence. • Parents or cares may fabricate how a child sustained its injuries.
Emotional abuse: also called psychological abuse	• The child is withdrawn, anxious or fearful of doing things wrong. • Parents ignore, blame or humiliate their children.	• Emotional abuse can take a long time to identify. It may include bullying (including online) by peers.
Sexual abuse: penetrative or non-penetrative sexual contact, or encouraging children to take or look at sexually explicit images	• The child displays an interest in or knowledge of sex, or uses sexual language inappropriate to their age. • The child behaves sexually, or encourages others to do so. • The child has physical, sexual health problems such as genital soreness.	• Many children who are victims of sexual abuse do not see themselves as such. • Sexual abuse is often but not exclusively committed by men. • Sexual abuse and harassment can take place between children, either between peers of the same age or between age groups.
Sexual exploitation: sexually exploiting children for money, status or power	• The child has unexplained gifts. • The child has an older boyfriend or girlfriend. • The child misuses drugs or alcohol. • The child is regularly absent, missing from home, or late home.	• By definition a child aged under 16 cannot consent to sex, even if they believe they have done so. • Young people aged 16 or over who consented may still have experienced abuse.
Neglect: failing to provide for children's needs resulting in impairment to the child's development	• The child is dirty or hungry. • The child lacks appropriate clothing (such as a winter coat). • The child is angry, withdrawn, volatile or self-harms. • The child does not receive basic health care.	• Children suffering from neglect are more at risk of other forms of abuse. • Parents and carers are less likely to be able to look after their child adequately if they suffer from substance abuse, mental health issues, or have a history of domestic violence.

This was arguably the case for David; however, others suggest that the system's black-and-white nature – children are either in care or not – reduces the options for more flexible arrangements. For example, some suggest that combining state and family care (perhaps by enabling children to spend more time with their families over the weekend) could be beneficial [21].

This speaks to a wider debate about the purpose of children's care. Does it exist to provide temporary refuge until a better alternative is found? Is it an alternative to family life? Should it serve to prepare children and young people for independence? Or should it provide a therapeutic setting in which children receive treatment? [29] Should there be a range of settings responsive to different needs? [30]

Setting England's approach in a wider international context, Petrie et al. suggest that differences in country's approaches to children's social care reflect wider socio-political philosophies. For example, England and the US's more market-orientated preferences mean the state plays less of a role in supporting children's care than in the socially democratic Nordic countries, and in Germany [31].

However, children's care is not only shaped by views on the role of the state. As Gilbert highlights, some children's care systems place greater emphasis on child protection, "correcting" or "compensating" for parenting (historically associated with the US, Canadian and English systems), while others – including those in continental Europe – employ "family service" models responsive to perceived psychological or socioeconomic difficulties [32]. Indeed, ongoing parental involvement is "taken as a given" in many countries [30], exemplified by the fact that adoption from care is not possible in Sweden, whereas this is comparatively common in England [33]. Over the last couple of decades, however, Gilbert argues that these conceptual models have begun to merge in some countries, for example with greater emphasis in England on family support [32]. However, England's approach to children's care remains relatively rigid in comparison with other countries, where "children are either in care – or not; in a foster or residential placement with distinct regulatory boundaries; in a secure or open setting" [34]. However, Hart et al. note these boundaries are more "blurred" in many other European countries [35].

6.2.5.2 Placement type

As we saw, above, foster care accounts for the highest proportion of care placements in England. The remainder are in settings including semi-independent living accommodation which are generally for older children aged 15 to 17 (such as Annie's homes), and children's homes which contain children of all ages. These can be extremely expensive to provide, and costs vary hugely by location. For example, in some local authorities placing children in care homes can cost less than £2,000 a week, but in some areas, this costs nearly five times as much [15, 36].

Indeed, a lack of suitable and affordable placements is one of the biggest challenges for children's social care, especially so for older children whose needs can be more extreme. However, while some attribute the growing costs of children's care solely to the emergence of private providers [37, 38], the truth is likely more complicated, with costs varying enormously by locality [39].

There has been a decline in the number of fostering households in England, and the number of vacancies available to children [40, 41]. This burden is not distributed evenly across the system: it affects certain regions more than others, and is particularly marked for children with more pronounced and complex needs (who require more skilled foster carers) [42]. Therefore, while the vast majority of children in need of foster placements receive them, often it is the neediest children that local authorities struggle to place [3]. This can mean local authorities rely on private provision (that is, private providers who recruit and train foster parents, as well as other forms of privately-provided provision such as care homes) [40]. Independent Fostering Agencies ("IFAs", most of which are privately operated) account for around a third of foster placements [3]. Some argue that this has dramatically increased the cost of securing foster placements for local authorities [10], although others counter that the comparison of costs is unfair because it is the most challenging children who cost the most to support who are placed in IFAs [3]. However, many foster carers do not feel they have adequate access to training and support, limiting their ability to take on young people with more complex needs, and this is clearly an area in which government could play a greater role [42].

6.2.5.3 Placement location

A little over half of all placements for children looked after are within their home local authority's own boundaries, and nearly three quarters of children are placed within 20 miles of their family home [13]. The APPG for Runaway and Missing Children and Adults highlights that the absolute number of children looked after placed within their home local authority has remained similar since 2012 (just under 30,000 children) but that the increasing number of children in care means the proportion placed outside their home local authority is growing [43]. This affects some parts of the care system more than others, and the APPG found that nearly 6 in 10 placements into secure homes, children's homes and supported accommodation were out-of-area placements, representing an increase of over 40% since 2012.

Children from certain parts of the country are more likely to be placed further from home. Children from London and the South West will be placed in a home that is, on average, more than 50 miles from their family, whereas children from the North West or Yorkshire and Humber will be less than 25 miles from their families on average [44]. This is because children's homes are not evenly distributed across the country: nearly a quarter of all homes (and 1 in 5 available places) are in the North West, and only 1 in 20 homes (and 1 in 18 places) is in London.

One reason cited for this is property prices and availability of affordable housing. Some argue it is cheaper to create and sustain provision in some regions than in others [43], although the National Audit Office has questioned this saying "there is no clear correlation between house prices and the costs of residential care" [39]. In fact, the NAO stated that neither government nor local authorities appear to have an adequate understanding of the drivers of costs.

The second reason is the proliferation of private provision: three quarters of children's homes are now privately run [44]. Local authorities argue that the presence of private provision reduces their control of placements, as private providers are not obliged to accommodate children and that have to be placed further from home outside the local authority's jurisdiction [45].

On the other hand, there is an active debate about the extent to which distance of placement is desirable or undesirable. Stephen Blunden, Chief Executive of Childhood First, said children who have experienced significant abuse and neglect or who face severe contextual safeguarding concerns "are generally best looked after at a significant distance from their home community, and preferably in a rural setting. Anything else is likely to be unsafe" [28]. Indeed, for some children, such as David, placements further away from home offer a necessary and important opportunity to escape danger.

However, for other children such as Karl, being nearer home means they can sustain important relationships with loved ones. Furthermore, some argue that proximity to family helps prevent children looked after from further harm. 70% of the 41 police forces contributing to the APPG for Runaway and Missing Children and Adults inquiry said that "placing children out of area increases their risk of exploitation and often results in them being coerced into going missing" [43].

Children looked after are already far more likely than their peers to go missing (that is, they are not at their placement setting or where they are expected to be, and their whereabouts are unknown) [46]. Children in care homes, semi-independent accommodation or secure units are most likely to go missing, perhaps because they tend to be older [13], and the situation is worsening, with both the number of children who go missing, and the number of incidents per child rising [43]. Children in foster care are also more likely than their non-looked after peers to go missing, albeit less likely than children in care homes.

The most commonly reported reason for going missing among foster children is contact with family or friends, accounting for over half of all incidents [41], and the same is said to be true for children in care homes [43].

Often, police and other professionals do not know which children are in care in their areas, meaning children who are already further from home are more likely to slip below the radar. This is exactly what happened to Karl.

6.2.5.4 Placement stability

Lisa Cherry has worked in the education and social care sectors, and experienced the care system herself first hand. In her book *The Brightness of Stars* she describes her experiences of moving frequently between foster carers and children's homes as follows:

> The overwhelming sensation again is one of difference. I can't connect. I am disconnected. Disconnection is a huge part of this experience.... By this stage I am disconnected from myself. There is no anchor from which to centre my existence. ...I do not belong anywhere or to anyone; I just come to stay. [47]
>
> *Lisa Cherry*

Experiences like Lisa's have been an important focus of research, with studies suggesting that a key determinant of outcomes for young people taken into care is the length and stability of their placement. For example, placement instability (irrespective of the type of care setting) is linked with worse mental health [48] and behavioural wellbeing [49], as well as lower levels of trust and ability to form relationships.

Internationally, Cameron shows that England's placement stability for children in care is lower and that children experience a greater number of placements than in Hungary, Spain, Denmark and Sweden [50]. However, Hart et al. show that lack of placement stability is far from a uniquely English problem and is a challenge in virtually every system [30].

In 2017 the Children's Commissioner launched the Stability Index, an annual measure of the stability of the lives of children in care. This suggests that rates of instability have remained relatively constant since 2016/17 [11]. While two thirds of young people that have been in care for two and a half years have been in the same placements for two years or longer, 1 in 10 children had three or more placements within a year [13].

Yet instability is not only caused by children's placements, but by changes in their home, social worker or school, and the 2019 Stability Index indicates that only 1 in 6 children in care experienced none of these changes over two years. 1 in 20 children experienced all three within the year, and many children experience multiple changes or physical moves within a year. If each of these elements of home, social worker and school are considered an anchor for these children, then it is clear how challenging it must be when they are subject to constant change and upheaval. Indeed, changes in social workers are the norm rather than the exception, and over half of children in care are subject to at least one of these destabilising shifts within a given year (over a quarter experience two or more). Recalling her own experiences of this, Lisa Cherry describes yet another "nameless and faceless social worker" [4], and the Children's Commissioner's "Children's Voices" also attests to the impact these frequent changes can have on young people:

> [You're] very on-edge for a good couple of months, if not a few years ... It took me a good year to settle in, to actually feel safe, and that had a really big impact on my life, because it just makes it difficult to make me feel safe with friends, and just makes me nervous whenever I go to meet anyone really, it makes me really nervous still. [51]
>
> *Female, 17*

As is the case in care provision more widely, instability is not felt evenly throughout the system. Instability varies greatly between local authorities, and social worker "churn" is more prevalent in local authorities facing greater difficulties with recruitment and retention. Children facing regular moves are less likely to attend a good school, and more likely to attend a worse one, compounding the impacts of placement instability [11]. Teenagers are more likely to change placements than younger children [52], and given their complex needs this may create a negative spiral whereby their needs are exacerbated by regular moves, in turn making subsequent moves more likely.

6.2.5.5 Medium-term destinations

Around a quarter of children leave care to return home to their parents, whilst others move into independent living (with or without support), special guardianship arrangements (which grants a carer parental responsibility without legally becoming a parent), or are adopted. In 2014 the government introduced "Staying Put", giving foster children the option to remain living with their foster parents after turning 18 (the age at which children are no longer "in care"). Around half of care leavers stay with their foster families upon turning 18, although only around a quarter are still there aged 20 [13]. As is explored below, longer-term outcomes for care leavers are an area of significant concern.

6.2.5.6 Assessing the options

Department for Education data indicates that children who have been referred to social services but not taken into care do slightly worse in school than children taken into care, although both groups achieve significantly worse results at Key Stages 2 and 4 than children not in need of social service support [53]. This is something that academic research on children's care has also examined, with studies indicating that children taken into care experience more positive outcomes than they likely might have done had they not been taken into care [54]. For example, in their meta-analysis of 27 studies from Western Europe, Australia and North America, Knorth et al. found that residential care programmes helped to improve children's psychological functioning in comparison with similar children not receiving this form of care [55]. This has a potentially vital implication: children on the edge of care face disadvantage if they remain with families struggling to look after them, in contrast with their peers who are taken into care.

Yet we must exercise caution before reaching generalised conclusions about an area as complex as children's care. As Lisa and Karl's experiences show, the care system is plagued by challenges. In their meta-analysis of therapeutic treatments in North America and Western Europe, De Swart et al. find that whether or not interventions are evidence-based is more important than whether or not these take place in a care setting [56]. Indeed, the authors suggest that "care as usual" for children with serious development and behaviour problems is not linked to a positive effect and could even make things worse. Describing her experience living in the Tiffield secure home in Northamptonshire, Lisa Cherry recalls an absence of management by adults resulting in hierarchies of power among the young people characterised by "sexual deviance, addiction capability, violence and offending" (the home was closed in 2007 after revelations that staff were abusing children in its care) [4].

De Sena et al. studied the Safe Homes programme in the US (a group care programme for children aged 3 to 12, seeking to improve placement stability) and found that while outcomes for these children did improve, children in foster care achieved better outcomes still [57]. Other studies have also shown that children in residential care experience worse outcomes across a range of measures including placement stability than their peers in foster care [58]. Young people's experiences "in care" are clearly not homogeneous and there are myriad forms of care provision.

Assessing outcomes from different forms of care is particularly difficult because there is rarely an opportunity to assess the counterfactual – that is, what an individual child's experiences would have been like had they taken a different path. In their review of the literature for the Department for Education, Hart et al. highlight how difficult it is for research to establish the impact care settings have [30]:

1. Many studies do not include a comparison group. This means that children and young people's progress is reported as "distance travelled" over a set period of time for the setting involved, but with no indication of what progress against similar outcomes children in different settings outside care might make.

2. Even with a control group studies encounter challenges because, in order to be comparable, children in both groups need to be as similar as possible in relation to their needs and circumstances. Children in care's experiences and outcomes are shaped by the reasons for them being in care, as well as factors such as placement history, age, gender and so on, making it particularly challenging to make comparisons with "similar" children. Many question whether it is children's pre-existing experiences that determine outcomes, or the system itself.

3. Studies tend to focus on isolating the impact of a specific intervention but frequently give insufficient attention to context.

4. Research that does compare outcomes for children in care tends to focus on shorter-term outcomes, over and above medium- and longer-term outcomes. Furthermore, the outcomes measured can be narrower than in other areas of children's policy research focusing for example on behavioural metrics (such as substance abuse or absence), and studies often insufficiently take into account children and parents' views.

6.3 Why does this group of young people matter?

6.3.1 Educational engagement

Children in need are three times as likely to be persistently absent from school, and two to four times as likely to be permanently excluded compared to their peers [7, 59]. Children in need of support from social services, but who are not in care, are more likely than their peers – both those in care, and not in contact with social services – to be absent from school [53], and this may be because children at the "edge" of care are frequently from families who, for a range of reasons, may be struggling to establish day-to-day routine. Meanwhile, children in secure units or semi-independent care are far more likely to go missing or be absent than children in other care provision, though this could be because they tend to be older [13].

Children in need but not in care are more at risk of permanent exclusion than children looked after, although the latter are more likely to face a fixed term exclusion [53]. They are also more likely to join a school at an unusual time of year sometimes due to them fleeing from violence or abuse at home. As was explored above, teenagers aged 13 and over are also more likely to face instability in their placements including moving school and this can drive the tendency to join school at an unusual time of year, with all the associated disruption this can cause [60]. Some also argue that children in need of support from social services can be seen as "trouble" by teachers and other professionals, driving a labelling effect which might lead them to go on and fulfil this stereotype [4]. This may play a part in the fact that children who have needed a social worker are 10 times as likely to be taught in Alternative Provision compared to their peers. As a result, these children make up over half the pupil population in over 80% of Alternative Provision settings.

6.3.2 Academic outcomes

Engagement is not always the problem. Ben entered Annie's house having been kicked out of his foster parents' house when they found cannabis in his room. This coincided with concerns being raised by Ben's school about his involvement in a local gang, leading him to be moved from London to Kent during his final year of GCSEs. Unsurprisingly, he did not get the results he wanted. Determined to improve his grades in order to go to college, Ben retook his GCSEs at a different school. Travelling from Kent, he needed funds to pay his train fare. Unfortunately, Ben's social worker was reluctant to give this to Ben without seeing him physically at the college. Ben felt self-conscious about this and refused to meet the social worker. Despite Annie vouching for Ben's dedication to his studies (demonstrated by his coursework), Ben lost out on his expense payments and his place at the college. Ben's experience exemplifies the additional hurdles children and young people in care experience, which simply do not exist for their peers. Unable to rely upon stable placements or adults who "have their backs", many children are pushed out of a system even when they actively want to engage with it.

Perhaps unsurprisingly given the educational experiences highlighted above, children who have needed a social worker do not do as well on average as their peers at school. Taking other factors such as SEND and parental income into account, research by the Department for Education shows that children who have needed a social worker are half as likely to pass English and maths GCSEs as those who have not [7]. These worse outcomes persist even where a child ceases to be in need. For example, children who needed a social worker up to four years prior to their GCSEs were still 25% to 50% less likely to pass English and maths.

Poorer educational outcomes extend beyond compulsory education with 6% of children who were in need during their final year of GCSE study going on to attend higher education at age 18, compared to 27% of their peers. Half of young people who were in need as children do not have level 2 qualifications by age 21, in contrast to 11% of their peers. They are also far more likely to be Not in Education, Employment or Training ("NEET") [13].

These outcomes are by no means inevitable, and results data show that some children currently in need or in need in the past go on to attain excellent GCSE results. Indeed, some care-experienced adults believe that the challenges they faced as children helped spur them on, giving them a sense of purpose and the emotional tools such as resilience that have supported success later in life. Pav, a trade union employment and equality lawyer, reflects on his time in care as giving him his sense of mission:

> When I reflect back, it was almost inevitable that I would respond to [the injustices I witnessed and experienced in care] with a long-term commitment to challenging bigotry and prejudice. ...It is connected to the perseverance I have shown in the face of tests that might have broken others. ...you quickly learn that self-reliance and self-sufficiency are your greatest assets. [61]
>
> *Pav*

However, the unfortunate fact is that statistics make it clear Pav's life outcomes are the exception rather than the norm, something Pav attributes in part to the low expectations held for children in care:

> I consider myself a positive case study [but...] the hallmark to survival for many in my "home" was rampant substance abuse; predatory emotional and sexual exploitation by [adults outside] ...as well as unchecked criminality. ... [I remember] the profound nihilism and poverty of ambition surrounding me and my prospects. The expectations were so low that it was easy to fall victim to the gloom that was predicted. [62]
>
> *Pav*

In their report on what works in education for children who have had social workers, Sanders et al. suggest "the needs of young people who have had a social worker in education may be different to their peers" [63]. While acknowledging the evidence-base does not permit robust conclusions, the study highlights interventions that show potential suggesting that programmes focusing on literacy and numeracy, and interventions targeting parents and carers are "particularly encouraging".

6.3.3 Crime and justice

Karl's story highlights an important theme relevant to the children's care system: children looked after are significantly more likely to be involved in the youth justice system [54]. This is unsurprising given that disrupted homelives and instability particularly during adolescence can make them vulnerable to exploitation, and to involvement in crime. Karl's circumstances – impending fatherhood, and the need to secure money to provide for his partner – were important in his decision to prioritise petty crime over college. Lisa Cherry's autobiographical account of her time in care highlights how children in care can become stuck in a cycle, feeling rejected by mainstream society and turning to crime (and other self-destructive behaviours) as a way to get by[113]. Strikingly, around a quarter of the adult prison population is care-experienced, and this group is also particularly likely to reoffend.

Returning to Ben's story we see several, sad ironies that underpin his experience. He lost his foster placement when his carers found cannabis in his room despite the fact that most children would not face eviction by their parents in the same situation. Meanwhile his school's concern about his involvement in a local gang meant he was re-housed outside London, a destabilising experience that added hours to his commute every week during the year of his GCSEs. Finally, Ben's understandable self-consciousness about meeting his social worker at college (something that would only add to his feelings of otherness and social alienation) and subsequent refusal to do so meant he lost access to the funding that made study possible. Annie does not know what happened to Ben, but paradoxically it was the fudged responses to Ben's initial, minor criminality that heightened his vulnerability to further, more serious crime.

Some research indicates that children in care settings are also more likely than their peers to be unfairly criminalised. For example, the Howard League for Penal Reform has raised alarms about high, and often unnecessary, police involvement in children's homes [64]. This is reflected elsewhere, for example in Lord Laming's independent review on children in care and involvement in crime for the Prison Reform Trust. This found that while the number of children in care receiving convictions, reprimands or warnings for committing offences has been declining since 2013, many are "sucked into the criminal justice system unnecessarily" for behaviours that would normally be dealt with without involving the police by a child's parents [65]. This was something Ruth, a social worker in East London, talked about, saying parents would be unlikely to report their child to the police for taking £20 without asking.

However, whether or not police get involved is often beside the point. Ruth and Annie both highlighted a paradox at the heart of the care system: while many young people feel as though no one cares for them and that they have been forgotten and alienated, their lives are scrutinised and recorded in far more detail than children living with parents. Both talked about how relatively minor behavioural infringements such as an argument with a peer or adult can be logged. Ruth said "everything is written down" partly out of a defensiveness whereby staff feel the need to cover themselves in the case of a serious incident. This affects semi-independent accommodation and foster placements as well as children's homes. This raises two issues:

1. Children are not being given the leeway parents might normally grant their own children.

2. While records are constantly made about children's lives, Ruth explained that these records are often inaccurate: "stuff gets written down wrong all the time. *All* the time. And it follows people around. ...It can't just be deleted".

Not everyone agrees with this characterisation. In his review of children's residential care settings, Sir Martin Narey argued that police generally become involved when it is necessary for them to do so, and that, in fact care settings often *avoid* involving them [28].

Research has explored whether children's care settings are criminogenic, that is, whether they make crime and criminality more likely and there are two possible components to this. Firstly, care settings are home to children whose conduct is more likely to be criminal, because their "pre-care experiences, including those of abuse, neglect and poor parenting, have a part to play in terms of their propensity for problematic behaviour and likelihood of youth justice involvement" [66–68]. Care settings might then reinforce criminal behaviours among these same children when they are brought together. Hayden (2010) also points out that the more settings such as care homes are seen as a last resort, the more likely it is that the children within them will be at risk [69].

Secondly, children in care are far more likely than their peers to be victims of crime and abuse, from their peers and also from staff. This is something that permeates many personal accounts of care experiences:

> [I was sent to a] teenage psychiatric centre .... Normally filled with girls with eating disorders, unfortunately for me when I was admitted it housed nine boys, all of whom were either schizophrenic or manic depressive. I was raped the first day I was there.
>
> I lasted ten weeks in a foster home, which should never have been allowed to have vulnerable children. I had just turned 15 and on the day my foster father and two of his friends decided to spend an afternoon raping me and beating me, I left. [70]
>
> *Caroline*

Reported levels of abuse and neglect experienced by children in care stand at around 2 to 3 cases per 100 children in the UK [71]. Yet despite this alarmingly high case-incidence, studies have found that they increase further when children report such crimes confidentially [72]. This highlights the critical importance of having confidential mechanisms by which children in care settings can report instances of abuse, and robust, swift mechanisms for dealing with these reports.

There is debate about whether care provision should reflect the "loving" environment one would expect to characterise parent/child relationships outside care settings. The literature is divided on this. Some argue that relationships in care settings should be "homely" [73]. Other research suggests that care settings have duty to acknowledge the young people within them likely have additional needs which require an additional degree of routine and boundaries [74].

6.3.4 Mental and physical health and wellbeing

All three of the children Annie told me about experienced profound issues in relation to their mental health and wellbeing. In their own ways, all three boys experienced feelings of anxiety, anger and alienation, reflecting a high prevalence of mental health needs amongst children in need. Analysis of the 1970 British Cohort Study found that children in residential care experienced worse outcomes on a range of wellbeing measures, including higher rates of depression and addiction, and lower rates of life satisfaction and self-efficacy [58]. Similar findings have been reported elsewhere [7, 75, 76].

As is explored above, a combination of childhood trauma and lower educational achievement can lead to worse job prospects, and make children in need – and particularly children looked after, vulnerable to exploitation, crime and homelessness. In some regions it has been estimated that half of female sex workers are care-experienced, and that a quarter of homeless people were in care as children (see Chapter 7). A lack of stable accommodation compounded by high costs of living and rent rises can mean care leavers are particularly likely to find themselves sofa surfing or rough sleeping [77] as part of what Lisa Cherry describes as an almost "inevitable" move from care into homelessness [4].

Children in need and especially those in care are more likely to have special educational needs or disabilities [53]. While children with disabilities are automatically considered in need of local authority support, this does not entirely explain the high prevalence of SEND among these children. Disability accounts for a small minority of primary need among children in care; social, emotional and mental health is by far the most common reason for SEND categorisation among children in need and children in care [78].

6.3.5 A growing crisis

The quality of children's care varies hugely. Ofsted is responsible for the inspection of children's social care services and does this at the local authority- and individual setting-level. While 4 in 5 children's homes were judged to be good or outstanding at the end of March 2019, under half of local authorities were judged to be good or outstanding in terms of their overall effectiveness [44]. However, effectiveness varies regionally: in 2019 London, the North East, Yorkshire and the Humber had the highest proportion of local authorities judged good or outstanding, and the West Midlands and South West the lowest [79].

Many factors shape local authorities' ability to meet children's needs. These include staff recruitment and retention, which can in turn be affected by a local authority's reputation. This can create a self-perpetuating cycle, since social workers may be put off working for local authority with a low Ofsted rating [10]. The cost of living, availability of affordable accommodation, and the salaries on offer in a particular local authority can all affect authorities' abilities to recruit and retain the right staff. Other factors include funding pressures (which have hit some local authorities harder than others), and the availability of suitable placements for children (which can put strain on local authorities' budgets) [80].

While Ofsted inspects Independent Fostering Agencies (4 in 5 of which are privately owned) [44], it does not inspect semi-independent accommodation. Ofsted explains that this is because such settings "should be used as a stepping stone to independence, and only ever when it's in a child's best interests" [81]. However, the quality of semi-independent care provision is a cause for concern. Ruth, a social worker in East London, said that while the quality of children's care in general can be extremely variable, semi-independent care is especially vulnerable to underperformance. This is because:

- The settings generally cater for older children (16 and above), and some will stay on until their late teens or even early 20s. As discussed earlier, teenagers can have more pronounced needs, making them harder to provide adequately for.

- The quality of staff in these settings is variable but often low. Many are not qualified and have "just fallen into it". They are often paid minimum wage, and receive little in the way of ongoing support or training. As Ruth put it, "It's not an easy job. You're working with kids who can be quite unpleasant towards you. If you're earning £9 an hour, you'd probably just think, 'fuck it'".

- Consequently, young people are often "left to their own devices", and can feel as though nobody in the setting really cares for them. Annie echoed many of these sentiments, recalling how her boss – the chief executive of the care homes Annie managed – had no professional experience of working with young people, which meant he was not able to provide much practical, day-to-day guidance or support.

The growing number of children identified as being in need has exacerbated these challenges [15]. While this increase partly reflects birth rates, which spiked during the 2000s [82], the *rate* of children entering care also grew by nearly 50% between 1994 and 2018 [18]. Four main factors lie behind this increase:

6.3.5.1 Child poverty

Poverty is one of the single most important factors leading to the involvement of children's social services in families' lives. Over 4 million children live in poverty, a figure that the Child Poverty Action Group believes will increase to over 5 million by 2022 [83].

The relationship between poverty and the likelihood that a child will be in need of support from social services is complex, but ultimately, it is clear that poverty makes the job of being a parent much harder.

Certain families are particularly likely to experience poverty, as evidenced by statistics compiled by the Child Poverty Action Group. For example, children in lone parent families or minority ethnic families are more likely to live in poverty (nearly half do).

The Association of Directors of Children's Services reports that parental mental ill-health, substance abuse and domestic violence among parents are rising [10]. All of these factors are associated with poverty in a reflexive relationship, that is, parental ill-health, substance abuse and domestic violence make poverty more likely, but also stem from it.

Over 40% of children in households containing three or more children live in poverty. Yet this is not because parents in these families are less likely to work; 7 in 10 children living in poverty have parents who are employed [83]. However, being a single parent, having a larger family or being from a minority ethnic background makes finding and keeping well-paid work more difficult.

In turn, living in poverty makes children more susceptible to physical and emotional ill-health, developmental delays and forms of SEND, social alienation, and curtailing of life chances [84].

Having a child who is facing these hurdles make the task of parenting more difficult, and increases the possible need for social service support.

6.3.5.2 Availability of support

In response to funding cuts, local authorities have dramatically scaled back their discretionary preventative services (sometimes called "early help") in order to maintain spending on statutory "reactive" children's social care which they are obliged to provide. This is well demonstrated by National Audit Office analysis [18].

Local authorities must also appoint Virtual School Heads (VSH) whose role is to ensure the authority fulfils its duty to promote the education of children looked after and children who were previously looked after. "Virtual Schools" do not physically exist. Rather, Virtual Schools will, for example, collate and maintain up-to-date information about children looked after in school or college (or who were previously looked after), advocate for these children, and liaise with professionals working with these children in order to provide suitable educational support [85]. However, in its 2012 review of Virtual Schools, Ofsted found that provision varied greatly between local authorities [86]. In some local authorities, small teams of two people primarily commissioned services; in others, Virtual Schools offered training and even teaching support. Ofsted notes that "budget constraints had led to a significant reduction in the capacity of the Virtual School in some local authorities" [87].

6.3.5.3 Changing legislative requirements

Reforms to SEND, and the introduction of initiatives such as "Staying Put" (giving care leavers the option to stay with their foster families) have increased the number of children and young people in need of support and consequent pressure on local authorities. These increases have not been adequately reflected in funding.

6.3.5.4 Attitude to risk

Some argue that a culture of defensiveness has developed among social workers, who work in a sector with a high emphasis on compliance and who want to "do things right" rather than "doing the right thing" [88]. Ruth talked about this in relation to monitoring and recording incidents of defiant behaviour, saying that staff are anxious to log "everything" without reflecting on whether recording the incident is beneficial, or taking the time to understand the reasons for the behaviour. Ben's social worker insisted on "doing things right" and meeting him at college, even though this was not something Ben wanted. Annie reflects that "doing the right thing" might have been seeking to compromise on the location in order to accommodate Ben's understandable self-consciousness.

Risk aversion can be exacerbated by tragic events such as those surrounding Victoria Climbié, Peter Connelly ("Baby P") and Daniel Pelka – cases in which horrific abuse was allowed to take place. Similarly, risk aversion is an understandable response to recognition that sex abuse cases in Rochdale, Bradford and Manchester were avoidable and that children had fallen through the cracks when social services, the police, education and health repeatedly missed opportunities to intervene.

Whilst such incidents rightly cause shock and alarm, in her review of child protection, Professor Eileen Munro highlighted how these events can sustain a blame culture (especially when the media or politicians get involved). This makes it harder to learn lessons because the cases are seen as someone's fault, rather than reflective of systemic practises. This can also mean professionals are less likely to admit to mistakes in future [89].

6.3.5.5 Pressures on the workforce

The residential workforce in England is underqualified and undervalued in comparison with many other European countries. Petrie et al. found that in contrast with Belgium, Germany, France and Denmark, England's residential workforce was the lowest qualified, typically to level 3 (A-level equivalent) rather than degree-level [31]. Furthermore, qualifications tend to focus more on mechanistic aspects of care giving, rather than supporting children's holistic development, something advocates of the social pedagogy model claim it offers. However, in his review of children's residential care, Sir Martin Narey contests the idea that higher qualifications are necessary, arguing instead that temperament is more important:

> The priority... should be to recruit staff with the right qualities, temperament and resilience and then help them to develop and, as part of that development, to gain an understanding of the type of children they care for. [90]

Others acknowledge that training and qualifications can make a difference, when they are the *right* training and qualifications [31]. However, there is some scepticism about the effectiveness of social care qualifications in England [28].

Practitioners working in children's care in the UK are more likely than their European counterparts to feel like technicians, with those working in England more likely to feel their job emphasises procedural tasks and behaviour management, over and above therapeutic work, and relational work with families [30]. This is perhaps reinforced by the fact that nearly half of all the 31,000 full time-equivalent children and family social workers in England are not in case-holder roles, instead holding managerial or supervisory positions [91]. This seems symptomatic of a system that prioritises accountability and paperwork (doing things right) over and above caring for children (doing the right thing).

6.4 Conclusion

As our coffee drew to a close, I asked Annie what her reflections are on her time working in children's care homes. Her answer summed up many of themes that are explored throughout this chapter.

Working with the young people was "not the difficult bit of the job", despite their often challenging, self-destructive behaviours and complex emotional needs. Looking into her empty coffee mug, Annie said that staffing structures and, namely, the high turnover of care home staff and social workers made it extremely difficult to provide young people with a consistent, quality experience.

Furthermore, Annie felt that staff were too often incentivised to focus on the "wrong things". Ben's social worker wanted to focus on Ben's drug use, rather than on his underlying issues (which Annie attributes to unaddressed trauma). The system encouraged the ticking of boxes, not doing the right thing for the young people under its care.

I asked Annie whether she still thinks about Karl, Ben and the other children that had lived in her care homes. "I still worry about them", she replied. Does she know what happened to them? "I Google them sometimes", she said, "but I really don't know. I can't help feeling the odds are stacked against them".

6.5 Taking Action

6.5.1 Practitioners

Teachers and other school-based practitioners need to be aware that the needs of children who have come into contact with social services may differ from other children's. Practitioners must ensure these children's core literacy and numeracy skills are developing in line with their peers', as evidence indicates reading, writing and maths provide a springboard for educational success for children in need [63]. Designated Safeguarding Leads and VSHs should support teachers to view safeguarding as everyone's responsibility, and not solely the responsibility of specific staff or social workers.

Social workers and local authorities should wherever possible provide families with early help, for example through support with issues like substance abuse, domestic violence and poor mental health. Rather than removing children once families have reached crisis point, this could tackle some of the underlying reasons why parents find parenting difficult, helping more families stay together. Family Group Conferences are sometimes used to help families discuss issues and identify their own solutions. These are arranged by an independent facilitator and not families' social workers [92]. Increased availability of such provision by local authorities could give families more agency and give them more control over the support they receive. Of course, there will remain instances where the child's wellbeing necessitates swift and more drastic action by local authorities.

There are promising findings from a pilot running in Lambeth, Southampton and Stockport, embedding social workers *within* schools [93]. During the pilot social workers supported children in school with Child Protection Plans, as well as offering early intervention for families. The pilot tentatively indicates that such a model can hold benefits for children, their families, and teachers, reducing the number of child protection enquiries in the boroughs in the pilot.

It is impossible to ignore the heightened risk of abuse that children in need, and especially those in care, face. More readily available mechanisms for reporting abuse and neglect confidentially, quickly and safely would help, as would improvements in record keeping and reporting by care giving staff. To reduce the influence of biases – unconscious or otherwise – staff should be supported to record incidents in a scrupulously fair manner, describing what has happened plainly and factually, rather than providing any additional information rooted in emotion or interpretation. Wherever possible, paperwork should be kept to a minimum in order to free up practitioners' time to focus on giving children and families support.

In their review of children's care (focused on children's residential care homes), Hart et al. highlight four principles they feel are important in supporting positive outcomes for children in care settings, four of which have important implications for children in need [30]:

1. Offer a continuum of care: support and provision should be needs-led, rather than service-led. In other words, children and their families should receive support in line with their specific needs rather than because of ease of providing it.

2. Develop positive relationships: these are the foundations of social care. One model that is widely used in continental Europe is social pedagogy, which emphasises relationships and listening. Petrie et al. (2006) describe social pedagogy as "education in the broadest sense of that term", encompassing personal, social and moral education and drawing together theories and concepts from related disciplines such as "sociology, psychology, education, philosophy, medical sciences and social work". In practice, this may mean involvement in therapeutic interventions, relational work with families, teaching, and promoting physical and mental health.

3. Work with families: having parents to visit, and undertaking whole-family support such as family therapy, is linked with improved outcomes for children in care.

4. Provide a "normal life" environment: this is characterised by smaller, more homely environments, providing good food, education and wider support including access to sport and leisure. First and foremost, these environments should be safe.

6.5.2 Policy makers

The suggestions for practice, above, depend on sufficient funding being available. This is the government's responsibility.

It is also important to provide alternatives to care, for example by providing care to whole families, and "part-time" care offering families with respite and the opportunity to have a break. This could help reduce the black and white nature of taking children into care, providing families with something that feels more like support than punishment. Helping to build parents' relationships with their children could increase family resilience helping more children to continue living with, or return to live with their families. This is policymakers' and legislators' responsibility in the first instance, as practitioners can only deploy the options legally available to them.

Another key theme that emerges throughout this chapter is training and support for providers of care in its many forms. Care providers, whether public, private or third-sector, should offer adults working with children and families access to high quality training and support. Foster carers, and staff working in residential and semi-independent care settings are particularly important priorities and training should be responsive to care givers' and children's needs. This training and support should be carefully evaluated, to ensure it is fit for purpose, and constantly updated and improved.

There is a particularly urgent need to improve foster carers' confidence in accommodating children (especially older children) with more challenging needs, and to support residential care staff in providing holistic care that improves children's wellbeing, over and above "firefighting".

These suggestions are not comprehensive, and will not "fix" children's social care. But they might help practitioners and other people working with children and families to offer the care they know is needed.

Further reading

The Brightness of Stars: Stories of Adults who came through the care System: Cherry, L. (2016). KCA Training

Notes

1 These children are also sometimes known as "looked after children".
2 These figures are an estimate, based on the government's CIN data.

References

1 Action for Children, & Jo Cox Loneliness Foundation. (2017). *It Starts with Hello,* Retrieved from https://www.actionforchildren.org.uk/media/9724/action_for_children_it_starts_with_hello_report_november_2017_lowres.pdf.
2 Holland, S. (2009). Looked after children and the ethic of care. *The British Journal of Social Work, 40*(6), 1664–1680. https://doi.org/10.1093/bjsw/bcp086.
3 Narey, M., & Owers, M. (2018). *Foster Care in England: A Review for the Department for Education,* Retrieved from https://assets.publishing.service.gov.uk/government/uploads/system/uploads/attachment_data/file/679320/foster_care_in_england_review.pdf.
4 Cherry, L. (2016). *The Brightness of Stars: Stories of adults who came through the care system.* Dursley: KCA Training.
5 Local Government Association. (2019). *Local Government Association Briefing: General Debate on Children's Social Care in England.* Retrieved from https://local.gov.uk/sites/default/files/documents/20190117%20LGA%20briefing%20-%20Children%27s%20Social%20Care%20in%20England%20FINAL.pdf.
6 Department for Education. (2019). *Children in Need of Help and Protection: CIN Review: Final Data and Analysis,* Retrieved from https://assets.publishing.service.gov.uk/government/uploads/system/uploads/attachment_data/file/809108/CIN_review_final_analysis_publication.pdf.
7 Department for Education. (2019). *Help, Protection, Education: Concluding the Children in need Review,* Retrieved from https://assets.publishing.service.gov.uk/government/uploads/system/uploads/attachment_data/file/809236/190614_CHILDREN_IN_NEED_PUBLICATION_FINAL.pdf.
8 Department for Education. (2019). *Characteristics of Children in need: 2018 to 2019,* Retrieved from https://assets.publishing.service.gov.uk/government/uploads/system/uploads/attachment_data/file/843046/Characteristics_of_children_in_need_2018_to_2019_main_text.pdf.

9 legislation.gov.uk (1989). *Children Act 1989*, Retrieved November 14, 2019, from http://www.legislation.gov.uk/ukpga/1989/41/section/17.

10 The Association of Directors of Children's Services. (2018). *Safeguarding Pressures Phase 6*, Retrieved from https://adcs.org.uk/assets/documentation/ADCS_SAFEGUARDING_PRESSURES_PHASE_6_FINAL.pdf.

11 Children's Commissioner. (2019). *Stability Index 2019*, Retrieved from https://www.childrenscommissioner.gov.uk/publication/stability-index-2019/.

12 Ibid.

13 Department for Education. (2019). *Children Looked after in England (including Adoption), Year Ending 31 March 2019*, Retrieved from https://assets.publishing.service.gov.uk/government/uploads/system/uploads/attachment_data/file/850306/Children_looked_after_in_England_2019_Text.pdf.

14 Francis-Devine, B., Booth, L., & McGuinness, F. (2019). *Poverty in the UK: Statistics. House of Commons Library*, Retrieved from https://researchbriefings.files.parliament.uk/documents/SN07096/SN07096.pdf.

15 Cromarty, H. (2019). Children's social care services in England. *House of Common Library*, Retrieved from http://researchbriefings.files.parliament.uk/documents/CBP-8543/CBP-8543.pdf.

16 Curtis, P., Newell, C., & Caruana Galizia, P. (2019). *The Poor Parents*, Retrieved November 21, 2019, from https://members.tortoisemedia.com/2019/04/27/punished-for-being-poor-what-the-numbers-tell-us-about-family-separation/content.html.

17 HM Government. (2018). *Working Together to Safeguard Children: A Guide to Inter-agency Working to Safeguard and promote the Welfare of Children*, Retrieved from https://assets.publishing.service.gov.uk/government/uploads/system/uploads/attachment_data/file/779401/Working_Together_to_Safeguard-Children.pdf.

18 National Audit Office. (2019). *Pressures on Children's Social Care*, Retrieved from https://www.nao.org.uk/wp-content/uploads/2019/01/Pressures-on-Childrens-Social-Care.pdf.

19 National Children's Bureau. (2018). *Storing up Trouble: A Postcode Lottery of Children's Social Care*, Retrieved from https://www.ncb.org.uk/sites/default/files/field/attachment/NCBStoringUp%20Trouble%5BAugustUpdate%5D.pdf.

20 Ward, H., Brown, R., & Hyde-Dryden, G. (2014). *Assessing Parental Capacity to Change when Children are on the Edge of Care: An Overview of Current Research Evidence*, Retrieved from https://dspace.lboro.ac.uk/dspace-jspui/handle/2134/18183.

21 Trowler, I., White, S., Webb, C., & Leigh, J. T. (2018). *Care Proceedings in England: The Case for Clear Blue Water*, Retrieved from https://www.sheffield.ac.uk/polopoly_fs/1.812157!/file/Sheffield_Solutions_Care_Proceedings.pdf.

22 Boddy, J., Statham, J., McQuail, S., Petrie, P., & Owen, C. (2008). *Working at the 'edges' of care? European models of support for young people and families*. London: Department for Children, Schools and Families.

23 Munro, E. (2011). *The Munro Review of Child Proetection: Final Report – A child-centred system*. London: Department for Education. https://doi.org/10.1375/jcas.36.3.164.

24 Rozenberg, J (2015). *Why the Judge was Right to Reunite a Child with his EDL-Supporting Father*, Retrieved November 14, 2019, from https://www.theguardian.com/law/2015/feb/18/judge-right-reunite-child-with-edl-father-english-defence-league-children-act.

25 Munby, J. (2015). *Approved Judgment*, Retrieved from https://www.judiciary.uk/wp-content/uploads/2015/02/re-a-child-2.pdf.

26 HM Government. (2015). *What to do if you are worried a Child is being Abused: Advice for Practitioners*, Retrieved from https://assets.publishing.service.gov.uk/government/uploads/system/uploads/attachment_data/file/419604/What_to_do_if_you_re_worried_a_child_is_being_abused.pdf.

27 Department for Education. (2019). *Keeping Children Safe in Education: Statutory Guidance for Schools and Colleges*, Retrieved from https://assets.publishing.service.gov. uk/government/uploads/system/uploads/attachment_data/file/835733/Keeping_ children_safe_in_education_2019.pdf.

28 Narey, M. (2016). *Residential Care in England: Report of Sir Martin Narey's independent review of children's residential care*, Retrieved from https://assets.publishing.service. gov.uk/government/uploads/system/uploads/attachment_data/file/534560/Residential-Care-in-England-Sir-Martin-Narey-July-2016.pdf.

29 Whittaker, J., Holmes, L., Del Valle, J., Ainsworth, F., Nor, T., Anglin, J., ... & Isr, A. (2016). Therapeutic residential care for children and youth: A consensus statement of the international work group on therapeutic residential care. *Residential Treatment for Children & Youth*, *33*, 89–106. https://doi.org/10.1080/0886571X.2016.1215755.

30 Hart, D., La Valle, I., & Holmes, L. (2015). *The Place of Residential Care in the English Child Welfare System*, Retrieved from https://assets.publishing.service.gov.uk/government/ uploads/system/uploads/attachment_data/file/435694/Residential_care_in_the_English_ child_welfare_system.pdf.

31 Petrie, P., Boddy, J., Cameron, C., Wigfall, & Simon. (2006). *Working with Children in Care: European Perspectives (First)*, Maidenhead: Open University Press.

32 Gilbert, N. (2012). A comparative study of child welfare systems: Abstract orientations and concrete results. *Children and Youth Services Review*, *34*(3), 532–536. https://doi. org/10.1016/j.childyouth.2011.10.014.

33 Bowyer, S., & Wilkinson, J. (2013). *Evidence Scope: Models of Adolescent Care Provision*, Retrieved from https://pdfs.semanticscholar.org/ef2d/e33e08fe665353a4e75de52d-dec85ff33c5e.pdf.

34 Hart, D., La Valle, I., & Holmes, L. (2015). *The Place of Residential Care in the English Child Welfare System*, Retrieved from https://assets.publishing.service.gov.uk/government/ uploads/system/uploads/attachment_data/file/435694/Residential_care_in_the_English_ child_welfare_system.pdf, p. 27.

35 Ibid.

36 Institute of Public Care (IPC). (2015). *Financial Stability, Cost Charge and Value for Money in the Children's Residential Care Market: Research Report*, London. Retrieved from https://ipc.brookes.ac.uk/publications/DfE_Childrens_residential_care_market_ report-June2015.pdf.

37 Bawden, A. (2018). *Councils Face Huge Bills as Foster Carers Jump Ship to Private Agencies*, Retrieved November 27, 2020, from https://www.theguardian.com/society/2018/ jan/30/councils-huge-bills-foster-carers-private-agencies.

38 Davies, R (2018). *Private Foster care Agencies Increasing Cost of Finding Children Homes*, Retrieved November 26, 2019, from https://www.theguardian.com/society/2018/ jan/30/private-foster-care-agencies-increasing-cost-of-finding-children-homes.

39 National Audit Office. (2014). *Children in Care*, Retrieved from https://www.nao.org.uk/ wp-content/uploads/2014/11/Children-in-care1.pdf.

40 Ofsted. (2019). *Fostering in England 2017 to 2018: Main Findings*, Retrieved November 21, 2019, from https://www.gov.uk/government/publications/fostering-in-england-1-april-2017-to-31-march-2018/fostering-in-england-2017-to-2018-main-findings.

41 Ofsted. (2020). *Fostering in England 2018 to 2019: Main Findings*, Retrieved January 21, 2020, from https://www.gov.uk/government/publications/fostering-in-england-1-april-2018-to-31-march-2019/fostering-in-england-2018-to-2019-main-findings.

42 House of Commons Education Committee. (2017). *Fostering: First Report of Session 2017–19*, 1–58. Retrieved from https://publications.parliament.uk/pa/cm201719/cmse-lect/cmeduc/340/340.pdf.

43 All Party Parliamentary Group for Runaway Missing Children and Adults. (2019). *No Place at Home: Risks facing children and young people who go missing from out of area placements*, Retrieved from https://www.childrenssociety.org.uk/sites/default/files/no-place-at-home.pdf.

44 Ofsted. (2019). *Children's Social Care in England 2019*. Retrieved November 27, 2019, from https://www.gov.uk/government/publications/childrens-social-care-data-in-england-2019/childrens-social-care-in-england-2019#childrens-homes.

45 The Guardian. (2019). *Moving Children far Away from Home in a Privatised Care System*, Retrieved December 17, 2019, from https://www.theguardian.com/society/2019/sep/18/moving-children-far-away-from-home-in-a-privatised-care-system.

46 Ibid.

47 Cherry, L. (2016). *The Brightness of Stars: stories of adults who came through the care system*. KCA Training, p. 57.

48 Rubin, D. M., Alessandrini, E. A., Feudtner, C., Mandell, D. S., Localio, A. R., & Hadley, T. (2004). Placement stability and mental health costs for children in foster care. *Pediatrics, 113*(5), 1336–1341, https://doi.org/10.1542/peds.113.5.1336.

49 Rubin, D., O'Reilly, A., Luan, X., & Localio, A. (2007). The impact of placement stability on behavioral well-being for children in foster care. *Pediatrics, 119*, 336–344. https://doi.org/10.1542/peds.2006-1995.

50 Cameron, C. (2014). "Our young people are worse": Family backgrounds, educational progression and placement options in public care systems. *European Journal of Social Work, 17*. https://doi.org/10.1080/13691457.2012.746285.

51 Children's Commissioner. (2019). *Children's Voices: Children's Experiences of Instability in the Care System*, Retrieved from https://www.childrenscommissioner.gov.uk/wp-content/uploads/2019/07/cco-childrens-voices-childrens-experiences-of-instability-in-the-care-system-july-2019.pdf. p. 3.

52 Wulczyn, F., Kogan, J., & Harden, B. (2003). Placement stability and movement trajectories. *Social Service Review – SOC SERV REV, 77*, 212–236. https://doi.org/10.1086/373906.

53 Department for Education. (2019f). *Outcomes for Childeren Looked after by Local Authorities in England, 31 March 2018 (Vol. 2)*, Retrieved from https://assets.publishing.service.gov.uk/government/uploads/system/uploads/attachment_data/file/794535/Main_Text_Outcomes_for_CLA_by_LAs_2018.pdf.

54 Oakley, M., Miscampbell, G., & Gregorian, R. (2018). *Looked-after children: the silent crisis*. London: Social Market Foundation.

55 Knorth, E., Harder, A., Zandberg, T., & Kendrick, A. (2008). Under one roof: A review and selective meta-analysis on the outcomes of residential child and youth care. *Children and Youth Services Review*, 123–140. https://doi.org/10.1016/j.childyouth.2007.09.001.

56 De Swart, J., Broek, H., Stams, G., Asscher, J. J., Laan, P., Holsbrink-Engels, G. A., & van der Helm, P. (2012). The effectiveness of institutional youth care over the past three decades: A meta-analysis. *Children and Youth Services Review, 34*, 1818–1824. https://doi.org/10.1016/j.childyouth.2012.05.015.

57 DeSena, A. D., Murphy, R. A., Douglas-Palumberi, H., Blau, G., Kelly, B., Horwitz, S. M., & Kaufman, J. (2005). SAFE homes: Is it worth the cost? An evaluation of a group home permanency planning program for children who first enter out-of-home care. *Child Abuse & Neglect, 29*(6), 627–643. https://doi.org/10.1016/j.chiabu.2004.05.007.

58 Dregan, A., & Gulliford, M. (2011). Foster care, residential care and public care placement patterns are associated with adult life trajectories: Population-based cohort study. *Social Psychiatry and Psychiatric Epidemiology, 47*, 1517–1526. https://doi.org/10.1007/s00127-011-0458-5.

59 Jay, M. A., & Mc Grath-Lone, L. (2019). Educational outcomes of children in contact with social care in England: A systematic review. *Systematic Reviews, 8*(1), 155. https://doi.org/10.1186/s13643-019-1071-z.

60 Children's Commissioner. (2019). *Children's Voices: Children's Experiences of Instability in the Care System*, Retrieved from https://www.childrenscommissioner.gov.uk/wp-content/uploads/2019/07/cco-childrens-voices-childrens-experiences-of-instability-in-the-care-system-july-2019.pdf.

61 Cherry, L. (2016). *The brightness of stars: Stories of adults who came through the care system*. KCA Training, pp. 155–157.

62 Ibid., p. 153.

63 Sanders, M., Sholl, P., Leroy, A., Mitchell, C., Reid, L., & Gibbons, D. (2020). What works in education for children who have had social workers? *Summary Report*, Retrieved from https://whatworks-csc.org.uk/wp-content/uploads/WWCSC_what_works_education_children_SWs_Feb20.pdf.

64 The Howard League for Penal Reform. (2019). *Ending the Criminalisation of Children in Residential Care* Retrieved from https://howardleague.org/publications/ending-the-criminalisation-of-children-in-residential-care/

65 Prison Reform Trust. (2016). *In Care, Out of Trouble*. Retrieved from http://www.prison-reformtrust.org.uk/Portals/0/Documents/In%20care%20out%20of%20trouble%20sum-mary.pdf.

66 Ibid.

67 Shaw, J. (2014). *Residential children's homes and the youth justice system: Identity, power and perceptions*. London: Palgrave Macmillan. https://doi.org/10.1057/9781137319616.

68 Shaw, J. (2016). Policy, practice and perceptions: Exploring the criminalisation of children's home residents in England. *Youth Justice, 16*(2), 147–161. https://doi.org/10.1177/1473225415617858.

69 Hayden, C. (2010). Offending behaviour in care: Is children's residential care a "crimino-genic" environment? *Child & Family Social Work, 15*, 461–472. https://doi.org/10.1111/j.1365-2206.2010.00697.x.

70 Cherry, L. (2016). *The Brightness of Stars: stories of adults who came through the care system*. KCATraining, pp. 144–146.

71 Biehal, N., Cusworth, L., Wade, J., & Clarke, S. (2014). *Keeping children safe: allegations concerning the abuse or neglect of children in care final report*. York: University of York. https://doi.org/10.13140/2.1.1991.2960.

72 Euser, S., Alink, L., Tharner, A., van IJzendoorn, M., & Bakermans-Kranenburg, M. (2013). Out of home placement to promote safety? The prevalence of physical abuse in residential and foster care. *Children and Youth Services Review, 37*. https://doi.org/10.1016/j.childyouth.2013.12.002.

73 Højlund, S. (2011). Home as a model for sociality in Danish children's homes: A question of authenticity. *Social Analysis, 55*(2), 106–120. https://doi.org/10.3167/sa.2011.550206.

74 Ward, A. (2006). Models of 'ordinary' and 'special' daily living: Matching residential care to the mental-health needs of looked after children. *Child & Family Social Work, 11*(4), 336–346. https://doi.org/10.1111/j.1365-2206.2006.00423.x.

75 Ford, T., Vostanis, P., Meltzer, H., & Goodman, R. (2007). Psychiatric disorder among British children looked after by local authorities: Comparison with children living in private households. *The British Journal of Psychiatry: The Journal of Mental Science, 190*, 319–325. https://doi.org/10.1192/bjp.bp.106.025023.

76 Hansen, R. L., Mawjee, F. L., Barton, K., Metcalf, M. B., & Joye, N. R. (2004). Comparing the health status of low-income children in and out of foster care. *Child Welfare, 83*(4), 367–380. Retrieved from https://search.proquest.com/openview/83eeb1358a224fe9a82d e427f7fdc14e/1?pq-origsite=gscholar&cbl=40853.

77 Noblet, P. (2017). *Care Leavers Risk Homelessness as Rents Continue to Rise*, Retrieved December 17, 2020, from https://www.childrenssociety.org.uk/news-and-blogs/our-blog/care-leavers-risk-homelessness-as-rents-continue-to-rise.

78 Ibid.

79 Ibid.

80 Ibid.

81 Ofsted. (2019). *Unregistered and Unregulated Provision – What's the Difference?* Retrieved December 18, 2019, from https://socialcareinspection.blog.gov.uk/2019/07/08/unregistered-and-unregulated-provision-whats-the-difference/.

82 Office for National Statistics. (2019). *Births in England and Wales: 2018*, Retrieved from https://www.ons.gov.uk/peoplepopulationandcommunity/birthsdeathsandmarriages/livebirths/bulletins/birthsummarytablesenglandandwales/2018#the-number-of-births-crude-birth-and-total-fertility-rates-decreased-in-2018.

83 Child Poverty Action Group. (2020). *Child Poverty Facts and Figures*, Retrieved January 21, 2020, from https://cpag.org.uk/child-poverty/child-poverty-facts-and-figures.

84 Child Poverty Action Group. (2020). *The Effects of Poverty*, Retrieved from https://cpag.org.uk/child-poverty/effects-poverty.

85 Department for Education. (2018). *Promoting the Education of Looked-after Children and Previously looked-after Children: Statutory Guidance for Local Authorities*, Retrieved from https://assets.publishing.service.gov.uk/government/uploads/system/uploads/attachment_data/file/683556/Promoting_the_education_of_looked-after_children_and_previously_looked-after_children.pdf.

86 Ofsted. (2012). *The Impact of Virtual Schools on the Educational Progress of Looked after Children*, Retrieved from https://assets.publishing.service.gov.uk/government/uploads/system/uploads/attachment_data/file/419041/The_impact_of_virtual_schools_on_the_educational_progress_of_looked_after_children.pdf.

87 Ibid.

88 Munro, E. (2011). *The Munro Review of Child Protection: Final Report – A child-centred system.* London: Department for Education. https://doi.org/10.1375/jcas.36.3.164.

89 Ibid.

90 Narey, M. (2016). *Residential Care in England: Report of Sir Martin Narey's Independent Review of Children's Residential Care*, Retrieved from https://assets.publishing.service.gov.uk/government/uploads/system/uploads/attachment_data/file/534560/Residential-Care-in-England-Sir-Martin-Narey-July-2016.pdf, p. 56.

91 Department for Education. (2020). *Official Statistics: Children and Family Social Work Workforce in England, Year Ending 30 September 2019*, Retrieved from https://assets.publishing.service.gov.uk/government/uploads/system/uploads/attachment_data/file/868384/CSWW_2018-19_Text.pdf.

92 Family Rights Group. (2020). *What is a Family Group Conference: A Guide for Families*, Retrieved April 15, 2020, from https://www.frg.org.uk/what-is-a-family-group-conference-a-guide-for-families.

93 What Works for Children's Social Care and Cardiff University. (2020). *Social Workers In Schools: An Evaluation Of Pilots In Three Local Authorities In England*, Retrieved from https://whatworks-csc.org.uk/wp-content/uploads/WWCSC_Social-Workers-in-Schools_pilot-study_full-report_May-2020.pdf.

7 Education without a place to call home

Kate Bowen-Viner

7.1 Introduction

I started to understand the relationship between home and education on my first day as a form tutor.

I had already been teaching for a year in a secondary school in West London, but still felt very nervous about meeting my new form. I had wanted to be a form tutor for quite a while and was determined to make a success of it. I therefore decided to collect tips from my more experienced colleagues. It struck me that a lot of strategies for being "a good form tutor" and providing pastoral support, involved home: calling home to speak to parents/carers; sending letters and post-cards home; talking to pupils about their home lives and even reviewing pupils' homework diaries.

Just as my colleagues had suggested, these approaches soon proved crucial to my role as a form tutor. I called home for almost half of my form who had turned up late, or forgotten their blazers, or lost their ties, or not brought a pen with them. I also established a reward system, involving a star-chart, stickers and me promising to send a postcard home for the young person with the most positive behaviour points each week. It certainly was not easy to build relationships with those young people and establish routines straight away, but the steps I took did help.

When it got to Easter, I was beginning to feel like I had cracked it. As a result of me consistently making contact with their parents and carers, my tutees were more likely to follow rules and we built up a really positive rapport. I concluded that "home" was the key!

Reflecting back now, I realise that I had not taken this insight to its logical con-clusion. I had not recognised what this means for young people who have no place to call home. That changed in 2017.

As part of a major research project with the Sage Foundation, entitled "A Place to Call Home", I met a group of ten young homeless people aged 16–24 and spent several months listening to their stories. By sharing their stories, the young people helped me to understand more about the critical role "home" plays in our lives and our experience of school. Their stories also revealed some of the ways we might tackle youth homelessness and improve the education system for young people at risk of, or experiencing homelessness.

This chapter draws on those young people's stories [1] as well as national data to explore young homeless people's marginalisation. It begins by setting out the current state of youth homelessness in the country and goes on to describe and examine young people's experiences of homelessness and education. Throughout the chapter, I present evidence to argue that urgent action is needed to improve young homeless people's access to, and experience of, education.

7.2 Who are the young and homeless in England?

7.2.1 Defining youth homelessness

In order to identify the young and homeless population, and to begin to understand young homeless people's experiences, we need a shared understanding of what "youth" and "homelessness" mean.

For the purpose of this chapter, I use the terms "youth" and "young people" to refer to 16–24-year olds. This is largely because experts and the government focus on this age bracket when discussing or researching young homeless people [2]. The fact that younger people are not included may seem surprising, but this is because the law dictates that under 16-year olds with no home should be supported through social services [3, 4]. They are therefore counted as being in state care. However, many younger children do experience life without a place to call home [5] and it should be acknowledged that they face many of the same challenges as homeless 16–24-year olds [6].

Defining "homelessness" can also be problematic because many people incorrectly equate homelessness solely with sleeping on the street. This means that large numbers of young people who live without a home are often forgotten about or hidden from view because their circumstances do not fit with stereotypical views of homelessness [7]. For example, a young person may be sofa surfing (staying with friends for short periods, often in an itinerant manner) and not recognised as homeless.

From a theoretical perspective, a home can be thought of as having three key domains. Therefore, a person who does not have access to one of the following might be described as homeless or as experiencing housing exclusion:

■ **Physical domain:** Physical space to meet the needs of a person/family.

■ **Social domain:** Ability to maintain privacy and enjoy social relationships.

■ **Legal domain:** Having legal access to, and possession of, a home [8].

Table 7.1 Types of homelessness [9]

	What does this mean?	Quality of official data collections
Statutory homelessness	A young person who approaches their local authority and qualifies for statutory support. A local authority will give a homeless person statutory support if: • They are deemed to be unintentionally homeless. • They are deemed to be eligible for assistance (i.e. meet immigration conditions). • They have a local connection. • They qualify as a priority need (for example, pregnant women, young people aged 16–17, care leavers who are aged 18 to 21).	Central government publish data collected from local authorities on the number of people who have been classified as "statutory homeless".
Non-statutory homeless	Young people who approach their local authority, but do not qualify for statutory support. Changes brought about through the Homelessness Reduction Act mean that this category can include young homeless people who qualify for "prevention and relief support" (i.e. support to find new accommodation or temporary accommodation).	Central government publish data collected from Local Authorities on the number of people who asked a Local Authority for assistance and were not deemed to be statutorily homeless. This is not always broken down by age. Central government also publish data collected from local authorities regarding the numbers of young people who were given "prevention and relief" by their local authority.
Hidden Homelessness	Young people who have not made contact with their local authority and are effectively "hidden" from official data collections – for example young people who are "sofa surfing" (temporarily staying with friends or family).	The government does not collect data on the numbers of hidden homeless young people. However, third sector organisations and researchers attempt to estimate how many hidden homeless young people there are in the country.
Rough sleeping	Young people who are sleeping on the streets.	Local authorities carry out "rough sleeper counts". The data is collated and published by central government. It can be difficult to accurately count the number of rough sleepers in a specific area. Therefore, official statistics about the number of rough sleepers are likely to be underestimates.

Figure 7.1 Photograph taken by Yasmin.

In England, homelessness is categorised (and measured) in certain established ways, and understanding this is important in order to understand the scale of the issue. Table 7.1 therefore sets out the four key categories of youth homelessness, as well as how valid and reliable data collections are.

Youth homelessness can also be understood through young people's first-hand experiences. Yasmin, a young person I met through our research, drew on her personal experience in defining youth homelessness. I come back to her words whenever I am reading or writing about youth homelessness (Figure 7.1).

> You don't have anyone that cares about you, friend or family, and it's not like you have to be sleeping on the streets, but you don't have a place to really just rest your head and be at peace. If you're living in a place where there's violence and there's things that you don't condone or you shouldn't even endure as a human, then you're homeless...

7.2.2 How many young people are homeless?

Official government data collections on youth homelessness are likely to be underestimates [10], yet the figures are still shocking. In 2018–19 for example, 71,589 young people in England approached their local authority because they were homeless or at risk of homelessness [11]. Only 3,676 were accepted as statutorily homeless and owed support and 41,127 were not supported into housing [12].

Estimates of hidden homelessness paint an even starker picture. Based on a survey of 2,011 16–25-year olds drawn from a representative survey of UK adults, Clarke [13] found that 703 16–25-year olds (35% of the sample of young people surveyed) had experienced sofa surfing at some point in their lives.

It is important to remember that thousands of young people's personal, troubling and complex stories lie behind these numbers.

7.2.3 Demographics

Popular rhetoric often suggests that homelessness "can happen to anyone" [14]. However, this is perhaps a misrepresentation. As Professor Suzanne Fitzpatrick points out, this narrative has been used by politicians "along with periodic eruptions of concern in the mainstream media about stories of middle-class homelessness" [15]. The discourse is damaging and unhelpfully shields the general public, including teachers and youth workers, from reality. The truth is that some groups of young people are more likely to be homeless due to the distribution of poverty, vulnerability and inequality in our society. In contrast, other groups are far better insulated from the risk of homelessness. As we will see further on in this chapter, the young homeless people I worked with shared vivid accounts of how the factors below contributed to their trajectory.

Poverty

- Suzanne Fitzpatrick and Glen Bramley's analysis reveals that the single greatest predictor of experiencing homeless in young adulthood is child poverty [16].

Black, Asian and Minority Ethnic groups

- Based on government statistics, Shelter report that 1 in 3 homeless households are black, Asian and minority ethnic, compared to around 1 in 7 in the general population [17].

LGBT+ community

- The Albert Kennedy Trust estimate that 24% of the young homeless population [18] are LGBT+ compared to 0.5% of young people nationally [11]. This figure is contested [19], but organisations consistently recognise that the LGBT+ community is over-represented in the youth homelessness population [20].

Offenders

- Estimated 14% of the young homeless population [21].
- 22% of the general homeless population [22].

Care leavers

- 17% of the young homeless population [23] compared to only 0.6% of the young population nationally [24].

Campaign groups have also highlighted that inadequate resources such as accessible and affordable housing options mean that young carers are at increased risk of youth homelessness [25]. Meanwhile, although data on the number of young homeless people who have a special educational need or disability (SEND) is limited, academics estimate that people with SEND are over-represented in the homeless population [26].

7.3 Why should the young and homelessness be a priority for the education and youth sectors?

Young people's journeys towards homelessness, and their actual experience of homelessness, can be traumatic. These events can exacerbate barriers that make it harder for young people to access, benefit from, or be supported within, the education system.

Clearly, the huge personal, long-term consequences for the individuals that experience homelessness is enough to demand action. Added to this though, homelessness also results in enormous costs to society. For example, youth homelessness prevents many young people from reaching their full potential and acts as a barrier between young people and the labour market [27].

7.4 How do young people become homeless?

Homeless Link identifies the following ten factors as the primary triggers for young people becoming homeless. This graph is based on the results from an online survey Homeless Link conducted with homelessness services and local authorities (Figure 7.2).

Existing research on youth homelessness suggests that a multitude of events and experiences in young people's lives contribute to their homelessness [16, 28].

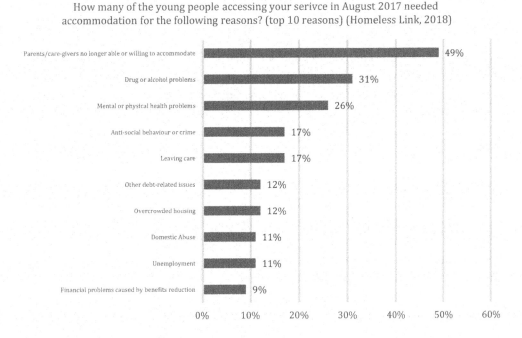

How many of the young people accessing your serivce in August 2017 needed accommodation for the following reasons? (top 10 reasons) (Homeless Link, 2018)

Figure 7.2 Young people's reasons for accessing services.

This was reflected in the stories of the young people I worked with. They tended to explain that events and experiences in their lives, often over extended periods, had come together to result in their homelessness. It is therefore essential to recognise the complex links between structural factors such as poverty, as well as personal factors such as family relationship breakdown in order to tackle the issue of youth homelessness.

Jerome's story

Before he became homeless, Jerome lived in poverty and was a young carer for his grandparents. This was whilst he was studying for his GCSEs and A-Levels. Jerome often found it difficult to manage school work alongside his responsibilities at home. He generally found that teachers at school were not aware that he was a carer and adjustments were therefore not made for him:

> It would have made a difference if the teachers actually knew that I was a young carer. Only a couple of the teachers knew I was a young carer but didn't act upon it.

As well as having little support from his school, Jerome was bullied. He felt let down by his school because he did not feel that they took appropriate action to stop the bullying. These experiences led Jerome to feel pushed out and isolated.

When his grandparents died, Jerome was devastated. He had lost his support network. He struggled to maintain his grandparents' house and his job and he felt he had no one to turn to. After a family member sold his grandparents' house, Jerome was forced to leave his home.

Jerome loved academic learning and was keen to find a job or course that would make use of his skills. However, he struggled to navigate the system and felt like information and support regarding further/higher education and employment was not readily available to him.

Living in poverty and being a young carer – particularly in the absence of effective support, pushed Jerome towards homelessness and left him isolated. However, more awareness amongst education professionals, and better signposting to appropriate services could have helped. Meanwhile, his struggle to access relevant education, training and employment opportunities once he was homeless illustrates the need for the education system to be easier to access and navigate.

Josh's story also shows clear links between structural factors and personal circumstances, a combination that has also been flagged in previous studies (Figure 7.3) [29].

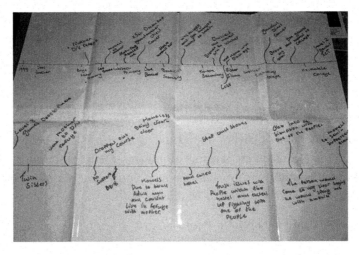

Figure 7.3 My Life's Timeline' by Josh.

Josh's story

Josh lived with domestic abuse during his childhood. When his mother went to stay in a refuge, Josh spent time living with different members of his extended family. However, limited material resources and overcrowding contributed to tense family relationships which in turn contributed to Josh's homelessness:

> I lived with my stepdad for a little bit but he kind of got sick of me. Because obviously, he's on benefits and that, and you've got to survive on the food that you've got, don't you? When you've got two adult men eating on one portion of food, he got annoyed about me eating his food. So, I went to live with my nanna... But she also got sick of me after a while and she then just called a hostel and sent me to a hostel. She said, "Look, you can't live here forever because it's a house with three other people living, well, five altogether".

Whether economic and social inequalities are manifested in families being on income support like Josh's stepfather, or through limited housing options as they were for Josh's grandmother, families living in such circumstances experience severe strain. It is no surprise that the burden of overcrowding, or the paucity of basic resources can then lead to relationship breakdown and ultimately homelessness, as it did for Josh.

7.5 The relationship between youth homelessness and education

The events that take place over the course of young people's journey towards homelessness can understandably create problems for their education. The factors that lead young people to become homeless can also contribute to their disengagement with education. I now explore the emotional and practical impacts of homelessness on young people's education, as well as how young people's experiences of the welfare system, low academic attainment and education interact.

7.5.1 The emotional impact of homelessness

Becoming homeless places severe emotional strain on young people. Those who are at risk of homelessness or become homeless often experience trauma [28]. Research shows that trauma impacts the way young people see themselves and relate to others [30]. This can lead to problems with:

- Attachment and building relationships.
- Emotional regulation.
- Cognition (problems with thinking and learning).
- Sense of safety and control [31].

The emotional impact of homelessness can also lead to problems in school or college, such as a lack of engagement, behavioural issues and poor relationships with staff and other pupils.

7.5.1.1 Dropping out

Young people who are homeless, or on the cusp of homelessness, can need considerable support from their school or college. This was certainly the case for Leila, who lived in an abusive home. Although her sixth-form supported her pastorally by putting her in touch with specialist services, this was ultimately insufficient because she felt she needed space and time away from full-time education to process the abuse she had experienced (Figure 7.4).

Figure 7.4 Photograph taken by Leila.

Leila's story

Leila suffered abuse at home and also struggled with the death of her grandmother, whom she was very close to. As she explained, the difficulties she was experiencing at home made it harder to concentrate on studying and eventually she dropped out of full-time education before she sat her A-Level exams:

> I did my first and second year of A-levels, but didn't finish [them] because I was just going through a lot at the time and it was hard to concentrate. But I did have the support from the school and they did support me a lot, but obviously, I just couldn't do it, it was getting too much for me to do the second year of A-levels.

7.5.1.2 Behaviour and exclusions

Unfortunately, the triggers for, and consequences of, youth homelessness can be manifested in poor behaviour, a lack of trust in adults such as teachers, and frequent school moves. Many of the young homeless people I worked with said that financial strain, familial relationship breakdown, abuse and sofa surfing led to them feeling stressed, angry and/or sad. In turn, these feelings contributed to behavioural problems at school, especially when they felt that teachers did not understand them or did not want to listen. In some cases, getting into trouble at school and changing location due to being homeless resulted in young people moving school multiple times. Frequent school moves made it more challenging for these young people to reach out to school staff and other pupils as they did not have time to form trusting and supportive relationships.

These experiences and feelings can result in young people being excluded from mainstream schools and, as we have seen in Chapter 1, once young people are excluded, their educational journeys, in many cases come to an end. This was the case for Emily (Figure 7.5).

Figure 7.5 Photograph taken by Emily.

Emily's story

Emily's home-life was chaotic. Her mother would often argue with her and ask her to leave the house. She also had a difficult relationship with her father and did not want to move in with him. She struggled to deal with her emotions and did not feel that she had a network of support that she could rely on. When her cousin died, Emily experienced profound grief which exacerbated her difficulties. This was manifested in increasingly problematic behaviour in school and worsening relationships with teachers, culminating in her being excluded from school. Unfortunately, this constituted a de facto end to her education:

> When I moved in to [Pupil Referral Unit], I started going with people who would cause trouble on a daily basis, and then I didn't want to get kicked out because that was the last school I would go to, so I changed, but then I ended up getting kicked out for something else. I didn't go to school then; I went to the library for forty-five minutes a day.

7.5.1.3 Education feeling irrelevant

The challenges young people face when they find themselves homeless and trying to live independently can seem very far removed from formal education. This can make young homeless people feel like there is no point in education or training because its links to their everyday lives are too tenuous.

They can then become disengaged from their school work or give up on education altogether. As Jerome's story demonstrates, young homeless people can lose enthusiasm for the traditional curriculum and feel like the education system let them down by not teaching them basic life skills.

Jerome's perspective on the relevance of education

Jerome felt like his school education had not given him basic life skills, such as knowing how to cook, clean and pay bills, or how to deal with life's emotional ups and downs.

When he became homeless, he realised he lacked many of the skills he needed and he had nowhere to turn to for advice. Jerome therefore believed that education should have a sharper focus on life skills and independent living:

> I think [education should include] basic things about life, life self-esteem, confidence, how not to be anxious. Things like getting a job. Things like how to deal with different people that you meet in life.

Jerome's experience demonstrates the need for young homeless people to have access to support when it comes to living independently in order to help them re-engage. There are of course questions as to who or which services are best placed to do this.

The Youth Homeless Parliament, made up of 16–25-year olds who have been homeless, feel that both housing and education sectors have a role to play. In 2019, they recommended that [32]:

- Practical life skills should be taught throughout each school year within citizenship or personal, social, health and economic (PSHE) lessons.

- Local authorities should write housing plans that build-in ways for young people to develop practical life skills throughout their homelessness journey.

7.5.2 The practical impact of homelessness

Young people's stories show that being homeless can create practical and logistical issues for accessing education. Without a safe, quiet place to sleep, how does one maintain concentration in school? How does one do homework? Is it even feasible to maintain the routine of attending school or college?

7.5.2.1 Mobility

Homelessness can involve frequent moves, between friends' sofas or to different relatives' houses or temporary accommodation – even if these are distant. These frequent moves can be highly disruptive when it comes to education with constant shifts of teachers and curriculum and difficulties forming firm and ongoing relationships.

Yasmin's story

When she became homeless, Yasmin started sleeping in friends' cars. She found moving from place to place wearing and this affected her engagement in education. She found it practically difficult to attend a college that was so far away from where she was sleeping. As well as this, the emotional drain of being homeless resulted in her losing her passion for her college course. Eventually, this led to Yasmin dropping out of college:

> I was kind of living in friends' cars… and I had a job at the time, and was in college, but because of all of the stuff that was going on, I kept calling in sick for my job, because I didn't want to explain, because I was embarrassed, and they were like already kind of a bit judgemental of me and stuff. So, I ended up losing my job, and then dropping out of college, because it was just a really far journey and I just didn't have any passion anymore.

7.5.2.2 Travel

If a young person qualifies for accommodation from their local authority, this can be far from their school or college, and travelling in can become difficult or expensive.

Amidst general disruption to their lives and attempts to settle into independent accommodation whilst experiencing emotional difficulties, managing complex journeys can become just one jigsaw piece too many to manage.

Yasmin's story continued...

As we saw previously, when Yasmin became homeless, she found it emotionally and practically difficult to attend a college that was so far away from where she was sleeping. Added to this, expensive bus fare made it challenging for her to continue with her college education:

> When I did go and speak to them [college staff] ... it was like, "I hope things get better", and that's it, and, "Still attend college". It's just like, "How am I meant to attend when I live miles away and have to pay about £5 every day to get here?"

Unfortunately, there are no publicly funded travel bursaries available for young homeless people who need help to continue attending their school or college once they have moved into temporary or supported accommodation. This is surely one practical problem that would be relatively simple to resolve.

7.5.2.3 Lack of "space to learn"

When a young person is homeless, things like completing homework and revising for exams become practically difficult. Without a quiet space and practical learning resources, it is hard, if not impossible, to learn at home. For example, some of the young homeless people we worked with explained that they did not have pens, paper or books outside of school because they had nowhere to keep them.

Josh's story

Before Josh became homeless, he had his own space at home to study and research his educational assignments online. However, once he began sofa surfing and moving frequently between his grandmother and his father's house, he no longer had a computer:

> Obviously I've got to go doorstep to doorstep, I can't carry a big PC around with me.

As a result, he struggled increasingly to focus and dedicate time to studying. Eventually, as his college work became more challenging, he ended up dropping out.

7.5.2.4 Lack of structure

A lack of structure and consistency can make it practically difficult to engage in education, as Ollie's story demonstrates.

Ollie's story

When Ollie became homeless, he was sofa surfing and stayed with various friends or random people he met. He did not know where he was going to sleep from one day to the next, meaning that his days lacked a steady structure, making it hard to adhere to timetables:

> I did have places where I could sofa surf, but there wasn't always guaranteed nights, so there actually was times when I had to go on the street, and I had to beg.

Ollie's homelessness became an insurmountable barrier to education.

7.5.2.5 Fatigue and inability to concentrate

Young people without a place to call home struggle to get adequate sleep. The physical and emotional discomfort of being homeless drain young people and can detract from their education. As we saw in Leila's story, the abuse that contributed to her homelessness and the lack of a consistent and safe place to rest meant that she was exhausted and found it difficult to concentrate at school.

7.5.3 Welfare and social security

Homelessness clearly creates personal challenges for young people wanting to gain academic credentials and training. However, on top of this, the benefits system can conspire against young homeless people and act as a wholly unnecessary and additional hurdle.

Individuals in part-time education, whether further or higher education, can claim Universal Credit. However, these young people are likely to need additional funds to support themselves through education (e.g. to eat, clothe themselves and buy study materials). While it should be possible for young people to fit part-time education alongside work-related requirements, Universal Credit guidance includes the caveat that claimants need to be available for work despite their part-time study [33] commitments. This can force young people to choose between honouring their Universal Credit requirements and their education, particularly when rules are badly implemented by poorly informed staff. Some young people are told that they will receive benefit sanctions if they miss job centre appointments because of their part-time study. As Andrzej explained:

> The job centre is constantly on my case to look for work, I'm in full-time education, I've shown them the thing to say I'm in college, but they said they were gonna sanction us, 'you've got to look for work because you're on Universal Credit and you're 18'... I had to look for work while I was still doing college, I had four days left of college... I got a job but because of that I then couldn't finish my first year, I failed that... so I can't do my second.

In Andrzej's case, his adviser later admitted that they had been mistaken in forcing Andrzej to work as he was a full-time student, but the consequences for him were already enormous.

Accessing Higher Education can cause further difficulties since it can result in Universal Credit payments being cut or stopped [34]. Most full-time students are expected to use their maintenance loans to cover the cost of their accommodation. However, a maintenance loan may not cover the cost of their current accommodation or general living expenses. Part-time students also have their student loans deducted from their Universal Credit payments, meaning that many young homeless people who want to study struggle to make ends meet. The National Union of Students has therefore highlighted the fact that Universal Credit is adversely affecting vulnerable students and dis-incentivising many from continuing with formal education [35].

The relationship between benefits regulations and education is clearly unjust. All young people deserve the right to education and the opportunity to achieve qualifications, yet the benefits system shows that public policy frequently acts against the interests of young people without a home.

7.5.4 Low attainment

A combination of emotional and practical difficulties impacts negatively on young homeless people's grades and this in turn makes it difficult to progress or transition successfully to the next stage of education or employment. Thus, low attainment can itself become an additional barrier to accessing education.

> ### Jess's Story
>
> Jess experienced abuse at home and had a difficult relationship with her mother. The emotional and practical impact of being homeless made it difficult for her to focus on school work and also contributed to her poor behaviour at school.
>
> Without a home, she struggled to sleep, was often tired, and struggled to concentrate. Her experiences had also worn her down emotionally, so she struggled to focus on school or to see the point in her education.
>
> She did not achieve C grade GCSEs and this made it harder to her to access further training and employment.
>
> > If I could change things, I would be good from the start of year 10 and I might have got my C's… it impacted my life a lot because it's always going to be there and I am going to struggle getting a job.

However, not all young homeless people have low educational attainment. For example, some of the young people we worked with achieved high grades in their

GCSEs and A-Levels whilst others had successfully completed BTECs and apprenticeships. On one hand, this shows that homelessness does not have to stand in the way of educational success. Less positively though, it also means that educational achievement is not enough to end homelessness.

7.6 Supporting young homeless people

7.6.1 Young people's aspirations

Young homeless people have no shortage of aspirations and hopes for the future, regardless of their circumstances. For example, Evan explained that his dream was to become a chef in an Italian restaurant.

> Hopefully in a couple of months' time I'll have my own tenancy, my own flat, so then I will need to get a job before that, so I can actually pay for the flat as well, instead of just being on benefits all my life. So, I want to actually get a job and then I want to be a head chef in an Italian restaurant, preferably.

Similarly, for Felix, a short placement working with autistic children had inspired him to work toward a career supporting young people with disabilities. He planned to take a relevant college course, achieve the grades he needed and work with disabled people in the future:

> If I get the right grades and all of that and the right studies, I want to work in a special needs school and help people.

Young homeless people, therefore, do not lack aspirations. However, they find themselves grappling with a pernicious mix of inequality and injustice, and challenging personal and family circumstances. Action is therefore needed to tackle the root causes of the challenges they face. Meanwhile, practical steps must be taken to make life easier, and education more accessible, for those caught in a deeply challenging and distressing situation. Below, I outline the key areas where young homeless people need support, as well as the role of education practitioners and policymakers.

7.6.2 Young people at risk of homelessness

Youth homelessness rarely happens without warning signs. A rapid response to challenges young people face could help reduce risks that eventually culminate in young people becoming homeless. Signs that a young person may be at risk of homelessness may include [7]:

- experiences of abuse;
- difficult behaviour;

- breakdown of support networks;

- substance misuse;

- mental health problems;

- LGBT+ phobic bullying and discrimination;

- living in poverty; and

- leaving care.

Where practitioners identify, or have the slightest concern about potential homelessness, they should immediately follow safeguarding procedures, since it is much better to be "safe than sorry". Safeguarding leads should then make contact with local services to implement targeted support, recognising that social services may not always have capacity to intervene below an extreme threshold, by which time it can be too late to take a preventative approach. This may mean that support needs to be brokered in from other organisations and providers. Policymakers should support safeguarding leads in doing this by providing all schools with up-to-date information on local services.

Policymakers have a major role to play in preventing youth homelessness. Alongside tackling the social and economic inequalities which underpin the challenges many young people on the fringes of homelessness face, they should prioritise greater investment in preventative work such as mental health support, family relationship support/mediation and counselling.

7.6.3 Young people experiencing homelessness

Teachers and education professionals see young people regularly and are therefore uniquely well-placed to identify those who may be experiencing homelessness.

Warning signs that a young person might be experiencing homelessness can include [36,37]:

- low or declining attendance;

- going missing;

- lack of engagement and concentration;

- disruptive behaviour;

- tiredness; and

- appearing "dishevelled".

As with warning signs regarding risks of youth homelessness, practitioners should flag their concerns using safeguarding procedures since legal frameworks mean that policymakers are obliged to provide many young homeless people with accommodation and support.

However, as this chapter demonstrates, policies do not adequately respond to the complexities associated with homelessness. For example, there is no specific policy-framework for providing any form of support to the hundreds of thousands of young people who are "hidden homeless". Furthermore, many young people who approach their local authority, or other services, do not receive adequate help and guidance. This needs to change. Policymakers must ensure that *no* young homeless person falls through the net.

7.6.4 Engaging young homeless people in education

Since homelessness has a detrimental impact on young people staying in and achieving in education, and thus on longer term life outcomes, keeping homeless young people in education and supporting them to achieve well is one of the most important forms of support that educational institutions and youth services can provide. As the young people I worked with argued, by providing pastoral support, being flexible and adapting practice to suit a young homeless person's individual needs, practitioners can help these young people to stay engaged in their education. This will in turn help to prepare them for future employment and training, as well as independent living.

Policymakers should reform welfare policies by ensuring that all young homeless people can retain Universal Credit if they enter full-time Higher or Further Education and choose to remain in supported housing. This change would emphasise the importance and value of education.

7.7 Conclusion

I look back on my time as a form tutor in West London fondly. I enjoyed supporting pupils and getting to know them and their families. Now, however, I wonder if I would have approached my role differently had I known more about the relationship between youth homelessness and education. Would I have looked out for the warning signs more? Would I have asked for specific training on schools and youth homelessness? Would I have spoken to my pupils about homelessness? Would I have written to my MP to argue that policy needed to change urgently?

As this chapter demonstrates, a huge number of young people experience homelessness. It disrupts and sometimes ends those young people's formal education. Policy is complicit in this. Teachers, youth practitioners and policymakers need to understand the youth homelessness landscape and take action by identifying the young and homeless, effectively safeguarding them and ensuring education remains accessible to them.

7.8 Taking action

The evidence presented in this chapter demonstrates that access to, and experiences of, education could be improved considerably for young homeless people and those at risk of it. The following recommendations, therefore, particularly focus on this theme.

7.8.1 Policymakers

■ The Department for Work and Pensions should adjust regulations to allow all young homeless people to retain Universal Credit if they enter full-time Higher or Further Education and choose to remain in supported housing. In such circumstances, young people should receive Universal Credit in place of a maintenance loan, but retain eligibility for Special Support Grants.

■ The Department for Work and Pensions should adjust Universal Credit regulations to ensure that part-time students in Further or Higher Education are not having Universal Credit payments capped unfairly (for example during the summer holidays).

■ The Department for Work and Pensions and the Department for Education should collaborate to create a database that tracks young homeless people through the system to ensure they are able to access Further and Higher Education.

■ The Department for Education should make the "16 to 19 Bursary Fund" available to all young people who are statutorily homeless or are receiving homelessness prevention and relief support. This existing fund helps young people who are facing barriers to remain in education.

■ The Ministry for Housing Communities and Local Government should ensure that local authorities offer young people information about applying for the "16 to 19 Bursary Fund".

7.8.1.1 Multi-academy trusts, schools and colleges

■ Education institutions need to play a role in preventing youth homelessness. Practitioners cannot be expected to deal with the problem, but they should:

● be aware of the prevalence of homelessness;

● know of how to spot the warning signs;

● signpost vulnerable young people to experts; and

● work with young people who are at risk of youth homelessness to help them remain constructively engaged with education.

■ Education institutions need to ensure they make arrangements for pupils and students who are experiencing homelessness to access emotional support to mitigate the risk of damage and to help them remain in education.

7.8.1.2 Universities

■ Universities should ensure all staff who work directly with students are aware of the prevalence of youth homelessness and be able to recognise the warning signs.

■ Pastoral and finance staff should flag-up support services to students who are experiencing homelessness, including advice services for claiming Universal Credit whilst receiving student loans.

■ Universities should offer Special Support Grants to students who are homeless to help cover living costs whilst studying at university.

Further reading

A Place to Call Home: Understanding Youth Homelessness: Mulcahy, E., Small, I., Viner, K. B., & Menzies, L., (2017) London: CfEY and Sage Foundation.
Homelessness in the UK: who is most at risk?: Bramley, G. & Fitzpatrick, S. (2018) *Housing Studies*, 33(1), pp. 96–116.
Hard Edges: Mapping Severe and Multiple Disadvantage in England: Bramley, G., Fitzpatrick, S., Edwards, J., Ford, D., Johnsen, S., Sosenko, F. and Watkins, D., (2015), London: Lankelly Chase Foundation.
Housing First in England: The Principles, Homeless Link (2018) London: Homeless Link.
Youth Homelessness in the UK: A Review for the OVO Foundation: Watts, B., Johnsen, C. and Sosenko, F. (2015), Edinburgh: Heriot-Watt University.

References

1 Mulcahy, E., Small, I. Bowen-Viner, K. and Menzies, L. *"A Place To Call Home: Understanding Youth Homelessness" [online]*, available from: https://cfey.org/wp-content/uploads/2017/09/FULL-RsEPORT.-A-Place-to-Call-Home.-Understanding-Youth-Homelessness.pdf (accessed: October 3 2019).
2 *ibid.*
3 Children Act, 1989, available at: http://www.legislation.gov.uk/ukpga/1989/41/contents.
4 G v London Borough of Southwark (2009) *UKHL 26 House of Lords*.
5 Digby, A. and Fu, E. *"Impacts of Homelessness on Children – Research with Teachers" [online]*, available from: https://england.shelter.org.uk/__data/assets/pdf_file/0011/1474652/2017_12_20_Homelessness_and_School_Children.pdf (accessed October 3 2019).
6 Centre Point (2020) *Real Homeless Stories [online]*, available from https://centrepoint.org.uk/youth-homelessness/real-stories/ (accessed April 20 2020).
7 Mulcahy, E., Small, I. Bowen-Viner, K. and Menzies, L. *"A Place To Call Home: Understanding Youth Homelessness" [online]*, available from: https://cfey.org/wp-content/uploads/2017/09/FULL-REPORT.-A-Place-to-Call-Home.-Understanding-Youth-Homelessness.pdf (accessed: October 3 2019).

8 Edgar, W., Doherty, J. and Meert, H. (2004). *Third Review of Statistics on Homelessness in Europe*, (Brussels: FEANTSA); Quilgars, D., Fitzpatrick, S. and Pleace, N. (2011). *Ending Youth Homelessness*, London: Centrepoint.

9 Mulcahy, E., Small, I. Bowen-Viner, K., and Menzies, L. *"A Place To Call Home: Understanding Youth Homelessness" [online]*, available from: https://cfey.org/wp-content/uploads/2017/09/FULL-REPORT.-A-Place-to-Call-Home.-Understanding-Youth-Homelessness.pdf (accessed: October 3 2019); Ministry of Housing Communities and Local Government (2019). *"Homelessness Statistics" [online]*, available from: https://www.gov.uk/government/collections/homelessness-statistics (accessed 3 October 2019); Homeless Link (2019) *"Hidden Homelessness" [online]*, available from: https://www.homeless.org.uk/facts/homelessness-in-numbers/hidden-homelessness (accessed 3 October 2019).

10 Munro, N. and Reeson, C. (2018) *Homelessness: Why New Statistics are Probably Underestimating the Problem [online]*, available from: https://theconversation.com/homelessness-why-new-statistics-are-probably-underestimating-the-problem-108840 (accessed April 16 2020).

11 Youth Homeless Databank (2020), *England 2018/2019*, [online] available at: https://centrepoint.org.uk/databank/England/2018-2019 (accessed April 16 2020).

12 *ibid.*

13 Clarke, A. (2016). The prevalence of rough sleeping and sofa surfing amongst young people in the UK. *Social Inclusion, 4*(4), 60–72.

14 Marsh, S. (2016) *'I am Well-spoken and not an Addict': How Homelessness can Happen to Anyone [online]*, available from: https://www.theguardian.com/commentisfree/2016/mar/10/i-am-well-spoken-and-not-an-addict-how-homelessness-can-happen-to-anyone (accessed April 16 2020).

15 *ibid.*

16 Bramley, G. and Fitzpatrick, S., 2018. Homelessness in the UK: Who is most at risk?. *Housing Studies, 33*(1), pp.96–116.

17 Garvie, D (2017) *BAME Homelessness Matters and is Disproportionately Rising- time for the Government to act (online)*, available at: https://blog.shelter.org.uk/2017/10/bame-homelessness-matters-and-is-disproportionately-rising-time-for-the-government-to-act/ (accessed April 16 2020).

18 Albert Kennedy Trust (2015). *LGBT Youth Homelessness: A UK National Scoping of Cause, Prevalence, Response and Outcome*, [online], available at: from: http://www.akt.org.uk/webtop/modules/repository/documents/AlbertKennedy_researchreport_FINALinteractive.pdf (accessed: April 16 2020); Cull, M., Platzer, H. and Balloch, S. (2006). *Out on my Own: Understanding the Experiences and Needs of Homeless Lesbian, Gay, Bisexual and Transgender Youth.* Brighton & Hove, England: Health and Social Policy Research Centre, Faculty of Health, School of Applied Social Science, University of Brighton.

19 Matthews, P., Poyner, C. and Kjellgren, R., 2019. Lesbian, gay, bisexual, transgender and queer experiences of homelessness and identity: Insecurity and home (o) normativity. *International Journal of Housing Policy, 19*(2), pp.232–253.

20 Centre Point (2020) *LGBTQ+ & Homelessness*, [online], available from: https://centrepoint.org.uk/about-us/blog/creating-safe-spaces-for-homeless-lgbtqplus-youths/ (accessed April 16 2020).

21 Homeless Link (2015) *Young and Homeless 2015*, London: Homeless Link.

22 *ibid.*

23 *ibid.*

24 Zayed, Y. and Harker, R. (2015) *Children in Care in England: Statistics*, London: House of Commons.

25 Wooley, S. (2017) *What Happens to Young Carers when they Grow up? [online]* available from: https://quakersocialaction.org.uk/taking-social-action/our-practical-work/homes-and-housing/move/what-happens-young-carers-when-they (accessed April 16 2020).

26 Mitchell, F., Neuburger, J., Radebe, D. and Rayne, R. (2004). *Living in Limbo: Survey of Homeless Households Living in Temporary Accommodation*, London: Shelter.

27 Bakos, P. (2007). Multiple barriers, multiple solutions: Inclusion into and through employment for people who are homeless in Europe. *Annual Theme 2007-Employment and Homelessness*. Belgium: FEANTSA European Report.

28 Bramley, G., Fitzpatrick, S., Edwards, J., Ford, D., Johnsen, S., Sosenko, F. and Watkins, D. (2015) *Hard Edges: Mapping Severe and Multiple Disadvantage in England [online]*, available at: https://lankellychase.org.uk/wp-content/uploads/2015/07/Hard-Edges-Mapping-SMD-2015.pdf (accessed April 16 2020).

29 Watts, B., Johnsen, S. and Sosenko, F. (2015) *Youth Homelessness in the UK: A review for the OVO Foundation*, Edinburgh: Heriot-Watt University.

30 Brennan, R. Bush, M and Trickey, D. (2019) *Adversity and Trauma Informed Practice (online)*, available at: https://youngminds.org.uk/media/3091/adversity-and-trauma-informed-practice-guide-for-professionals.pdf (accessed April 18 2020).

31 National Child Traumatic Stress Network (2020) *Effects (online)*, available at: https://www.nctsn.org/what-is-child-trauma/trauma-types/complex-trauma/effects.

32 Youth Voice (2019) *Youth Homeless Parliament Report (online)*, available at: https://youth-voice.co.uk/wp-content/uploads/2019/11/YHP-Final-2019.pdf (accessed: April 18 2020).

33 Department for Work and Pensions (2020) *Universal Credit and Students*, [online] available at: https://www.gov.uk/guidance/universal-credit-and-students#universal-credit-if-youre-studying-full-time (accessed on: April 16 2020).

34 *ibid.*

35 Clements, C. (2018) *Universal Credit 'hits students harder'*, [online], available at: https://www.bbc.co.uk/news/uk-scotland-46452653 (accessed on: April 16 2020).

36 *ibid.*

37 Missing People (2014) *Missing and Homeless*, (online), available at: https://www.missingpeople.org.uk/about-us/about-the-issue/research/77-relatedissues2.html (accessed April 18 2020).

8 Conclusion

Loic Menzies

In 2019, England's Children's Commissioner published a report entitled *"The Children Leaving School with Nothing* [1]". The report highlighted the nearly 100,000 pupils a year who leave school without basic qualifications, a number that had been rising since 2015. A large proportion of these young people are affected by the issues explored in this book; a third of pupils from poor families (FSM eligible) leave school without five good GCSEs, and according to the report, pupils with special educational needs and disabilities are the most likely to leave education "with nothing".

"Leaving with nothing" is an oversimplification, and does not do these pupils justice. Many young people overcome huge hurdles in order to achieve qualifications below the magic A*–C threshold used in the Children's Commissioner's Report, and they should not be told they have "achieved nothing". When Francis, (whom I describe in Chapter 2) achieved his sub-C pass in Humanities this was certainly not "nothing". However, the fact remains that in 2018, 1 in 10 16–24-year olds were not in education, employment or training (NEET) [2] and pupils like these tend to fall into the group highlighted by the Children's Commissioner. For these young people, and many of those we focus on in this book, the estimated £100,000 that the state has spent on their education [1], has not achieved the bare minimum that one might hope for.

This book has its genesis in the fact my co-authors and I have spent much of the last ten years researching specific groups of young people who are at increased risk of becoming NEET or "leaving with nothing". Between us, we have written about Latin American young people and the challenges they face in progressing to university, working-class boys and their aspirations or expectations, pupils in the capital and how they seem to buck the trend, and innumerable other discrete groups. Yet, the challenges these groups have told us about have not differed greatly, and neither have the solutions we have ended up proposing.

Each group might, on its own, represent a minority of young people, and therefore be a peripheral concern for most policy makers, or a niche area of teacher expertise. However, as the Children's Commissioner and NEET figures above show, the consequences of their combined marginalisation are immense, and the curtailing of their collective life chances means there is a powerful case for reducing the extent to which our system pushes them to the margins.

The promise and optimism that lies behind the arguments made throughout this book is that society can, collectively, bring young people in from the margins. Moreover, the approaches that benefit one group are also likely to benefit others.

Fundamentally, time and again, young people tell us they want to be known and they want to be understood. In the Introduction, I quote James Pye who refers to "cracking the enigma" of Alasdair. In Chapter 1, I go on to share Jarlath O'Brien's touching account of how he cracked the enigma of Dean's reaction to the Bunsen Burners. Meanwhile, Jerome, a young homeless person described by Kate Bowen-Viner in Chapter 7, picks up the same theme saying:

> It would have made a difference if the teachers actually knew that I was a young carer. Only a couple of the teachers knew I was a young carer but didn't act upon it.

Similarly, in Chapter 4, Sam Baars points out that, unfortunately:

> The effort expended on identifying target areas for intervention outweighs the time spent getting under the skin of exactly how young people respond to spatial environments.

The recurring importance of curiosity about pupils' life stories takes me back to my first academic publication after leaving the classroom as a teacher. Kerry Jordan-Daus at Canterbury Christ Church University had decided to take a chance on me, a young, untested newbie in the world of research, offering me an opportunity to lead a project reshaping how the university approached the government's requirement to prepare trainees for "teaching in diverse settings".

As the project developed, we worked ever harder to move away from what we termed a "strand based approach" to diversity [3], where trainees received discrete training on different categories of young people. Instead we defined diversity as "the variety in pupils' sense of self and the background that has gone into making them who they are [4]". The work eventually culminated in a resource and associated training entitled *"What's your Story? Teaching for Diversity"* [5, 6]. One of my favourite case studies I heard whilst working on the project was of a teacher who, every year, after a term with a new class, tried to write down the name of all her pupils from memory. She then checked her list against the official list and picked out any pupils she had forgotten, noting down their names and determining to find out more about them from then on. I wonder how many pupils like Alasdair and Jerome might have benefited from that teacher's approach. That teacher's commitment to engaging with her pupils' stories and identities certainly differed from that of one of my former colleagues, who had told me it was too late in the year for pupils to put on a play about their identity "because black history month was last month".

On the other hand, whilst this book sets out a number of micro-level steps practitioners can take to minimise marginalisation, this is also a book about the big picture. The root cause of young people's marginalisation is, more often than not, a failure of policy and in most cases, the poverty and structural inequality that result from this, whether due to underinvestment in mental health services or through decades of "area-based policy making" that have misfired after a failure to engage with the substance of deprivation and how this interacts with a community's day-to-day life.

Thus, bringing young people in from the margins is possible, but requires action at a macro and micro level. Only through action on both levels can the negative outcomes that are catalogued throughout this book, be avoided – whether in terms of educational achievement, financial well-being, incarceration or poor health. More importantly though, both types of action are needed if we are to avoid inexcusable damage to human potential and flourishing. Thus, we finish with four overarching themes which we we believe would help bring young people in from the margins.

8.1 Get to know each young person's life story

As James Pye argues [9], an inquisitive stance on the part of all professionals, combined with professional conversations about each young person can help spot issues early and guide practitioners towards the most effective response.

8.2 Early intervention

Elevated "thresholds of need" mean that by the time support is put into place, unnecessary damage has been done. As Ellie Mulcahy and Kate Bowen-Viner argue in their 2020 report on preventative approaches to tackling youth homelessness:

> By the time a young person approaches their local authority for support, they have often reached crisis point. This is why preventing youth homelessness through early intervention is so important. It reduces harm to the young person and carries a lower cost to the public pursue [10]

Throughout this book we highlight a range of early warning signs, including poor school attendance, family difficulties and disruptive events such as bereavement. Watching out for these and responding fast can nip issues in the bud.

8.3 More than just schools

Having a foot on both sides of what sometimes seems an impregnable barrier between the "youth sector" and "schools sector" makes me keenly aware of how little teachers, youth workers, social workers and children's services know about (and respect) each-others' work. As Will Millard reflects in Chapter 6:

> I taught some young people like Karl, but did not really understand the world of children's social care even though it affects a large number of families. This chapter therefore serves an introduction to the world of children's social care, for those who, like me, could do with knowing a bit more about lives like Karl's.

It is striking how much my co-authors and I might have benefited from learning more about these groups and the professionals who work with them before we entered the classroom or completed our teacher training. Initiatives to collocate social workers, youth workers and mental health experts within schools therefore hold great promise.

8.4 Child poverty

Child poverty has risen sharply in recent years and is projected to continue increasing, both in absolute and relative terms [7, 8], yet most of the issues we describe in this book have poverty at their root. However, there is no inevitability to this; policymakers have pledged to reduce (or end) child poverty in the past, and it has been shown to be a feasible policy goal [11]. Tackling child poverty therefore needs to become a priority once again, since it is our greatest hope for bringing many young people in from the margins.

Figure 8.1 Child Poverty in the UK, Child Poverty Action Group (cpag.org.uk) p6.

References

1 Children's Commissioner for England (2018). *Briefing: the children leaving school with nothing*, Available at https://www.childrenscommissioner.gov.uk/wp-content/uploads/2019/09/cco-briefing-children-leaving-school-with-nothing.pdf.

2 Department for Education (2019). *NEET Statistics Annual Brief: 2018, England 28 February 2019*. Retrieved July 5, 2020, from 2019 website: https://assets.publishing.service.gov.uk/government/uploads/system/uploads/attachment_data/file/781544/NEET_statistics_annual_brief_2018_statistical_commentary.pdf.

3 Menzies, L., & Jordan-Daus, K. (2012). "The Importance of schools and HEIs in Initial Teacher Training: How Collaboration Between Canterbury Christ Church University and its Partnership of Schools Changed Trainees' Understandings of Diversity". *Tean Journal*, 4(2), February [Online]. Available at: http://insight.cumbria.ac.uk/id/eprint/1365/1/113-455-1-PB.pdf.

4 Menzies, L., & Curtin, K. (2010). *What's Your Story? Teaching for Diversity*, Unpublished. Canterbury Christ Church University, Canterbury.

5 ibid.

6 Menzies, L. (2010). *What's Your Story? – Teaching for Diversity – CfEY*, Retrieved July 4, 2020, from https://cfey.org/2010/12/whats-your-story-teaching-for-diversity/.

7 Hood, A., & Waters, T. (2017). *Living standards, poverty and inequality in the UK: 2017–18 to 2021–22*, Retrieved from http://www.ifs.org.uk.

8 Tucker, J., et al. (2017). *The Austerity Generation: the impact of a decade of cuts on family incomes and child poverty*, Child Poverty Action Group, Retrieved from https://cpag.org.uk/sites/default/files/files/Austerity%20Generation%20FINAL.pdf.

9 ibid.

10 Mulcahy, E., & Bowen-Viner, K., (2020). *Preventing youth homelessness through whole family, community led working*, Sage Foundation and The Centre for Education and Youth.

11 The Institute for Public Policy Research (2018). *Move On Up?* Social mobility, opportunity and equality in the 21st century, IPPR London.

Index

[**bold**=table; *italics*=figure]